Interlibrary Loan/ Document Delivery and Customer Satisfaction: Strategies for Redesigning Services

Interlibrary Loan/ Document Delivery and Customer Satisfaction: Strategies for Redesigning Services

Pat L. Weaver-Meyers
Wilbur A. Stolt
Yem S. Fong
Editors

The Haworth Press, Inc.
New York • London

Interlibrary Loan/Document Delivery and Customer Satisfaction: Strategies for Redesigning Services has also been published as *Journal of Library Administration* Volume 23, Numbers 1/2 1996.

The development, preparation, and publication of this work has been undertaken with great care. However, the publisher, employees, editors, and agents of The Haworth Press and all imprints of The Haworth Press, Inc., including The Haworth Medical Press and Pharmaceutical Products Press, are not responsible for any errors contained herein or for consequences that may ensue from use of materials or information contained in this work. Opinions expressed by the author(s) are not necessarily those of The Haworth Press, Inc.

Cover design by Monica L. Seifert

The Haworth Press, Inc., 10 Alice Street, Binghamton, NY 13904-1580 USA

Library of Congress Cataloging-in-Publication Data

Interlibrary loan/document delivery and customer satisfaction : strategies for redesigning services / Pat L. Weaver-Meyers . . . [et al.].
  p. cm.
  Includes bibliographical references and index.
  ISBN 0-7890-0013-X (alk. paper).–ISBN 0-7890-0304-X (pbk. : alk.paper)
  1. Interlibrary loans–United States. 2. Document delivery–United States. 3. Research libraries– United States. 4. Greater Midwest Research Library Consortium. 5. Libraries–User satisfaction– United States. 6. Interlibrary loans–Middle West. 7. Document delivery–Middle West. 8. Research libraries–Middle West. 9. Library user satisfaction–Middle West. I. Weaver-Meyers, Pat.
Z713.5.U61574 1996
025.6'2–dc20   96-33324
                                 CIP

INDEXING & ABSTRACTING

Contributions to this publication are selectively indexed or abstracted in print, electronic, online, or CD-ROM version(s) of the reference tools and information services listed below. This list is current as of the copyright date of this publication. See the end of this section for additional notes.

- *Academic Abstracts/CD-ROM,* EBSCO Publishing, P.O. Box 2250, Peabody, MA 01960-7250

- *Academic Search: database of 2,000 selected academic serials, updated monthly:* EBSCO Publishing, 83 Pine Street Peabody, MA 01960

- *AGRICOLA Database,* National Agricultural Library, 10301 Baltimore Boulevard, Room 002, Beltsville, MD 20705

- *Cambridge Scientific Abstracts,* Environmental Routenet (accessed via INTERNET), 7200 Wisconsin Avenue #601, Bethesda, MD 20814

- *CNPIEC Reference Guide: Chinese National Directory of Foreign Periodicals,* P.O. Box 88, Beijing, People's Republic of China

- *Current Articles on Library Literature and Services (CALLS),* Pakistan Library Association, Quaid-e-Azam Library, Bagh-e-Jinnah, Lahore, Pakistan

- *Current Awareness Bulletin,* Association for Information Management, Information House, 20-24 Old Street, London EC1V 9AP, England

- *Current Index to Journals in Education,* Syracuse University, 4-194 Center for Science and Technology, Syracuse, NY 13244-4100

- *Educational Administration Abstracts (EAA),* Sage Publications, Inc., 2455 Teller Road, Newbury Park, CA 91320

(continued)

- ***Higher Education Abstracts,*** Claremont Graduate School, 231 East Tenth Street, Claremont, CA 91711

- ***IBZ International Bibliography of Periodical Literature,*** Zeller Verlag GmbH & Co., P.O.B. 1949, d-49009 Osnabruck, Germany

- ***Index to Periodical Articles Related to Law,*** University of Texas, 727 East 26th Street, Austin, TX 78705

- ***Information Reports & Bibliographies,*** Science Associates International, Inc., 6 Hastings Road, Marlboro, NJ 07746-1313

- ***Information Science Abstracts,*** Plenum Publishing Company, 233 Spring Street, New York, NY 10013-1578

- ***Informed Librarian, The,*** Infosources Publishing, 140 Norma Road, Teaneck, NJ 07666

- ***INSPEC Information Services,*** Institution of Electrical Engineers, Michael Faraday House, Six Hills Way, Stevenage, Herts SG1 2AY, England

- ***INTERNET ACCESS (& additional networks) Bulletin Board for Libraries ("BUBL"), coverage of information resources on INTERNET, JANET, and other networks.***
  - JANET X.29: UK.AC.BATH.BUBL or 00006012101300
  - TELNET: BUBL.BATH.AC.UK or 138.38.32.45 login 'bubl'
  - Gopher: BUBL.BATH.AC.UK (138.32.32.45). Port 7070
  - World Wide Web: http: / / www.bubl.bath.ac.uk./BUBL/ home.html
  - NISSWAIS: telnetniss.ac.uk (for the NISS gateway)
  The Andersonian Library, Curran Building, 101 St. James Road, Glasgow G4 ONS, Scotland

- ***Journal of Academic Librarianship: Guide to Professional Literature,*** Grad School of Library & Information Sciences/Simmons College, 300 The Fenway, Boston, MA 02115-5898

(continued)

- *Konyvtari Figyelo-Library Review,* National Szechenyi Library, Centre for Library and Information Science, H-1827 Budapest, Hungary

- *Library & Information Science Abstracts (LISA),* Bowker-Saur Limited, Maypole House, Maypole Road, East Grinstead, West Sussex RH19 1HH, England

- *Library Literature,* The H.W. Wilson Company, 950 University Avenue, Bronx, NY 10452

- *MasterFILE: updated database from EBSCO Publishing,* 83 Pine Street, Peabody, MA 01960

- *Newsletter of Library and Information Services,* China Sci-Tech Book Review, Library of Academia Sinica, 8 Kexueyuan Nanlu, Zhongguancun, Beijing 100080 People's Republic of China

- *OT BibSys,* American Occupational Therapy Foundation, P.O. Box 31220, Rockville, MD 20824-1220

- *PASCAL International Bibliography T205: Sciences de l'information Documentation,* INIST/CNRS–Service Gestion des Documents Primaires, 2, Allee du Parc de Brabois, F-54514 Vandoeuvre-les-Nancy, Cedex, France

- *Public Affairs Information Bulletin (PAIS),* Public Affairs Information Service, Inc., 521 West 43rd Street, New York, NY 10036-4396

- *Referativnyi Zhurnal (Abstracts Journal of the Institute of Scientific Information of the Republic of Russia),* The Institute of Scientific Information, Baltijskaja ul., 14, Moscow A-219, Republic of Russia

- *Trade & Industry Index,* Information Access Company, 362 Lakeside Drive, Foster City, CA 94404

Book reviews are selectively excerpted by the *Guide to Professional Literature of the Journal of Academic Librarianship.*

SPECIAL BIBLIOGRAPHIC NOTES

related to special journal issues (separates)
and indexing/abstracting

☐ indexing/abstracting services in this list will also cover material in any "separate" that is co-published simultaneously with Haworth's special thematic journal issue or DocuSerial. Indexing/abstracting usually covers material at the article/chapter level.

☐ monographic co-editions are intended for either non-subscribers or libraries which intend to purchase a second copy for their circulating collections.

☐ monographic co-editions are reported to all jobbers/wholesalers/approval plans. The source journal is listed as the "series" to assist the prevention of duplicate purchasing in the same manner utilized for books-in-series.

☐ to facilitate user/access services all indexing/abstracting services are encouraged to utilize the co-indexing entry note indicated at the bottom of the first page of each article/chapter/contribution.

☐ this is intended to assist a library user of any reference tool (whether print, electronic, online, or CD-ROM) to locate the monographic version if the library has purchased this version but not a subscription to the source journal.

☐ individual articles/chapters in any Haworth publication are also available through the Haworth Document Delivery Services (HDDS).

Interlibrary Loan/Document Delivery and Customer Satisfaction: Strategies for Redesigning Services

CONTENTS

ABOUT THE EDITORS

Pat L. Weaver-Meyers, MLS, PhD, is Professor of Bibliography, and Access Services Department Head at the University of Oklahoma Libraries. A member of the American Library Association and the Oklahoma Library Association, she frequently participates in university and state committees. Recently Chair of the Faculty Senate at the University of Oklahoma, she is currently serving on its Executive Committee and is a member of the Steering Committee for the Oklahoma Library Technology Network. An active speaker, Professor Weaver-Meyers regularly presents her research at state and national conferences and workshops. Her most recent work has included research on interlibrary loan and customer satisfaction, cutting costs while improving materials accessibility, and modeling change strategies in public affairs programs.

Wilbur A. Stolt, MA, MS, is Director of Library Public Services and Associate Professor of Bibliography at the University of Oklahoma Libraries where he has coordinated the automated systems program since 1987. He has also served as Co-Director of the Oklahoma Library and Information Research Center. Mr. Stolt is active in many professional organizations including the Advisory Council of the Oklahoma Library Technology Network, the Interlibrary Cooperation Committee of the Oklahoma Library Association, and the Automation Subcommittee of the Oklahoma Council of Academic Library Directors. He is also a member of the editorial board of the *Journal of Library Administration.*

Yem S. Fong, MLS, is Head of Information Delivery Services at the University of Colorado at Boulder Libraries. She is a professor in the University Libraries and an adjunct professor in the Ethnic Studies Department. Ms. Fong is also Director of the University of Colorado Technical Research Center and is a consultant on information delivery and database development. Engaged in library management and resource sharing for over 17 years, she is the author of numerous articles on fee-based services and interlibrary loan/document delivery.

Introduction

The rising interest in interlibrary loan operations now occurring comes at a time when the tenets of Total Quality Management and customer satisfaction are the focus of many managers. At the same time, interlibrary loan and document delivery are transforming from peripheral services into primary services in the academic library. This volume reflects the ongoing transformation by examining customer perceptions and interlibrary loan activities.

The volume was conceived as a byproduct of a 1995 customer satisfaction survey on interlibrary loan conducted by members of the Greater Midwest Research Library Consortium (GMRLC). Several of the papers analyze the results of the study from different perspectives and the volume includes a detailed appendix of the survey responses. Other papers focus on issues of interest to interlibrary loan (ILL) document delivery (DD) specialists such as: examining ILL workloads, comparing current ILL management software, empowering ILL customers and redesigning library operations within the current conditions of rapid growth in ILL/DD. Many library administrators will find these discussions crucial to mastering the fast-paced changes impacting this area.

Cherie Geiser and Rachel Miller provide the background and discuss the development of an interstate courier among GMRLC members. Their findings and impressions of the courier service's effect on shipping costs, delivery speed, staff productivity and lending policies will be invaluable to any libraries embarking on the same challenge.

The next three papers examine data and information from the GMRLC customer satisfaction survey. Pat Weaver-Meyers and Wilbur Stolt analyze how delivery speed and selected variables relate to customer satisfaction. The conclusions confirm some earlier findings that undo a common

[Haworth co-indexing entry note]: "Introduction." Weaver-Meyers, Pat L., Wilbur A. Stolt, and Yem S. Fong. Co-published simultaneously in *Journal of Library Administration* (The Haworth Press, Inc.) Vol. 23, No. 1/2, 1996, pp. 1-3; and: *Interlibrary Loan/Document Delivery and Customer Satisfaction: Strategies for Redesigning Services* (ed: Pat L. Weaver-Meyers, Wilbur A. Stolt, and Yem S. Fong) The Haworth Press, Inc., 1996, pp. 1-3. Single or multiple copies of this article are available from The Haworth Document Delivery Service [1-800-342-9678, 9:00 a.m. - 5:00 p.m. (EST). E-mail address: getinfo@ haworth.com].

1

assumption; speed is not the most important factor in satisfying ILL customers. Yem Fong uses survey respondents' comments to expand ón the survey's quantitative analysis. Her qualitative approach develops an interesting picture of how customers value ILL services. Lee-Allison Levene and Wayne Pedersen take the same data and present it as a case study. They compare operations at University of Arkansas-Fayetteville and Iowa State University and examine how different operations and policies may impact customer satisfaction.

Nancy Paine and John Ward turn their focus to ILL operations, examining the transaction to staff ratios in 1990s ILL departments. Their comparison of current data with an earlier study gives the reader insight into the effect of increased transactions rates and improved ILL operations' effectiveness. The paper proceeds with an excellent examination of other ILL activities that influence productivity.

Of high interest to ILL managers will be the paper by Yem Fong, Penny Donaldson and Enid Teeter which compares three conceptually different ILL management software packages. This article provides valuable information for decision-making and freezes for posterity a snapshot of ILL software history.

Molly Murphy and Yang Lin examine customers' willingness to pay fees for ILL services. The authors analyze customer responses from a sample of requests which required lending fees. The analysis is an intriguing picture of ILL customers' unrealistic beliefs about costs. Their conclusions suggest that pass-through charging on a per request basis is counterproductive.

Barbara Preece and Susan Logue describe projects at Southern Illinois Libraries which, by developing web access and links to OCLC and state networks, have given ILL customers the power to make requests and reduce staff workload. With this description comes a discussion of the interdepartment collaboration and institutional support required to make software development projects like this one a success. Tom Delaney chronicles the development of patron-initiated request software at Colorado State University and discusses the statewide adoption of software initially conceived for local use.

In the last paper, Brice Hobrock issues a call to radically rethink libraries and library functions such as ILL. He calls for a paradigm shift that takes ILL operations into new types of partnerships with other libraries and into new partnerships with library customers.

Woven throughout the volume are analyses of customer satisfaction and the transformation of ILL services. Improving ILL services requires that customers are consulted and understood. New developments and creative redesign of ILL processes cannot be effective without a successful partnering between the service provider and the customer. This volume is a tapestry richly woven by that partnership.

The editors would like to thank the GMRLC member libraries for their financial support of the survey and the staff in the ILL operations at each participating institution for their time and effort. Studies like these provide much more useful data when they are undertaken by several institutions. Because of this cooperation, this data is a worthy benchmark for all academic libraries. A special thanks to Greg Lambert, graduate assistant at the University of Oklahoma, for his assistance with the various data tables and Bob Schull, statistical software consultant, for his help with SAS programming.

Finally, we thank our contributors. These GMRLC librarians are innovative leaders in ILL/DD and represent, in our opinion, exceptional colleagues.

Pat L. Weaver-Meyers
Wilbur A. Stolt
Yem S. Fong

GMRLC Negotiations
for an Interstate Courier:
History, Results, and Trends

Cherie Geiser
Rachel Miller

SUMMARY. In the fall of 1994, the Greater Midwest Research Libraries Consortium (GMRLC) negotiated a contract with Federal Express for expedited delivery of interlibrary loan materials within the consortium. This paper describes the negotiation of the contract for interstate courier services, reviews the implementation process, noting lessons learned, and discusses the effects of the new service on interlibrary loan shipping costs, delivery speed, staff time, policies, and procedures. *[Article copies available from The Haworth Document Delivery Service: 1-800-342-9678. E-mail address: getinfo@haworth.com]*

INTRODUCTION

Librarians agree that resource sharing among libraries cannot succeed without effective delivery of materials. Indeed, the quality of libraries is measured increasingly not by the size of local collections but rather by the

Cherie Geiser is Head of Interlibrary Loan Services, Farrell Library, Second Floor, Kansas State University Libraries, Manhattan, KS 66506-1200.
Rachel Miller is Head of Acquisitions/Serials/Interlibrary Services, 210 Watson Library, University of Kansas Libraries, Lawrence, KS 66045-2800.

[Haworth co-indexing entry note]: "GMRLC Negotiations for an Interstate Courier: History, Results, and Trends." Geiser, Cherie, and Rachel Miller. Co-published simultaneously in *Journal of Library Administration* (The Haworth Press, Inc.) Vol. 23, No. 1/2, 1996, pp. 5-22; and: *Interlibrary Loan/Document Delivery and Customer Satisfaction: Strategies for Redesigning Services* (ed: Pat L. Weaver-Meyers, Wilbur A. Stolt, and Yem S. Fong) The Haworth Press, Inc., 1996, pp. 5-22. Single or multiple copies of this article are available from The Haworth Document Delivery Service [1-800-342-9678, 9:00 a.m. - 5:00 p.m. (EST). E-mail address: getinfo@haworth.com].

effective delivery of wanted information, wherever it resides.[1] Despite advances in bibliographic access and in communications technology, users of interlibrary loan services today still face "the unpredictability of timeliness."[2] If libraries are to build users' willingness to forego local ownership and depend instead on remote collections, libraries must provide rapid and reliable physical delivery of research materials. Ultimately, their ability to do so will determine their success or failure in meeting library users' information needs.[3]

This paper describes the efforts of the Greater Midwest Research Library Consortium (GMRLC) to improve the physical delivery of materials within the consortium by establishing an interstate courier service.

HISTORY OF GMRLC INTERLIBRARY COOPERATION

GMRLC emerged from a group that consisted originally of eight libraries whose parent universities belonged to the Association of Big Eight Universities (ABEU), plus five additional university libraries in the region. These thirteen libraries were known as "ABEU Plus" and their deans and directors met regularly for a number of years. In October 1992 the group took the new name of Greater Midwest Research Library Consortium, and formalized its existence through bylaws, a governance structure, and a mission statement. In November 1994, it expanded to include four Texas libraries whose parent institutions joined with the Big Eight Athletic Conference to form the Big 12. Current membership stands at eighteen libraries distributed over twelve states:

- University of Arkansas, Fayetteville
- Baylor University, Waco
- University of Colorado, Boulder
- Colorado State University, Fort Collins
- Iowa State University, Ames
- University of Kansas, Lawrence
- Kansas State University, Manhattan
- Linda Hall Library, Kansas City, Missouri (adjunct member)
- University of Missouri, Columbia
- University of Nebraska, Lincoln
- University of New Mexico, Albuquerque
- University of Oklahoma, Norman
- Oklahoma State University, Stillwater
- Southern Illinois University, Carbondale

- University of Texas at Austin
- Texas A&M University, College Station
- Texas Tech University, Lubbock
- University of Wyoming, Laramie

Primarily state and land grant universities with similar missions and academic programs, GMRLC institutions share an interest in cooperative programs. In 1990 they initiated an OCLC union list (BIGU), which has since foundered due to several sites' inability to support union list maintenance costs in addition to local serials check-in. To encourage cooperative collection development, information on subscriptions to expensive journals and on serials cancellations is shared within the group. Reciprocal interlibrary loan, based on the idea that members are "first recourse" libraries for each other, is a cornerstone of GMRLC. Although reciprocal lending had been in place for decades within the Big Eight, it was first formalized in October 1991. At that same time statistics on lending within the group began to be collected. Recognizing effective delivery of materials as a key to resource sharing, the deans and directors promoted ARIEL for transmission of articles as soon as this new technology became available, and also began discussing the possibility of establishing an interstate courier service to expedite delivery of returnable materials.

THE INTERSTATE COURIER PROPOSAL

Background

A review of the literature suggests that there are many successful *intrastate* courier systems–Colorado, Alabama, Pennsylvania, Illinois, Oregon, Washington, Kansas, and others.[4] In 1991, however, when GMRLC leaders initiated the process of creating an *interstate* courier service, few precedents existed, although members of the Research Libraries Group were using United Parcel Service (UPS) for interlibrary loan as early as 1981.[5]

From the beginning, GMRLC deans and directors expected that an interstate courier service would help achieve three key objectives:

- It would provide quick and reliable delivery of materials within the consortium;
- By assuring the safety and security of shipments, it would enable member libraries to loan materials they would previously not have been willing to share due to fear of loss or damage in transit;

- Through the use of recyclable plastic containers, the courier service would significantly reduce staff time spent in wrapping and handling and thereby would increase staff productivity.[6]

The Request for Proposal (RFP) Timetable

- *The Initial Recommendation (May 1991):* A proposal that ABEU Plus establish an interstate courier service was formally presented to the deans and directors by Brice Hobrock, Dean of Libraries at Kansas State University.
- *Preparation of Bid Specifications (May 1991-November 1992):* Deans and directors decided to proceed on the assumption that the State of Kansas' negotiated bid process (i.e., a process not requiring acceptance of the lowest bid), would produce a contract that the entire ABEU Plus membership could adopt. Draft specifications, prepared under Hobrock's leadership, were presented and discussed at each subsequent ABEU Plus meeting and shared with interlibrary loan staff. Each library was expected to consult with its own campus and state purchasing agents to determine if institutional and state regulations would allow adoption of a contract negotiated by the State of Kansas. Although early draft specifications were based on the courier service used at the time by the Kansas Regents system, these quickly evolved to reflect additional service options.
- *Preparation of RFP (November 1992-December 1993):* In November 1992, a final draft of the specifications was formally endorsed by the deans and directors as well as by interlibrary loan representatives. One year later, after additional consultation with interlibrary loan, purchasing, and legal staff at each site, an official State of Kansas Request for Proposal was issued to vendors for bidding, with a December 1993 deadline. A "pre-bid conference" held shortly after the RFP was issued provided all parties an opportunity to clarify their understanding of the services needed. The conference was attended by the GMRLC Courier Negotiating Team (composed of representatives from Kansas State University and the University of Kansas), prospective vendors, and campus and state purchasing agents.
- *Summary of the RFP:*[7] The major requirements contained in the document were the following:

  The contract would provide service to the fourteen academic libraries that were members of GMRLC at that time, as well as five satellite campuses.

Non-consortium libraries could adopt the GMRLC contract if at least 10 percent of their total borrowing and lending activities were with consortium libraries. (This specification was added because some members were interested in using this contract to develop courier subsystems in their regions; however, this has not materialized to date.)

Each member could have the option of declining or dropping courier service at any time.

Delivery turnaround time could not exceed three business days between any two sites.

Charges would be based on actual shipping volume, rather than on a flat monthly rate, to avoid inequities between net borrowers and lenders. (Estimates of the volume, expressed both in terms of numbers of packages as well as their weight, were included in the document.)

Each library would be permitted to select its own preferred shipping container.

- *Review of Technical Proposals (February 1994-March 1994):* Four vendors submitted bids. As required by the State of Kansas, these were in the form of separate technical and cost proposals. Each GMRLC site received a copy of the technical proposals for comment along with an evaluation worksheet developed by the Negotiating Team. Vendor evaluations were completed in February 1994.
- *Bid Negotiation Meetings and Review of Final Cost Proposals (March 1994-May 1994):* To clarify the technical and cost information the four vendors had provided, the State of Kansas Division of Purchases scheduled a bid negotiation meeting with each. As a basis for vendors' submission of final cost offers in May, the Negotiating Team provided additional information on anticipated shipping volume.
- *Final Negotiations and Vendor Selection (June 1994-July 1994):* After review of the final cost proposals, the Negotiating Team met with two vendors in June, 1994 to discuss remaining questions and to hear each vendor's best and final offer. Following these meetings, the Negotiating Team recommended Federal Express as the vendor which would best meet the needs of GMRLC. The Team based its choice on this company's superior customer service record, as well

as its provision of free shipping supplies, pre-printed manifests and labels, statistical reports, and on-site access to an automated tracking system.[8] The contract and prices were negotiated specifically for GMRLC libraries, exclusive of other Federal Express contracts in place at individual university campuses. The team considered the negotiated prices to be reasonable considering the emphasis on expedited delivery and the twelve-state territory covered by the consortium. (Specific prices are confidential.)

- *Contract Approval (August 1994-October 1994):* The State Division of Purchases approved the selection of Federal Express on August 5, 1994. The Negotiating Team and Federal Express then developed the actual contract, attempting to make its provisions sufficiently generic that other states could adopt it with only slight modifications. This contract was approved and signed by Division of Purchases personnel on October 5, 1994. GMRLC libraries were then notified that Federal Express would be contacting them to discuss implementation, pricing and any requirements needed beyond those included in the Kansas contract.

IMPLEMENTATION OF THE INTERSTATE COURIER CONTRACT

Summary of the Kansas Contract

The Federal Express contract with GMRLC members, as negotiated by the State of Kansas, contains the following major provisions:

- Delivery options are economy two-day, standard overnight (delivery by next business afternoon), and priority overnight (delivery by next business morning).
- Federal Express provides free shipping supplies (boxes, map tubes, and envelopes in several sizes). The contract also allows for use of recyclable plastic containers. (As explained below, however, these proved not to be cost-effective at current interlibrary loan traffic levels within GMRLC.)
- Packages must be delivered to and picked up from the library itself, rather than a drop-off or pick-up point elsewhere on campus.
- Participating libraries may not use express mail services offered by other vendors.
- The Federal Express Powership 3 workstation is available free of charge to any GMRLC library shipping at least three packages per

day. It produces mailing labels, invoices, a summary of daily deliveries, on-site tracking of lost or missing materials, and reports. While in use for shipment preparation or tracking, it requires a dedicated phone line. A digital scale for weighing shipments is also required.

"Beta Test" at Kansas State University

Kansas State University was the first GMRLC member to implement the contract, on October 5, 1994. A Federal Express representative provided on-site instruction in basic procedures and in the use of Powership 3 (this required less than one hour). Customer service personnel were accessible by phone and staff could also make use of well-written manuals. The University of Kansas was next to implement the contract, later in October, and Oklahoma State University followed in November, but KSU staff took the lead in "beta testing" the Federal Express service.

Cherie Geiser, Head of Interlibrary Loan Services at KSU, assembled an informational packet to help other sites with their implementation process. The packet included basic information on the provisions of the contract, a summary of advantages and disadvantages, equipment needed, a comparison of Federal Express and U.S. Postal Service shipping costs based on KSU's experience, as well as Geiser's proposals regarding delivery standards and an implementation plan. An important early finding of the KSU staff was that the volume of interlibrary loan shipments within GMRLC was not distributed evenly enough to justify the use of recyclable plastic boxes. Because they would incur a shipping fee if returned empty, their use would not be cost-effective.

Presentation to GMRLC Deans and Directors (November 1994)

At the deans' and directors' next meeting, Hobrock and Geiser distributed the information packet as well as a statement of purpose for the courier service which reiterated the basic objectives of (a) providing rapid delivery, (b) increasing lending of library materials, and (c) reducing staff costs by streamlining wrapping and mailing procedures. The discussion emphasized that successful implementation of the Federal Express contract depended on full participation by the GMRLC membership. Failure to use the contract by several members could compromise the effectiveness of consortial resource sharing. In support of quick implementation, the deans and directors recommended that the GMRLC ILL representatives meet in January 1995 to develop a delivery system agreement and protocols.

Meeting of ILL Representatives (January 1995)

On January 6-7, 1995, ILL representatives from sixteen of the eighteen GMRLC libraries and deans or directors from six sites attended the Federal Express implementation meeting.

David Morales, Government Sales Executive for Federal Express, provided an overview of the provisions of the contract. He explained that the GMRLC contract was a trial arrangement and that the contract's favorable rates were dependent upon speedy implementation by all members and a minimum daily average of one hundred packages per day shipped throughout the consortium. The contract's rates could be used by any library department–not just the interlibrary loan office–but could not be exported beyond the library. Morales recommended a target date of February 15, 1995 for implementation at all sites.

The assembled GMRLC ILL representatives then proceeded to develop "The GMRLC Inter-Library Delivery Systems Agreement," which outlines a baseline of delivery service within the group. By this agreement, full GMRLC members provide each other with expedited delivery via Federal Express, ARIEL, and fax, to the best of their abilities. (Satellite campuses are excluded from this agreement.) The group agreed to observe the following guidelines routinely:

- Nonreturnables: Send via ARIEL or fax if less than 20 pages; send via Federal Express if over 20 pages. If other materials are being sent by Federal Express to the same destination, consider sending via Federal Express rather than ARIEL or fax. However, deliver rush requests using the method indicated by the borrower.
- Returnables: Send via Federal Express at the economy two-day rate, cost billed to the lending library. If the borrowing library wishes a higher level of service for rush items (priority or standard overnight), the cost is billed to the borrowing library. Return loaned periodicals, microforms, audiovisual and other special materials via Federal Express at the economy two-day rate, billed to the borrowing library. Return other loans via U.S. mail, except if requested otherwise by the lending library. Consider returning via Federal Express when other materials are being sent by this method to the same destination.

At this meeting (and again at a second meeting held November 9-10, 1995), considerable discussion was devoted to ways of exploiting the potential of the courier service to improve resource sharing within GMRLC. The following options were among those suggested:

- Using the Federal Express account to expedite delivery of rush returnables borrowed from non-GMRLC libraries;
- In light of the greater security provided by Federal Express, modifying local policies to encourage the loan of unbound and bound periodicals (as an alternative to payment of copyright and photocopying fees) and even to permit the occasional loan of some rare and/or fragile materials; and
- Using Federal Express for delivery during the Christmas holiday season when the U.S. mail service is more likely than usual to be slow and unreliable.

Although the primary objective of the January 1995 meeting was to encourage the rapid implementation of the Federal Express contract, it also marked the beginning of additional initiatives. The GMRLC ILL Group (GIG) was established formally with a mission statement and officers. To promote day-to-day communication by all ILL-related staff at member libraries, the group also produced a directory and initiated a listserv. An effort to document each institution's lending policies was also begun.

Implementation at Individual Sites

Implementing the contract across all GMRLC libraries proved far more complicated than originally anticipated, due chiefly to the inability of several states to utilize the generic contract negotiated by the Kansas institutions. Despite GMRLC's original intention that the contract between Federal Express and the State of Kansas would lend itself to being adopted quickly by all other sites, in most cases each GMRLC member ultimately had to negotiate a separate contract with Federal Express.

Nevertheless, most consortium members adopted the contract as quickly as they could. By July 1995, all but three had done so; by November 1995 only Colorado State University and the University of Texas at Austin had not been able to begin using the GMRLC contract. Figure 1 shows the increase in the volume of Federal Express shipments month by month from January 1995 through September 1995. By September, the average number of packages per day had risen to 80.75, still slightly short of the Federal Express goal of 100 per day.

Lessons Learned from the Process

More than four years elapsed between May 1991, when the GMRLC deans and directors endorsed formally the idea of an interstate courier

FIGURE 1. GMRLC Shipments by Federal Express
January-September 1995

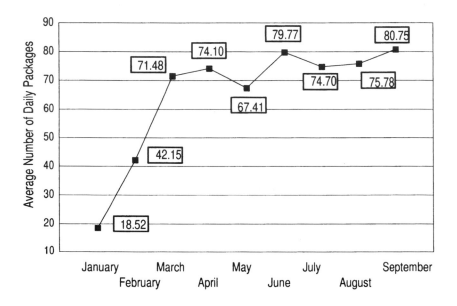

Data provided by David Morales, Government Sales Executive, Federal Express

proposal, and the spring of 1995, when the majority of GMRLC members actually signed the contract with Federal Express. The development and implementation of the interstate courier service was a slow process due to many obstacles:

- The concept of an interstate courier service for consortial ILL operations was new, both to libraries and to vendors. Specifications were initially drafted on the model of an existing service and required extensive modification through many months of consultation within the group, before the draft RFP could meet the needs of the consortium. The RFP prompted the vendors to create a service that did not previously exist.[9]
- The negotiated procurement process was new within the State of Kansas at that time. Purchasing agents' lack of experience with it

may have contributed to some delays. On the other hand, the negotiated bid process made it possible for all parties to discuss and clarify the provisions of the RFP, especially important in light of the fact
that none of the vendors had experience providing an interstate courier service.[10]

- Not surprisingly perhaps, implementing a contract by a consortium
consisting of many institutions governed by different state laws
proved not to be simple. Procurement officers and legal staff in each
state had difficulty dealing with a contract that crossed state lines. As
noted above, in most cases modifying the generic contract prepared
for the State of Kansas proved not to be an option. This greatly
lengthened the implementation process.

- The task of coordinating communications among the eighteen
GMRLC libraries—regarding preparation of the RFP, contract negotiations, and implementation—placed extraordinary demands on the
KSU library staff who led the process. The timeline might have been
shortened had it been possible for GMRLC to formally assign two
library staff members (one administrative and one interlibrary loan)
to coordinate the overall effort, and if all libraries could have
assigned one individual to manage all aspects of implementation at
each site. However, the complexity of the contract specifications,
combined with the need to consult with several procurement and
legal staff at each site, made all stages of the process intrinsically
cumbersome and difficult to manage.

- The consortium leadership's strong commitment to the value of a
courier service, as reflected in deans' and directors' willingness to
invest library funds and staff time in supporting this experiment, was
critically important. Concerns that shipping costs might be too great
for budgets to bear, complicated in some cases by state, university, or
even library restrictions on the source of funds used to pay for Federal Express charges, contributed to implementation delays at some
institutions. Clear and frequent communication among all those
involved—the library leadership, ILL staff, and external procurement
and legal staff—proved essential.

- The GMRLC experience also demonstrates that formalized interlibrary loan delivery agreements, based on shared expectations
regarding how Federal Express will be integrated into the existing
mix of interlibrary loan delivery strategies, are a crucial component
of the implementation process.

RESULTS OF INTERSTATE COURIER IMPLEMENTATION

Shipping Costs

During the October 1994 "beta test," as noted above, KSU staff compiled and shared with the rest of the consortium a comparison of FedEx costs with U.S. Postal Service costs (library rate). Based on actual shipments during a three-week period, they estimated that FedEx charges would be 434 percent higher than library rate for the same shipments (255 percent higher after January 1, 1995 when library rates increased substantially).

Despite concerns about costs, most of the eighteen member libraries proceeded to adopt the contract as quickly as they could. Figure 2 shows each library's expenditures on Federal Express for the January 1995-September 1995 period. Beyond the basic fact that each library adopted the contract at a different time, several reasons account for the differences in levels of use among sites. For example, GMRLC members vary in the overall volume of ILL transactions, and also in the percentage that GMRLC ILL transactions constitute of their total lending and borrowing. Practices vary considerably. Some libraries ship by Federal Express only to other GMRLC libraries, others use it more broadly. Some libraries use Federal Express to return materials borrowed from other libraries, others do not.

In the nine-month period illustrated by this graph, Federal Express expenditures were greatest at the Kansas State University, where they totalled $7,188.87, and at the University of Kansas, where they totalled $7,086.07. In this period KSU shipped both loans and borrowing returns by Federal Express to all GMRLC libraries. KU shipped both loans and borrowing returns to all GMRLC libraries except one. Over the nine-month period, this consisted of 1914 loaned items and 833 returned borrowed volumes, for a total of 2,747 volumes, shipped by Federal Express at an average cost of $2.58 per volume.

Delivery Speed

At the November 1995 GMRLC Interlibrary Loan Group meeting, David Morales reported that 83 percent of GMRLC shipments in the January 1995-September 1995 period were made at the economy two-day rate and 17 percent at the standard overnight rate.[11]

In an informal survey attached to the March 1995 semi-annual lending statistics collection form, KU staff asked GMRLC colleagues the follow-

FIGURE 2. GMRLC Expenditures for Federal Express
January-September 1995

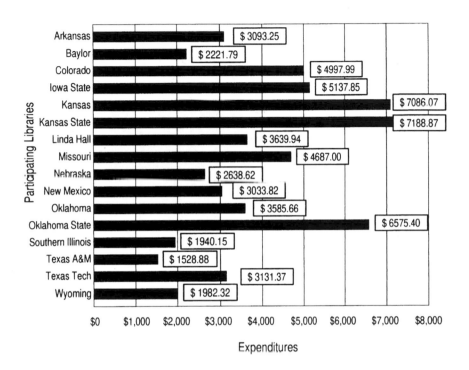

Data provided by David Morales, Government Sales Executive, Federal Express

ing question: "What effect has the use of Federal Express had on your borrowing time?" Thirteen libraries reported improvement in turnaround. For most, this statement was based on impressions only, but four libraries that attempted to sample transactions before and after reported a two-day reduction in delivery time. (One library reported no change in turnaround and three had no information to report.)

A formal user satisfaction survey carried out cooperatively at all GMRLC libraries in April 1995, also collected data on delivery speed.[12] Of 712 items supplied to users in GMRLC libraries in the month of February, 50 had been shipped by Federal Express. Mean delivery time for these items was 12 days, compared with 18.6 for items delivered by U.S.

mail, 5.2 days for items delivered by fax, and–perhaps most interest-ing–11.5 days for items delivered by ARIEL.

The University of Kansas and Kansas State University also sampled delivery time of books borrowed (i.e., returnables only) from other GMRLC libraries at two time periods: in September 1994 (before the use of Federal Express began) and in September 1995. At KU, turnaround time averaged 12 days in September 1994, and 9 days in September 1995. At KSU, the figures were 10 days and 9 days respectively.

Although these figures are suggestive, turnaround time is affected by many variables. Even assuming that the improvement can be attributed to Federal Express at least to some extent, actual delivery times within GMRLC still remain rather long. Use of Federal Express reduces transit time from the lending library to the borrowing library, but does not by itself result in fast interlibrary loan. Obviously, many other variables con-tribute to actual delivery speed: the time involved in verification and ordering; whether the request can actually be filled by the first library in the lender string, or must be passed on; the time required at each library to receive a request, page and ship an item.

An informal survey of GMRLC members in October 1995 also attempted to assess perceptions of the effect that the Federal Express pickup and delivery location has had on turnaround time. Of the seven libraries that accept deliveries in a library location other than the interli-brary loan office, two believe turnaround time suffers as a result.

Staff Time

Because staff represent the most significant cost of interlibrary loan operations,[13] increasing their productivity was one of the key objectives of establishing the courier service. The deans and directors anticipated that a container-based courier system would decrease staff time spent on sorting, wrapping, taping, and labelling packages. However, as noted earlier, use of re-usable plastic containers proved unfeasible due to the cost of return-ing them empty to keep them in circulation throughout the consortium. In the future, if interlibrary loan traffic increases or distribution patterns change, recyclable plastic containers may offer a way to achieve labor cost savings. In the meantime, some staff time may be saved through use of standard Federal Express packaging and labelling.

In responses to the October survey, GMRLC libraries were divided in assessing the impact of Federal Express on staff time: five libraries indi-cated that use of Federal Express produced savings in this area, five noticed no change, and five said Federal Express required more staff time (although several of these interlibrary loan operations had not previously had the responsibility of preparing packages for shipment).

Changes in Interlibrary Loan Policies and Procedures

The October 1995 survey sheds some light on the extent to which use of Federal Express is influencing changes in interlibrary loan policies and procedures within the group. Of the sixteen GMRLC libraries that had adopted the contract by then, nine rated the service provided by Federal Express as "exceptional," six as "above standard," and one as "standard." During the nine-month period between January and September 1995, 99.4 percent of the 12,448 GMRLC packages shipped were delivered on time (i.e., within the delivery time requested by the customer—either economy two-day or standard overnight). Of 161 delayed packages, 79 were attributed to error by Federal Express, and 82 to customer error (e.g., wrong address). No claims for lost or damaged packages were filed during the entire nine-month period.[14]

No doubt based on this excellent service record, six GMRLC libraries indicated in the October 1995 survey that they would be changing their lending policies and would be more willing to lend periodicals, audiovisuals, and rare or fragile items. Two may consider lending these materials. However, eight libraries did not anticipate that use of the interstate courier would lead them to make any changes at all in lending policies. This result may simply reflect the fact that such policies are usually not under the control of interlibrary loan staff but rather are determined by collection managers and library administrators. Nevertheless, liberalized policies made possible by secure and rapid delivery mechanism could significantly strengthen resource sharing in the consortium. In the area of periodical loans, for example, the impact could be significant, considering the savings in fees for copyright ($6-$9 per article) and for commercial article delivery (averaging $12-$15 per article) that could be achieved if bound and unbound journals were loaned. The cost of shipping a periodical issue, especially when combined with other items in a single package going to the same destination, is far less than the cost of obtaining an article from a commercial supplier.

Though the costs of shipping by Federal Express are not insignificant, much of the GMRLC group uses Federal Express more extensively than called for by the guidelines agreed to in January 1995. Eight libraries return borrowed materials by Federal Express, no doubt having realized that it is often more economical to bundle loans and returns together in a single package than to ship one item by Federal Express and another through the U.S. Postal Service. In addition, processing is streamlined when staff are able to send all GMRLC shipments by Federal Express, thus avoiding the extra time involved in sorting items for shipment by different methods.

Whenever ARIEL is unavailable, virtually all libraries ship copies of articles by Federal Express. Twelve libraries use Federal Express at least occasionally for rush borrowing of returnable items from non-GMRLC libraries. Although none routinely ship loans by this method to non-GMRLC libraries, one library is considering this option for loans to members of the Association of Research Libraries (ARL). In most institutions, the Federal Express account is used not only by the interlibrary loan office but also by other units in the library (e.g., acquisitions, administration).

Interest in using Federal Express for international shipments is particularly high. Without adequate insurance or reliable tracking systems many libraries cannot afford the risks of international loans. At present, use of Federal Express and other vendors is not financially feasible for international lending because of the cost and paperwork involved in customs duties. However, Federal Express has announced plans to introduce two-day rates for Canada and customs authority for duty-free entry to other countries.[15]

CONCLUSIONS

Is GMRLC's interstate courier achieving the results desired and expected from it? According to the very preliminary data reported here, delivery times are reduced. Shipping costs, though significant, have not risen beyond the levels anticipated, and those libraries that have had the highest expenditures–Kansas State University and the University of Kansas–remain committed to maintaining and possibly expanding expedited delivery. Expectations for quality of service and security of delivery have been met. However, few GMRLC libraries appear willing to liberalize their lending policies even though there have been no claims for losses or damages. The effects of Federal Express on staff productivity still remain to be measured, and in the meantime librarians' opinions on this question differ.

Although further study of all these issues is required, the GMRLC experience makes evident that the interstate courier is a key component in the mix of delivery technologies used for interlibrary loan within the consortium. An excellent courier service cannot by itself surmount all the obstacles that stand in the way of effective resource sharing, however. GMRLC members recognize that continual attention to process, workflow, and policy issues remains essential. In the coming months, the group will be participating in Phase 2 of a study to investigate interlibrary loan performance measures, planned by Mary E. Jackson of the Association of Research Libraries (ARL) and supported by the Andrew W. Mellon Foundation.

Consortium members agree that expedited delivery mechanisms for interlibrary loan can only grow in importance as individual institutions purchase fewer library materials and depend more heavily on cooperative collection development agreements. Standards-compliant library systems will make it easier for users in one GMRLC library to request the items they need directly from other GMRLC libraries, and will probably increase their expectation that requested materials will be delivered quickly. Although electronic delivery mechanisms and commercial document suppliers may replace libraries as sources for some journal articles, in the foreseeable future only other libraries will be able to supply most of the monographs needed by users. Effective on-demand access to monographs is possible only with rapid delivery services like Federal Express.

Recent events demonstrate that GMRLC libraries are not alone in seeking to expedite delivery of materials. In the months since GMRLC negotiated its contract with Federal Express, the Association of Research Libraries (ARL) has also secured an agreement with the same company to provide discounted rates for quick delivery of interlibrary loan materials among member libraries.[16] In addition, the Committee on Institutional Cooperation (CIC) negotiated a contract with Pony Express which provides for daily stops at all campuses of the Big Ten and the Center for Research Libraries and a 24-48 hour delivery time.[17] Through all these initiatives, rapid and reliable delivery of library materials to users is increasingly recognized as essential to libraries' resource sharing programs.

NOTES

1. Eleanor Mitchell and Sheila A. Walters, *Document Delivery Services: Issues and Answers* (Medford, NJ: Learned Information, Inc., 1995), 11-12.

2. Shirley K. Baker and Mary E. Jackson, *Maximizing Access, Minimizing Cost: A First Step Toward the Information Access Future* (Washington, DC: Association of Research Libraries, 1993), 4.

3. Barbra Buckner Higginbotham and Sally Bowdoin, *Access Versus Assets: A Comprehensive Guide to Resource Sharing for Academic Librarians* (Chicago: American Library Association, 1993), 202-207.

4. Susan Fayad, "Document Delivery: You Can Get It There From Here," *Colorado Libraries* 16 (December 1990): 13-14; John Campbell, "The Serendipitous Courier," *Colorado Libraries* 16 (December 1990): 19-20; Sue O. Medina, "Improving

Document Delivery in a Statewide Network," *Journal of Interlibrary Loan & Information Supply* 2, no. 3 (1992): 7-14; Peter Deekle, "Document Delivery Comes of Age in Pennsylvania," *Wilson Library Bulletin* 65, no. 2 (1990): 31-33; "Excerpts from the Illinois Interlibrary Loan Delivery System Review," *Illinois Libraries* 75, no. 2 (March 1993): 96-127; Sue A. Burkholder, "By Our Own Bootstraps: Making Document Delivery Work in Oregon," *Computers in Libraries* 12, no. 11 (December 1992): 19-24.

5. Barbara Brown, "Interlibrary Loan in the Research Libraries Group," *Prospects for Improving Document Delivery: Minutes of the 101st Meeting, October 13-14, 1982, Arlington, Virginia* (Washington, DC: Association of Research Libraries, 1983), 90-92.

6. Brice Hobrock, interview by authors, Manhattan, Kansas, August 18, 1995.

7. Copies of the RFP are available on request from Cherie Geiser.

8. Nancy Karabatsos, "Absolutely, Positively Quality," *Quality Progress* 23, no. 5 (May 1990): 24-28; "How to Have Satisfied Employees," *Library Personnel News* 6, no. 2 (1992): 3, 6.

9. Hobrock, interview by authors.

10. *Ibid.*

11. David Morales, "GMRLC and Federal Express: Interlibrary Loan Delivery Program Update," Presentation to the GMRLC ILL Group, Iowa State University, Ames, Iowa, November 9, 1995.

12. Pat Weaver-Meyers and Wilbur Stolt, "Analysis of Delivery Speed and Other Measures of Satisfaction with ILL Services," *Journal of Library Administration*, 23(1/2).

13. Marilyn M. Roche, *ARL/RLG Interlibrary Loan Cost Study: A Joint Effort by the Association of Research Libraries and the Research Libraries Group* (Washington, DC: ARL, 1993), 19-29, 34.

14. Morales, "GMRLC and Federal Express."

15. *Ibid.*

16. For information on ARL's contract with Federal Express, contact Mary E. Jackson, Access and Delivery Consultant, Association of Research Libraries, 21 Dupont Circle, Washington, DC 20036 (email: mary@cni.org).

17. "New CIC Delivery Initiatives Use Pony Express, Networks," *Library Hotline* 24, no. 50 (December 18, 1995): 4.

Delivery Speed, Timeliness
and Satisfaction:
Patrons' Perceptions About ILL Service

Pat L. Weaver-Meyers
Wilbur A. Stolt

SUMMARY. An investigation of Interlibrary customer satisfaction at Greater Midwest Research Libraries Consortium member libraries reveals highly satisfied customers. Through correlation and regressional analysis the study verifies that customers' satisfaction is only minimally dependent on actual delivery speed. Customer perceptions about timeliness suggest that materials received within two weeks satisfy the average academic's "window of usefulness" for loaned items. The implication of these findings on investment of resources to improve delivery speed and on the importance of determining other factors which influence "complete customer satisfaction" are discussed. *[Article copies available from The Haworth Document Delivery Service: 1-800-342-9678. E-mail address: getinfo@haworth.com]*

What is most convenient to measure is often the most frequently measured characteristic of any population or service. The easily measured

---

Pat Weaver-Meyers is Head of the Access Services Department at University of Oklahoma Libraries, Norman, OK. E-mail address: patwm@uoknor.edu.

Wilbur Stolt is Director of Public Services at University of Oklahoma Libraries, Norman, OK. E-mail address: wstolt@uoknor.edu.

The authors wish to acknowledge the contributions of Bob Schull, Statistical Software Consultant; Robert Swisher, Professor of Library and Information Studies; and Greg Lambert, Graduate Assistant, Department of Access Services, University of Oklahoma.

[Haworth co-indexing entry note]: "Delivery Speed, Timeliness and Satisfaction: Patrons' Perceptions about ILL Service." Weaver-Meyers, Pat L., and Wilbur A. Stolt. Co-published simultaneously in *Journal of Library Administration* (The Haworth Press, Inc.) Vol. 23, No. 1/2, 1996, pp. 23-42; and: *Interlibrary Loan/Document Delivery and Customer Satisfaction: Strategies for Redesigning Services* (ed: Pat L. Weaver-Meyers, Wilbur A. Stolt, and Yem S. Fong) The Haworth Press, Inc., 1996, pp. 23-42. Single or multiple copies of this article are available from The Haworth Document Delivery Service [1-800-342-9678, 9:00 a.m. - 5:00 p.m. (EST). E-mail address: getinfo@haworth.com].

23

factors, however, may not be the best information to have when trying to decide how to improve service to a particular population. Delivery speed for interlibrary loan and other document delivery services is easy to measure and has been repeatedly used in the assessment of service quality.[1] Commercial document delivery providers tout it as a reason to select their service over competitors.

Delivery speed is certainly an important measure that affords easy comparison among service providers. It is useful to managers analyzing the efficiency of office staff. It can be used as a signal of an overload and should be part of any review of delivery services.[2] Average turnaround, and length of time to receipt are part of the monthly statistical reports provided by OCLC and Research Libraries Group interlibrary loan subsystems, respectively. Such figures are evidence that delivery speed is considered important in the evaluation of reciprocal services. Recent studies of document delivery vendors have also focused on delivery speed, comparing vendor claims and library performance.[3]

How important, though, is rapid delivery to the end user? How fast must delivery be to qualify as "rapid" in the mind of the customer? In a 1994 study of one academic interlibrary loan department, a survey of users revealed no correlation between delivery speed and user satisfaction.[4] This somewhat surprising result stimulated an expansion of that study. The larger study uses a similar customer satisfaction survey (see Appendix Figure A.1). The population of customers surveyed here is drawn from member libraries of the Greater Midwest Research Library Consortium (GMRLC). Ten of the 18 member institutions participated. This article reports the results of that survey, describing what correlations exist between delivery speed and survey responses about user satisfaction and user perceptions of timeliness. In addition, multiple regression analysis helps identify those variables contributing most to any significant relationship. The data were examined further using Analysis of Variance to determine what differences could be attributable to individual institution performance.

Unusual in this study is the calculation of delivery speed. Except for a study by Anna Perrault and Marjo Arseneau, in which patrons categorized how long they *perceived* it took them to get an item, most studies calculate delivery speed from the date of the request to the date of the receipt of the item by the requesting library.[5] In this study, we calculated delivery speed from the date of the request to the date of the receipt of the item *as reported by the patron.* Therefore, average delivery speed in this study may appear longer than delivery speed in some previous studies because it includes the time elapsed between the requesting library's receipt of the item and the receipt of the item by the customer.

The focus in this study, therefore, is on the user's perception of the quality of service, not on the actual comparative performance of the libraries. Procedures unique among institutions can slow the ordering or on-site delivery of a document, changing the actual delivery speed from the customer's perspective. Such changes influence the customer, but might not be evident in a study that measures only the actual turnaround between ordering and receipt. Such turnarounds may not be proportional to the delivery speed perceived by the user, particularly in loans. Notification of availability and the patrons' time schedules, which may delay pickup of the item, contribute to their perception of how long it takes to get what they want.

BACKGROUND

Higginbotham and Bowdoin provide a thorough and recent literature review of interlibrary loan and document delivery issues.[6] In particular, their chapter entitled "Approaches to Document Delivery" points out the emphasis given to delivery speed even though there is a notable absence of any substantive research on its real value to library customers.[7] Their review lacks only the most recent three years of studies, which look primarily at commercial document delivery vendors and raise a controversy about their ability to deliver as promised.

Wayne Pedersen and David Gregory fill this three-year gap by summarizing the more recent findings comparing library services with commercial services.[8] At the same time, these authors provide their own data on the use of vendors, reporting a best average turnaround of nine days with a vendor and a best average of four days for select instate libraries. However, their study calculated the fastest times by eliminating the time between the patron's submission of the request and the placement of the request on OCLC. Pedersen and Gregory conclude by suggesting that the integration of vendor and library services will provide the most flexibility and the best service for patrons.

Durniak and Kurosman, on the other hand, maintain that libraries provide faster, cheaper delivery service.[9] Some of the difference between the conclusions of these two studies is based on the different interpretation of the cost and value of mediating and routing requests by ILL staff. Both studies look at comparable service efficiency among providers, as do previous studies. Most previous studies look at efficiency from the library's perspective. Patron's perceptions of service quality were briefly addressed in the late 1970s and have just recently become part of the literature again.

Perrault and Arseneau's study describes a series of works in the 1970s that look at perceived inconvenience and satisfaction with document delivery service. Perrault and Arseneau's study reports descriptive statistics on satisfaction and patrons' perceptions of how response time met their expectations. For both faculty and graduates, only about 15 percent reported the response time as less than satisfactory, even when their expectations for delivery speed were higher. Faculty selected speed more than 32 percent of the time as their most important priority.[10] This suggests, as do older studies, that satisfaction is somewhat independent of delivery speed. Unfortunately, Perrault and Arseneau's study did not go beyond descriptive analysis.

A recent study completed at Emory University is summarized in an Internet Web document. Questions on this survey, created with focus group opinion, are more detailed than the questions used in this study.[11] However, they touch on the same issues: convenience in placing a request, convenience of pickup, staff availability, obtaining the correct item, and so forth. The results are summarized on the Internet and include recommendations for service improvement.[12] Patrons rated the importance of delivery speed as urgent; these responses were not compared with actual delivery speed, making it difficult to determine if the service speed met their need for urgency.

METHODOLOGY

Survey

The original 1994 survey was designed for the pilot study by selecting some of the evaluation criteria suggested by Higginbotham and Bowdoin that could be easily queried. These included questions about delivery speed, timeliness and usefulness of the item provided, perceived convenience and ease of use, as well as satisfaction with the transaction. That survey design was reviewed by a select group of frequent ILL customers to insure validity and revisions were made when necessary. In this study, the same form was circulated to all the potential participating Interlibrary Loan personnel and additional suggestions were incorporated. Wording was changed to make the survey more generic. In addition, two questions were added at the request of one participant. Both questions:

This item was valuable to my research; and

The average cost of ILL transactions to the library is about $18. This material was worth that investment;

are attempts to have the customer assign some additional measure of value to the transaction; a quality emphasized by Peter Hernon and Charles McClure in their research on performance measures.[13] Relating these questions to delivery speed, it was assumed, would illuminate further the importance of speed to individual researchers.

Table A.1 in the Appendix lists the Cronbach coefficient alpha for the total sample and for the individual institutions.[14] Survey reliability of all responses was calculated by SAS software to be .7183. Reliability for the individual institution responses ranges from .6711 to .7592 with the exception of institution F. Alpha of institution F survey responses, .5124, was disproportionately lower than the others. As all the other institutions' reliability estimates are comparable, we concluded that administration of the survey accounted for the outlying value, and not the instrument itself. Total number of responses from institution F represent only 9.1 percent of the total. Since removing these responses from the alpha calculations raises the reliability to only .7295, we chose to include these responses in the complete analysis. However, this low level alpha should be remembered in any interpretation of individual institution data.

Participants

Participants in this study were self-selected. All members of GMRLC were invited to participate in a January 1995 meeting; ten institutions chose to do so. Although this was not a random selection of institutions, a review of the participating institutions revealed them to be representative according to high, medium and low volume ILL providers. Table A.2 in the Appendix shows interlibrary loan borrowing and lending activity for all GMRLC members, the population from which the participants came. Included also are institutions with large, medium and small collection expenditures among the GMRLC members (see Appendix, Table A.2). Given the number of Association of Research Libraries members among the GMRLC membership, results may be reasonably interpreted as relevant to that group of academic libraries.

Distribution

Each participating institution was sent a master copy of the survey form and asked to reproduce it with their return address on the reverse side. Instructions specified that a total of 200 forms were to be distributed. A form was inserted with every third ILL item received in the mail for distribution to customers, and customers were assured of anonymity. The survey was distributed with both books and photocopies. Return envelopes were included for patrons with off-campus addresses. On-campus patrons were instructed to return the survey in campus mail. No effort was made to prevent the same patron from receiving more than one survey form. Instructions to respondents asked them to complete all they received and evaluate their satisfaction with each specific transaction. It was assumed customers might be satisfied with the service in one situation and dissatisfied with a different transaction.

RESULTS

During distribution, which took place over two weeks in April 1995, ILL personnel completed the bottom section of the survey form. Actual delivery speed was calculated by determining the number of days between the date requested and the receipt date reported by the customer. The date requested was provided in the office use section of the form completed by ILL personnel. The date provided by the patron was in answer to the question, "When did you receive the attached interlibrary loan item?"

Table A.3 (see Appendix) shows the number of responses received from each institution and the percent return rate. Table A.5 (see Appendix) depicts the breakdown of respondents by patron type. The patron type distribution compares with independent institutional distributions of the breakdown of patrons served. Despite modest return rates, such a breakdown suggests the sample is unskewed by patron type.

The mean delivery speed for all respondents, depicted in Table 1, is 15.46 days. Individual institution means range from 8.38 to 19.14 days.

TABLE 1. Delivery Speed in Days

Institution	N	Mean	S.D.	Min.	Max.
A	71	18.94	17.17	7	97
B	101	18.34	31.25	1	313
C	37	12.89	8.31	4	48
D	93	18.62	15.26	4	126
E	59	11.22	5.86	1	28
F	66	15.57	8.10	5	53
G	78	15.17	10.26	5	63
H	77	8.38	5.94	0	32
I	78	13.89	12.23	1	67
J	54	19.14	14.06	6	101
All Institutions	714	15.46	16.32	0	313

Delivery speed ranged from zero or same-day delivery to 313 days.[15] Approximately 50 percent of all requests were received in 12 days or less. Ninety percent of all requests arrived in the patron's hands in 27 days or less. Since this study includes the time between the requesting library's receipt of the item and the patron's receipt, it is important to note the mean of the difference. The mean of the number of days between these two dates is 2.67 days.

In Table 2, satisfaction levels are high, with a mean of 1.45 on a scale of 1 = strongly agree to 5 = strongly disagree. Perceptions of timeliness were also quite positive, although slightly lower with an overall mean of 1.69 (see Table 3). Ninety-three point two percent of all respondents agreed or strongly agreed they were satisfied and 86.9 percent agreed or strongly agreed they received the item in a timely manner.

Confirming the perceived timeliness of the delivery, responses to the question, "Because it took so long to receive this item, it was no longer useful to me," averaged 4.42 (Table 4). Customers clearly felt their items were useful, although their support of the worth of the library's investment of $18 was less strong, averaging 2.00 with a standard deviation of 1.13 (Table 5).

Although these figures provide a general picture of the respondents, more complex analyses of the data are required to determine how satisfaction and perceptions of timeliness relate to the actual delivery speed. Based on the previous pilot, we assumed there would be no correlation between delivery speed and either satisfaction or timeliness. Table 6 is a report of the significant correlation coefficients among all the numerical

TABLE 2. Responses to "Based on This Transaction, I Am Satisfied with Interlibrary Loan Services" (Satisfaction)

Institution	N	Mean	S.D.
A	79	1.55	0.87
B	101	1.40	0.66
C	56	1.58	0.84
D	93	1.32	0.51
E	61	1.34	0.65
F	67	1.49	0.76
G	79	1.50	0.93
H	79	1.35	0.64
I	77	1.41	0.61
J	53	1.71	0.88
All Institutions	745	1.45	0.74

Scale
1 = Strongly Agree, 2 = Agree, 3 = Neutral, 4 = Disagree, 5 = Strongly Disagree

TABLE 3. Responses to "I Received This Item in a Timely Manner" (Timeliness)

Institution	N	Mean	S.D.
A	79	1.86	1.10
B	101	1.62	0.92
C	57	1.84	0.92
D	92	1.45	0.71
E	61	1.78	0.98
F	70	1.75	0.92
G	81	1.75	1.11
H	78	1.46	0.65
I	77	1.72	0.95
J	54	1.90	0.93
All Institutions	750	1.69	0.93

Scale
1 = Strongly Agree, 2 = Agree, 3 = Neutral, 4 = Disagree, 5 = Strongly Disagree

TABLE 4. Mean Response to "Because It Took So Long to Receive This Item,
It Was No Longer Useful to Me"
(Took Too Long)

Institution	N	Mean	S.D.
A	76	4.25	1.02
B	98	4.38	0.94
C	54	4.40	0.81
D	88	4.64	0.72
E	61	4.40	0.80
F	62	4.43	0.78
G	76	4.36	1.12
H	77	4.58	0.87
I	70	4.30	1.04
J	51	4.37	0.82
All Institutions	713	4.42	0.91

Scale
1 = Strongly Agree, 2 = Agree, 3 = Neutral, 4 = Disagree, 5 = Strongly Disagree

survey responses for the total respondent group and delivery speed.[16] Note that there is a significant correlation between both satisfaction and delivery speed and timeliness and delivery speed. The strongest correlation is with timeliness.

Tables 7 and 8 report the significant correlations for satisfaction and timeliness, respectively, and all other numerical survey responses. These correlations reveal relationships with other variables. However, because

TABLE 5. Responses to "The Average Cost of ILL Transactions to the Library Is About $18. This Material Was Worth That Investment." (Worth Investment)

Institution	N	Mean	S.D.
A	73	1.98	1.23
B	93	2.01	1.07
C	55	1.89	0.91
D	90	1.81	0.95
E	60	1.96	1.20
F	61	2.09	1.16
G	74	1.89	1.09
H	77	2.12	1.33
I	70	2.24	1.18
J	50	2.14	1.12
All Institutions	703	2.00	1.13

Scale
1 = Strongly Agree, 2 = Agree, 3 = Neutral, 4 = Disagree, 5 = Strongly Disagree

TABLE 6. Significant Pearson Correlation Coefficients for Delivery Speed and Other Survey Responses

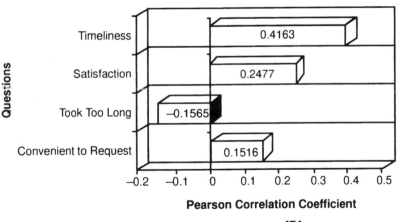

n = 474
p < .05 = significant

the sample is so large (n = 474) all relationships are statistically significant (non-zero order) if not practically significant. A quick review of the individual institution correlations for delivery speed and satisfaction (Table 9) indicates that under the conditions of much smaller sample sizes, there is no consistent indication of significant correlations among these same variables.

TABLE 7. Significant Pearson Correlation Coefficients for Satisfaction and Other Survey Responses

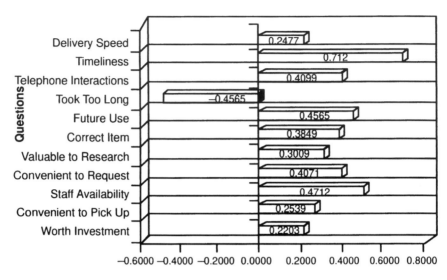

Pearson Correlation Coefficient

n = 474

p < .05 = significant

To better identify the strength of the relationship among these variables, three multiple regressions were calculated using the dependent variables of delivery speed, satisfaction and timeliness.[17] The results, reported in Tables 10-12, respectively, suggest that some of the statistically significant correlations are practically trivial.

For example, in Table 10 where delivery speed is the dependent variable, timeliness accounts for about 17 percent of the variance. Although that is a reasonably strong predictive relationship, it also indicates that other unknown factors account for the majority of the variance and suggests that perceptions of timeliness are based on much more than actual delivery time. Satisfaction with the transaction, surprisingly, explains less than 1 percent of the variance and is less influential than satisfying telephone interactions or perceived convenience in the placing of requests.

Tables 11 and 12 show a very strong relationship between satisfaction

TABLE 8. Significant Pearson Correlation Coefficients for Timeliness and Other Survey Responses

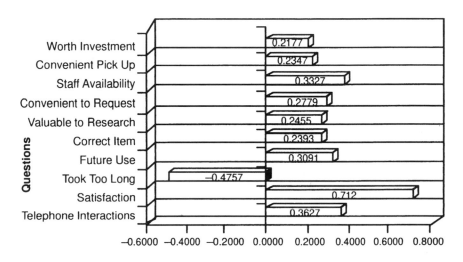

Pearson Correlation Coefficient

n = 474
p < .05

TABLE 9. Significant Pearson Correlation Coefficients Between Delivery Speed and Satisfaction at Individual Institutions

Institution	R
A	0.2841
B	N/S
C	N/S
D	N/S
E	0.3307
F	N/S
G	0.3897
H	0.2844
I	N/S
J	0.4144

p < .05 = Significant
N/S = Not Significant

TABLE 10. Multiple Regression
Dependent Variable = Delivery Speed

Variable	Partial R2	C(p)	F	Probability
Timeliness	0.1733	23.42	98.96	0.0001
Telephone Interaction	0.3680	3.43	21.96	0.0001
Convenient to Request	0.0048	2.54	2.90	0.0892
Staff Availability	0.0044	1.89	2.66	0.1030
Willingness to Pay	0.0043	1.32	2.59	0.1080
Number of Requests	0.0034	1.32	2.03	0.1545
Valuable to Research	0.0016	2.36	0.96	0.3265
Satisfaction	0.0008	3.87	0.50	0.4797

n = 474
No other variable met the .5 significance level for entry into the model

TABLE 11. Multiple Regression
Dependent Variable = Timeliness

Variable	Partial R2	C(p)	F	Probability
Satisfaction	0.5070	127.14	485.00	0.0001
Delivery Speed	0.0613	54.84	66.92	0.0001
Took Too Long	0.0247	26.97	28.48	0.0001
Telephone Interactions	0.0105	16.26	12.41	0.0005
Number of Requests	0.0050	12.15	6.02	0.0144
Correct Item	0.0032	10.34	3.78	0.0522
Value	0.0026	9.15	3.18	0.0751
Willingness to Pay	0.0016	9.20	1.94	0.1639
Worth Investment	0.0013	9.67	1.53	0.2167
Vendor Use	0.0010	10.51	1.16	0.2806
Convenient to Request	0.0009	11.44	1.06	0.3026
Convenient to Pick Up	0.0012	11.96	1.48	0.2242
Future Use	0.0006	13.29	0.67	0.4118

and timeliness. More than 50 percent of the variance for timeliness is accounted for by satisfaction, while delivery speed accounts for about 6 percent. Patrons' perceptions that the transaction took too long to be useful accounted for less than 3 percent of the variance. All three factors together account for almost 60 percent of the variance in the model and begin to draw a picture of what contributes to the customer's perception of timeliness.

Similarly, almost 63 percent of the variance for satisfaction is ascribable to timeliness, patron's willingness to use the service in the future, perceived staff availability and patron's assessment that the item received

TABLE 12. Multiple Regression
Dependent Variable = Satisfaction

Variable	Partial R2	C(p)	F	Probability
Timeliness	0.5070	170.65	485.47	0.0001
Future Use	0.0618	92.38	67.46	0.0001
Staff Availability	0.0435	37.91	52.66	0.0001
Correct Item	0.0011	25.36	13.94	0.0002
Convenient to Request	0.0055	20.20	6.94	0.0087
Vendor Use	0.0047	16.10	5.98	0.0148
Took Too Long	0.0051	11.44	6.61	0.0104
Telephone Interactions	0.0036	8.79	4.64	0.0316
Value	0.0023	7.82	2.98	0.0848
Number of Requests	0.0011	8.44	1.39	0.2388
Willingness to Pay	0.0006	9.62	0.82	0.3629

was the item ordered. All other variables contribute less than 1 percent. Clearly, the strongest correlations and predictive relationship exist between patrons' perception of timeliness and their level of satisfaction.

Although delivery speed plays a significant role in patrons' perception of timeliness in this study, it has only a trivial impact on customers' satisfaction. These findings confirm the pilot study's conclusion that patron satisfaction is not dependent on delivery speed. The speed of delivery and timeliness, on the other hand, are interdependent. F. W. Lancaster's suggestions that patrons have a definition of usefulness prompted us to conclude that perceptions of timeliness may depend on whether an item is received while it is still deemed useful.[18] Stuart defined this as "urgency of demand" and concluded it was more important than actual turnaround.[19] Our objective was to look at the data in a way that might pinpoint a "window of usefulness" common among academic library customers.

Analysis of variance and the Ryan Einot Gabriel Welsch Multiple Range test were used to distinguish a common "window of usefulness."[20] Independent variables were defined as institution and delivery speed. Delivery speed was grouped into quartiles to create variables with an equal number of responses in each category (delivery speed categories are: 0-8 days = short, 9-12 days = medium, 13-18 days = long, 19 or more days = longest).[21] Dependent variables were defined as means of patron responses to:

- "Based on this transaction, I am satisfied with interlibrary loan";
- "I received this item in a timely manner"; and
- "It took so long to receive this item, it was no longer useful to me."

Tables 13-15 show the results. The three dependent variables do not vary significantly according to which institution filled the request; nor is

TABLE 13. ANOVA and Multiple Range
Test for Timeliness

| | ANOVA for Timeliness | | | |
	Type III SS	Mean Square	F Value	Pr > F
Institution	12.92	1.43	1.75	0.0737
Delivery Speed	24.81	8.60	10.51	0.0001
Institution * Delivery Speed	20.97	0.77	0.95	0.5403
n = 772				
	Multiple Range Test for Timeliness			
	Grouping	Mean	N	
Longest	a	2.05	163	
Long	b	1.75	192	
Medium	b&c	1.63	163	
Short	c	1.45	232	
n = 710				

Note: MSE = .8186
Longest = 19 or More Days, Long = 13-18 Days, Medium = 9-12 Days, Short = 0-8 Days

TABLE 14. ANOVA And Multiple Range
Test for Satisfaction

| | ANOVA for Satisfaction | | | |
	Type III SS	Mean Square	F Value	Pr > F
Institution	6.04	0.6719	1.25	0.2637
Delivery Speed	7.69	2.5664	4.76	0.0027
Institution * Delivery Speed	10.39	0.3850	0.71	0.8569
n = 772				
	Multiple Range Test for Satisfaction			
	Grouping	Mean	N	
Longest	a	1.66	166	
Long	b	1.47	191	
Medium	b	1.40	158	
Short	b	1.33	230	
n = 745				

MSE = .5394
Longest = 19 or More Days, Long = 13-18 Days, Medium = 9-12 Days, Short = 0-8 Days

there a significant interaction effect between institution and delivery speed with respect to these same three variables. Delivery speed, though, does exhibit a significant relationship with all three dependent variables (satisfaction, timeliness, and delivery-in-time-to-be-useful). Correspondingly, the multiple range test consistently identifies the "longest" category as significantly different from the other delivery speed categories in all three

TABLE 15. ANOVA and Multiple Range
Test for "Took Too Long"

| | ANOVA for "Took Too Long" | | | |
	Type III SS	Mean Square	F Value	Pr > F
Institution	11.49	1.27	1.67	0.0914
Delivery Speed	16.59	5.53	7.25	0.0001
Institution * Delivery Speed	32.23	1.19	1.57	0.0349
n=772				
	Multiple Range Test for "Took Too Long"			
	Grouping	Mean	N	
Longest	b	4.16	157	
Long	a	4.44	180	
Medium	a	4.57	154	
Short	a	4.51	220	

n = 711
MSE = .7629
Longest =19 or More Days, Long = 13-18 Days, Medium = 9-12 Days, Short = 0-8 Days

tables. The remaining delivery speed categories vary among the tables. In Tables 13 and 14, the categories of "long" and "medium" are indistinguishable from one another. However, the category "short" differs significantly from "medium" only in Table 14.

It is clear that items received in 19 or more days do not meet the "window of usefulness" for the average academic patron. The analysis becomes fuzzier when the delivery speed is quicker. However, the strongest F values in Tables 13 and 15 show that the medium and short categories are indistinguishable. Therefore, a conservative interpretation would suggest that delivery speed should be 12 or fewer days to meet the "window of usefulness" for the average academic patron.

CONCLUSIONS

Although several statistical procedures were needed to establish our results, a summary can be stated quite simply.

- Our study confirms that patron satisfaction has little relationship to actual delivery speed.
- Patron satisfaction and patron perceptions of timeliness are strongly correlated.
- Only 17 percent of a patron's perception about timely receipt of an item can be predicted from actual delivery speed.

- Variances in responses to satisfaction, perceptions of timeliness and delivery-in-time-to-be-useful suggest that a delivery speed of 8-12 days is indistinguishable from shorter delivery times. Delivery times longer than 12 days, however, are significantly different.

These findings are important for many reasons. First, they confirm similar findings by Kinnucan in which he concluded that academic library faculty did not attach great importance to the difference in delivery time for material that arrived within one day or within two weeks.[22] Kinnucan's findings did reveal greater delivery speed sensitivity among graduate students.

Perhaps, though, the greatest importance of these results relates to cost. Defining an acceptable "window of usefulness" helps control costs by identifying when enough resources have been spent to improve delivery speed. In times of ever-decreasing resources, knowing when one can stop spending and still satisfy customers will become ever more vital. Debunking the belief that delivery speed is the best measure of document delivery service forces librarians to seek a greater understanding of their customers. Practitioners may begin to take another look at similar long-standing assumptions in an effort to decide what library patrons value and where librarians' limited resources should be concentrated.

The study also suggests factors other than cost are important. For example, convenient placement of requests is a current trend. Many institutions are developing World Wide Web access and non-mediated request placement. These developments and the discussion in the literature of models for document delivery that eliminate mediation, underlie an assumption that convenience is the highest of priorities.[23] The results in Table 12 support convenience as a factor, but suggest it is of minor importance. Of course, there are other reasons librarians pursue non-mediated request placement. Savings in staff time is one and matching service convenience with vendors is another.

Staff availability and telephone interactions with staff affect customer perceptions. These factors and their impact contradict the push to eliminate staff in the request placement scenario. Although it is not clear from this study what type of interaction contributes to an increase in satisfaction, the value of that personal contact is evident when noting Tables 10-13. All include telephone interactions. One explanation may be that staff interactions provide an increased opportunity for the patrons to adequately communicate their "window of usefulness." This allows staff to rank transactions to meet individual needs. These exchanges may also improve the patron's understanding of limitations and problems that characterize a particular request, reducing any negative interpretations of delays. If true, increased contact may increase satisfaction for the more difficult requests.

The value of this study is not limited to the identification and ranking of customer concerns. This research provides solid benchmarking on the speed and quality of services now offered at academic libraries. It is one contribution in a number of recent studies that provides comparative data. However, it provides some information that is not available in most other research. In particular, the length of time between receipt of the item by the borrowing library and the customer's receipt is an issue previously unexamined. Clearly, though, reducing that time can make a significant difference in the net delivery speed. Assuming responsibility for "complete delivery" (delivery from the point of request to the receipt by the patron) moves the examination of customer satisfaction to a new level.

In a recent issue of *Harvard Business Review*, Thomas Jones and Earl Sasser raise a new concern about the limitations of knowing when a customer is satisfied versus when customers are "completely satisfied."[24] In their discussion, the authors analyze customer loyalty and report that completely satisfied customers are six times more likely to repeat their business than customers who are merely satisfied. Why should this be a growing concern among librarians? Jones and Sasser analyzed data from highly competitive businesses and monopolies. In particular, the hospital market, which often has little or no competition, mirrors libraries. Due to developments in HMOs, hospitals may soon find themselves in a much more competitive atmosphere. Due to rapid growth in document delivery vendors, libraries are beginning to compete more than ever before. When competition develops in previously unchallenged markets, Jones and Sasser maintain that long-established services may quickly decline in popularity because their customer's satisfaction was based on a non-competitive model. Businesses which face growing competition will lose if their customers are merely satisfied. Loyalty, the authors maintain, is the result of complete satisfaction.

Why do academic libraries need loyalty when their services are free? Such might be the first question posed by academic librarians, who usually run the only library on campus. However, it is an inadequate answer for university administrators looking at options to fund library collection development or purchase document delivery vendor contracts. Without customer loyalty, libraries may see customers defect when vendors become viable alternatives. Although many arguments can be offered that indicate vendors have a long way to go before they can substitute for the variety and complexity of services offered by libraries, the viability of document delivery vendors is undeniable. Librarians should be positioned to give up a market if they determine it is not cost effective, rather than losing a market they would rather provide. To guarantee that position, librarians must know how to completely satisfy customers.

This study is one effort in what is a growing need to find out what customers want and how well libraries provide. More research is essential to establishing customer loyalty. Such research must include non-customers to incorporate latent demand in our calculations for providing service. The importance of retaining current customer loyalty and of increasing the customer base is emphasized in recent debates among interlibrary loan discussion groups. Richard Dougherty, in response to comments on the ILL-L discussion group about the future of interlibrary loan, exhorts librarians to take charge.

> Decide what is the unit's preferred service and then figure out how to achieve it. Involve stakeholders who can influence the outcome, e.g., other public service librarians, current and potential customers, etc. In point of fact this is what companies that are reengineering themselves are doing. The successful ones are those that are taking a proactive approach.[25]

NOTES

1. Richard Boss, *Document Delivery in the United States: A Report to the Council on Library Resources* (Washington, DC: Council on Library Resources, 1983).

2. Pat Weaver-Meyers, Shelley Clement and Carolyn Mahin, *Interlibrary Loan in Academic and Research Libraries: Workload and Staffing* (Washington, DC: Office of Management Services, Association of Research Libraries, 1988).

3. Kathleen Kurosman and Barbara Ammerman Durniak, "Document Delivery: A Comparison of Commercial Document Suppliers and Interlibrary Loan Services," *College and Research Libraries* 55 (March 1994): 129-139.

4. Wilbur Stolt, Pat Weaver-Meyers and Molly Murphy, "Interlibrary Loan and Customer Satisfaction: How Important is Delivery Speed?" in Richard Amrhein (Ed.) *Continuity and Transformation: The Promise of Confluence* (Chicago, IL: Association of College and Research Libraries, 1995), 365-371.

5. Anna H. Perrault and Marjo Arseneau, "User Satisfaction and Interlibrary Loan Service: A Study at Louisiana State University," *RQ* 35 no. 1 (Fall 1995):90-100; Wayne Pedersen and David Gregory, "Interlibrary Loan and Commercial Document Supply: Finding the Right Fit," *Journal of Academic Librarianship* 19 (Nov. 1994): 263-272. In this case, the calculations went further and eliminated the additional time required between patron submission of the request and the actual ordering date.

6. Barbara Buckner Higginbotham and Sally Bowdoin, *Access Versus Assets: A Comprehensive Guide to Resource Sharing for Academic Libraries* (Chicago, IL: American Library Association, 1994), 275-280.

7. Higginbotham and Bowdoin, 205.

8. Wayne Pedersen and David Gregory, "Interlibrary Loan and Commercial Document Supply: Finding the Right Fit, 263.

9. Kathleen Kurosman and Barbara Ammerman Durniak, "Document Delivery: A Comparison of Commercial Document Suppliers and Interlibrary Loan Services," 138.

10. Anna H. Perrault and Marjo Arseneau, "User Satisfaction and Interlibrary Loan Service: A Study at Louisiana State University."

11. Emory University ILL User Survey Form can be found at URL: http://www.emory.edu/LIB/survey.htm

12. A Summary report of the results of the Emory University ILL User Survey can be found at URL: http://www.emory.edu/LIB/execsum.htm.

13. Peter Hernon and Charles McClure, *Evaluation and Library Decision Making* (Norwood, NJ: Ablex, 1990), 34.

14. Cronbach coefficient alpha is a standard measure of reliability that varies between zero and 1.00. A perfectly reliable instrument has a reliability of 1.00. The higher the coefficient the more the instrument is free of error variance and the stronger confidence one can have that the instrument is a measure of the true differences among respondents.

15. It is worth noting that the patron who received the item in 313 days agreed with the statement, "Based on this transaction, I am satisfied with interlibrary loan service." The patron disagreed with the statement, "I received this item in a timely manner." This confirms the findings of a 1978 study: M. L. Herman, *Idaho Interlibrary Loan: A Study of Fill Rate, Turnaround Time, Patron Satisfaction and Characteristics of Requests* (Denver, CO: Graduate School of Librarianship, University of Denver, 1978), ED 165749.

16. All correlations described here were generated with SAS procedure: proc corr no miss alpha.

17. All regressions described here were generated with SAS procedure: proc reg/method = forward.

18. F. W. Lancaster, *The Measurement and Evaluation of Library Services*, 235.

19. M. Stuart, "Some Effects on Library Users of the Delays in Supplying Publications," *ASLIB Proceedings* 29 (January 1977): 35-45.

20. All ANOVA described here were generated with SAS procedure: proc glm/regwq.

21. Categories were determined by dividing the responses to delivery speed into frequency quartiles 0-25 percent, 26-50 percent, 51-75 percent, 76-100 percent using SAS frequencies procedures. Although the categories were of equal size initially, the N of some categories changed when missing dependent variables were encountered. Institution was included so that it could be factored out, if proven to be a significant influence.

22. Mark T. Kinnucan, "Demand for Document Delivery and Interlibrary Loan in Academic Settings," *Library and Information Science Research* 15 (1993): 355-374.

23. Mary E. Jackson, "Integrating ILL with Document Delivery: Five Models," *Wilson Library Bulletin* 68(1993): 76-78.

24. Thomas O. Jones and Earl Sasser, Jr., "Why Satisfied Customers Defect," *Harvard Business Review* 73(Nov-Dec 1996): 88-99.

25. Richard M. Dougherty, "The(re) is a future for ILL," *ILL-L@usc.edu*".

The Value of Interlibrary Loan: An Analysis of Customer Satisfaction Survey Comments

Yem S. Fong

SUMMARY. An analysis of comments drawn from a customer satisfaction survey assesses how users value interlibrary loan services in research environments. This study reveals that value and general customer satisfaction are given high marks when staff interactions are experienced positively, and when services are considered convenient and easy to use. Most respondents are unwilling to pay for expedited delivery and are surprised at the average cost to borrow an item. These comments support the theory that customer satisfaction relies on multiple characteristics of service and not on turnaround time alone. *[Article copies available from The Haworth Document Delivery Service: 1-800-342-9678. E-mail address: getinfo@haworth.com]*

INTRODUCTION

In 1994 the American Library Association adopted a revised National Interlibrary Loan Code that reflected a major shift in how librarians view interlibrary loan (ILL). Recognizing that information technology has significantly enhanced interlibrary cooperation, the code states "Interlibrary

---

Yem S. Fong is Assistant Professor and Head of Information Delivery Services at the University of Colorado at Boulder.

[Haworth co-indexing entry note]: "The Value of Interlibrary Loan: An Analysis of Customer Satisfaction Survey Comments." Fong, Yem S. Co-published simultaneously in *Journal of Library Administration* (The Haworth Press, Inc.) Vol. 23, No. 1/2, 1996, pp. 43-54; and: *Interlibrary Loan/Document Delivery and Customer Satisfaction: Strategies for Redesigning Services* (ed: Pat L. Weaver-Meyers, Wilbur A. Stolt, and Yem S. Fong) The Haworth Press, Inc., 1996, pp. 43-54. Single or multiple copies of this article are available from The Haworth Document Delivery Service [1-800-342-9678, 9:00 a.m. - 5:00 p.m. (EST). E-mail address: getinfo@haworth.com].

borrowing is an integral element of collection development for all libraries, not an ancillary option."[1] Increasingly acknowledged by library administrators, the notion of access and the principals of resource sharing take on greater importance for libraries in setting budgets and defining collection policies. It is safe to assume then that interlibrary loan and document delivery as a service is "valued" in the profession. But what of the consumers of this service? Do they also place value on interlibrary loan?

Value can be defined as: (1) monetary worth of something; (2) relative worth, utility, or importance: degree of excellence.[2] Traditionally libraries, viewed as 'good' and 'free,' are valued in Western culture. Extending beyond libraries, information is valued as a resource and a commodity. Do users attribute these same qualities to library services such as interlibrary loan? Recent customer satisfaction studies of interlibrary loan have begun to shed light on users' perceptions of this service. Survey comments from a customer satisfaction study among the Greater Midwest Research Libraries Consortium (GMRLC) provide additional answers to these questions.

MEASURING VALUE

There are relatively few works in the library literature that explicitly measure value from the perception of the consumer. Typically evaluations of library services are based on performance measures and levels of use rather than on subjective perceptions of how a service benefitted the user. In a study comparing user expectations and user satisfaction at Louisiana State University faculty and graduate students were asked to rank the following priorities in ILL: (1) speed (2) cost (3) obtaining materials regardless of speed and cost. Results indicated that obtaining the materials regardless of speed or cost ranked as the highest priority by both groups.[3] This supports the assumption that ILL is necessary and important to users.

The concept of value is more thoroughly examined in market and business research where managers seek to identify the economic value of information, information systems and information services. Value is most often related to use and to cost/benefits. The literature reveals that there are numerous approaches to assessing the value of information and problems with these approaches as well. Kemp in an article on the changing value of information notes:

> The complicating factor for the providers of library and information services is the uncertainty of the value of a piece of information. The

value varies according to the customer, the certainty of the information, its immediate future relevance and applicability, and the structural or political factors surrounding its reception. Thus, the ultimate value of information to the user comes from its expected use at some future point and is influenced by the circumstances of its use.[4]

Ahituv notes that the value of information, which he distinguishes from data, is based on multiple attributes that may be categorized as: (1) Timeliness–recency, response time, frequency; (2) Contents–accuracy, relevance, exhaustiveness; (3) Format–the way information is displayed; (4) Cost of providing the information.[5] In a study on information delivery, Broadbent and Lofgren utilize the perceived value approach based on subjective evaluations by both managers and users.[6]

Jose-Marie Griffiths of King Research Inc. has identified three different types of value that we can extrapolate to interlibrary loan: (1) Willingness to pay–not only in monetary terms but also in terms of the actual time a user has. (2) What would users do if the ILL service was not available–difference between what it would cost to go elsewhere and what it costs to run the service internally. (3) Benefits from having access to an information service–savings in time, dollars and duplicate research.[7] Findings indicate that organizations receive a high rate of return on their investment in a library or information service. Griffiths estimates that it would cost an organization almost twice as much per professional if they did not have a library or service in house.[8] In these studies information services are perceived as valuable by both the organizations and their users. These findings lend support to the belief that interlibrary loan is a valuable service. The in-depth analysis of customer comments that follows corroborates this perception.

CUSTOMER SATISFACTION SURVEY

The GMRLC customer satisfaction survey was implemented in 1995 among ten consortia participants. It contains two questions that specifically focus on value (see Appendix Figure A.1).

Question #9. This item was valuable to my research.

Question #15. The average cost of ILL transactions is about $18. This material was worth that investment.

Question nine seeks to link value to research while question 15 relates value to monetary worth. Survey results for all institutions show a mean of 1.3456 on question nine (see Appendix Table C.9). Using the ranking scale 1-5, with 1 = strongly agree and 5 = strongly disagree, this indicates strong agreement with the statement. A mean of 2.0099 for question 15 shows that there is significant acknowledgement of the monetary worth of the borrowed material (see Appendix Table C.15).

In the section available for 'Comments' users freely and anonymously wrote opinions, suggestions or criticisms of their institution's interlibrary loan service. From analyzing these comments answers to the following emerge: (1) What are users' perceptions of the value of interlibrary loan? (2) What issues were raised most often in the comments? (3) Did the comments support survey results?

The customer comments were difficult to classify into single categories. They often referred to several points raised in the survey. Sometimes comments were short and sweet, such as "Great job." In one instance an entire typed letter was attached to the survey expounding on the user's many thoughts and feelings about ILL. The comments were classified as closely to the variables in the survey as possible (see Appendix Table A.4). Other categories were added to encompass the scope of the comments. The majority fit into the following categories:

- Speed/Timeliness
- Value
- Staff Interactions
- Request Process
- Delivery
- Reliability/Quality
- Communications with ILL Office/Notification
- Access vs. Acquisitions/Library or University Policies
- Costs/Worth $18
- Satisfaction

ANALYSIS

Table 1 shows the results of the customer comments by categories. A total of 349 respondents wrote comments out of 770 completed surveys administered by the GMRLC Libraries. Since comments often referred to more than one question or idea, 513 comments, partial comments or points were identified (see Appendix F.1). Users were overwhelmingly positive about the value of interlibrary loan, satisfaction with the service and staff interaction. Critical comments fell mostly under the categories of speed, cost, communication and access vs. acquisitions issues. The remaining categories pointed to trends and concerns that will be useful for re-designing interlibrary loan and document delivery.

TABLE 1. 1995 GMRLC Customer Satisfaction Survey Respondent Comments by General Subject Category

Subject Category	Number of Responses
Speed	63
Value	98
Staff Interaction	72
Request Process	20
Delivery	15
Reliability	35
Communication	26
Access vs. Acquisition	55
Cost	55
Satisfaction	74

VALUE

The largest number of comments fell under the category of value. Since the comment section followed the last question on the survey referring to whether the material was worth $18, the placement of this question seems to have influenced what users said. Users mostly perceived ILL as valuable, using terms such as "essential to research," "indispensable," "necessary," vital." Comments range from: "The ILL service is very useful and helpful to me" to "Without this service, I could not do necessary research." Respondents clearly acknowledged the value of ILL to their research. In some instances users noted that it was difficult to determine beforehand if an item would be relevant.

> The biggest problem I've had with ILL is that I have ordered things that end up being useless because I had too little information when I ordered it . . . It is very difficult to tell what titles to order on the online abstracts or synopsis.

Representative of 10% or more of the comments was the recognition of the need for ILL in place of owning a journal subscription.

> ILL is the only way I can perform a comprehensive literature review. I would prefer immediate access to journals, but I can live with the inconveniences of ILL. Thank you for providing the service.

While users perceived value in ILL services, they also questioned the libraries collections policies.

ACCESS VS. ACQUISITION

Fifty-five comments were related to a library or university's collection policy or funding. Many of these remarked on the lack of available materials:

> Given the Library's poor collection, investment in databases and ILL is the only practical way to maintain a research capability. It is a prudent investment.

Several users challenged libraries' purchasing choices when commenting on the cost of interlibrary loan:

> Subscription to journal would be more cash effective.

> I think the library, as a whole, might do better to monitor texts requests on ILL, then order them for the permanent collection.

> Library needs to look at costs of ILL vs. having complete collection–I have to use ILL often with this journal because the library doesn't have some years.

These responses indicate that libraries might do a better job of communicating to users how collection policies work and how funding mechanisms affect libraries. Other comments regarding acquisitions policies and costs reinforce the belief that library services should be free:

> A fee of $10 would put this service out of my reach. Many of the books I order (and articles) should be in our library. A better investment of your money would be to buy and process books in a timely manner.

> That seems like an outrageous overcharge rip-off ($18) by somebody. Why does this administration not give a fixed % of grant indirect cost directly to the library? That would provide incentive to write grant proposals.

COST

Two questions on the survey addressed the cost of ILL, Question 10, Willingness to pay $10 for speedier service, and question 15, Worth $18 investment. These figures were eye opening and generated some contentious comments.

> $18 seems high.

> A resource more directly related would probably be worth $18.

> $18? That's insane. If I and a few other faculty request 10 or so articles per year it would cost more than the journal subscription. Why so expensive?

Out of 55 comments related to cost only six indicated willingness to pay.

> Sometimes I would like to pay for faster delivery.

These sentiments are in line with survey results which found that users were not willing to pay $10 (see Appendix Table C.10). While library users pay for information, i.e., purchase textbooks, newspaper subscriptions, electronic services and equipment, the cost of library services continues to remain essentially hidden. The Association of Research Libraries provided an immense service to libraries by calculating the average unit cost of borrowing and lending an item at almost $30 per request.[9] Consumers for the most part are uneducated about the range and depth of library costs, continuing to view library services as ones that should be "free."

SPEED/TIMELINESS

Customer comments regarding turnaround time indicated a strong desire for speedier delivery of an ILL request. Nearly half of the comments in this group expressed opinions such as,

> Sometimes requests take too long.

> I would like faster service, but I do not intend to pay fees.

> I had good luck this time, but my last ILL request was returned without me ever being contacted, and had to be re-requested (a 6 week wait).

These comments support the literature's claims that users want speedier service. Conversely, in the GMRLC survey users were satisfied with time frames met (see Appendix Table C.3). A minority perception is expressed by this user who was unsatisfied with turnaround time and felt that ILL was not beneficial.

> It took over 2 months to get this article. I finally wrote the author and he faxed me a copy and I've been doing research from this information for 6 weeks now. ILL is not useful to me. A fee of $10 is pretty steep!

STAFF INTERACTION

ILL services have commonly involved a great deal of interaction between staff and customers depending on how offices are configured, i.e., centralized or decentralized, and whether electronic request systems are in place. Library studies that attempt to measure customer satisfaction recognize the relationship between customer expectations and perception of satisfaction. Francoise Hebert's study of ILL in 38 large public libraries in Canada uses service quality measures to compare ILL from the perspective of both the library and the library customer. One interesting result indicates that how services are provided may, in some instances, outweigh the "technical quality" dimension, i.e., speed, cost, etc., of what services are delivered.[10] Interactions with staff make up a large part of this perception.

In this study, customers gave high marks to staff and usually did not distinguish between phone and personal interactions.

> ILL staff is always helpful and friendly. I'm very satisfied with their service.

Comments on staff interaction ranked third following value and satisfaction, 72 out of 513. They were mostly appreciative and complementary, describing staff as excellent, exemplary, courteous, efficient, etc. Those who valued ILL frequently commented on positive staff interactions and general satisfaction with the service. This lends credence to the theory that satisfaction is independent of speed.

COMMUNICATION

Comments regarding communication by the ILL office were more mixed than those on staff interaction. These included concerns about the lack of notification regarding the status of requests.

With multiple requests it is difficult to keep track with the current system. Notification varies, sometimes I get a call, sometimes the article is mailed . . .

I would like to be notified of the progress of my other requests.

Other communication issues had to do with e-mail request systems.

With the new ZAP system it is not convenient to check on ongoing loan requests. There is no need to notify the recipient via regular mail at his/her private address. How about e-mail or campus mail?

Communication comments indicated a need for keeping users informed of the progress of their requests. As offices move to comprehensive ILL management software packages accessible via the Internet these issues will lessen. More efficient ways of communicating with users about their requests seems to be the major concern.

REQUEST PROCESSING

Related to communications is the request process. Comments on the convenience of e-mail requesting ranked high.

I appreciate the e-mail service. I found the old forms somewhat inconvenient, but the ability to use e-mail requests will greatly increase my ILL use.

Critical comments had to do with the need to supply the same information when making multiple requests, presumably filling paper requests.

I use ILL primarily for journal articles–it is time consuming to fill out the "card" with the same information time after time.

DELIVERY

Positive comments on delivery appeared when institutions mailed items to home addresses and when picking up materials at branch libraries was an option. These two options were also listed as desired services in institutions that did not offer them.

RELIABILITY

In the article by Hebert, reliability is listed as the number one performance measure of satisfaction.[11] Her study reports that customers frequently rated satisfaction with ILL as high even if a request was unfilled, and conversely, users were often dissatisfied after receiving a filled request.[12] In the GMRLC survey reliability in terms of receiving the correct item was high (see Appendix Table C.8). It is interesting to note that comments from users at the same institution often generated completely different experiences: "Screwed up! Please get this right the next time." At the same institution: "I am very pleased with the service I received." Included in this category are comments on quality problems, usually poor photocopies. In general customers had experiences such as these:

> On most occasions this service works very well. This was one where it didn't. Some of the articles never came to me.

> This request was handled promptly and was 'in time.' I have made requests that never were completed and was disappointed.

SATISFACTION

Seventy-four comments fell into this category. Frequently they were 'short and sweet' in nature such as,

> ILL provides excellent service.

> I am very pleased with the work of ILL. I make many requests, and have always been quite satisfied.

Satisfaction indicators correlated mostly with comments on value. Expressions of overall satisfaction agreed with survey results that reported a mean of 1.4563 for all institutions on satisfaction with the individual transaction (see Appendix Table C.5). Given the mix and range of comments in other categories the fact that positive comments on ILL service and general satisfaction ranked second to value confirms Hebert's belief that

> Customer expectations of what a service should be exist at two levels: a desired level and an adequate level, separated by a zone of tolerance which varies across customers and expands or contracts within the same customer.[13]

CONCLUSIONS

When reviewing these comments it is important to keep in mind the context of the survey, which focuses on different measures of customer satisfaction. These comments are essentially given by a random group of ILL users picking up or receiving requested material. Only those who chose to comment did so. Comments may have been significantly different if the survey had included all potential users which would bring in those who rarely use the service or dissatisfied customers who choose not to use ILL for specific reasons. The customer comments are very subjective with the user's attention drawn to the individual transaction.

What do these customer comments tell us about their perceptions of interlibrary loan? Users tell us it is difficult to know in advance the value or quality of the information received as a result of an ILL transaction. As noted by Kemp, the ultimate value of information to the user lies in the expected use at some future point. Kemp further points out that in order to fully assess the value of ILL we would need to determine: the critical importance to the user, the type of information sought, the cost of service, and whether the user had other options.[14] The user's level of need and the availability of alternative sources are additional factors to consider. As Web resources increase and vendor costs decrease interlibrary loan may cease to be the only viable option for obtaining research material.

The comments do indicate that users perceive the value of interlibrary loan as essential and important for research given their library's collections. Most are unwilling to pay for this service and view the libraries as having a responsibility to carry the materials needed for their work. Users would prefer that the library purchase subscriptions for immediate access but are willing to rely on the "inconvenience" of ILL when necessary.

Other indicators from these responses tell us that $18 sounds extremely high. Only a handful of users would pay for expedited delivery. E-mail request systems and communication are popular among ILL users, and notification via e-mail would be preferred to mail. Although there were some reliability problems, customers were pleased with staff interactions and generally satisfied with interlibrary loan service.

While these comments are subjective impressions and evaluations they are informative. This qualitative aspect of the larger customer satisfaction study provides a fuller picture of user's perceptions than can be assessed by quantitative methods alone. The conclusions reached here should be included with the descriptive and inferential data presented elsewhere in this volume when drawing complex conclusions about patrons' perceptions.

NOTES

1. Interlibrary Loan Committee, Management and Operation of Public Services Section, Reference and Adult Services Division, American Library Association, *National Interlibrary Loan Code for the United States, 1993.* RQ 33 no. 4 (Summer 1994): 1.

2. *Webster's Ninth New Collegiate Dictionary* (Springfield: Merriam-Webster, Inc., 1983), 1303.

3. Anna H. Perrault and Marjo Arseneau, "User Satisfaction and Interlibrary Loan Service: A Study at Louisiana State University," *RQ* 35, no. 1 (Fall 1995): 97.

4. Susan Kemp, "The Changing Value of Information in a Global Economy," *The Value of Library Information Services* (Australia: CSIRO Publications, 1992), 4.

5. Niv Ahituv, "Assessing the Value of Information: Problems and Approaches," *Proceedings of the Tenth International Conference on Information Systems* (Boston: December 4-6, 1989), 317.

6. Marianne Broadbent and Hans Lofgren, "Information Delivery: Identifying Priorities, Performance, and Value," *Information Processing & Management,* v. 29, no. 6 (1993):684.

7. Jose-Marie Griffiths, "How Library and Information Services in the US Indicate Value," *The Value of Information Services* (Australia: CSIRO Publications, 1992), 36-37.

8. Ibid., 40.

9. Marilyn M. Roche, *ARL/RLG Interlibrary Loan Cost Study, Association of Research Libraries* (June 1993), 4.

10. Francoise Hebert, "Service Quality, An Unobtrusive Investigation of Interlibrary Loan in Large Public Libraries in Canada," *Library & Information Science Research,* v. 16, no. 1 (Winter 1994): 18.

11. Ibid., 17.

12. Ibid., 15.

13. Ibid., 13.

14. Susan Kemp, "The Changing Value of Information in a Global Economy," 4.

Patron Satisfaction at Any Cost?
A Case Study of Interlibrary Loan
in Two U.S. Research Libraries

Lee-Allison Levene
Wayne Pedersen

SUMMARY. Data from a survey on interlibrary loan customer satisfaction conducted among Greater Midwest Research Library Consortia members is compared to institution-specific data from two of the participating libraries. Results are discussed in the context of office procedures and service policies at Iowa State University Library and University of Arkansas Library. Contrasts in policies at each institution are discussed in light of results that show significant differences in supplier charges per request and delivery speed, but little difference in patron satisfaction. *[Article copies available from The Haworth Document Delivery Service: 1-800-342-9678. E-mail address: getinfo@haworth.com]*

INTRODUCTION

In terms of performance evaluation, interlibrary loan (ILL) has to be one of the most studied and analyzed public services offered by libraries

---

Lee-Allison Levene is Head of Interlibrary Loan and Document Delivery at the University of Arkansas, Fayetteville.
Wayne Pedersen is Head of Resource Sharing at Iowa State University.

[Haworth co-indexing entry note]: "Patron Satisfaction at Any Cost? A Case Study of Interlibrary Loan in Two U.S. Research Libraries." Levene, Lee-Allison, and Wayne Pedersen. Co-published simultaneously in *Journal of Library Administration* (The Haworth Press, Inc.) Vol. 23, No. 1/2, 1996, pp. 55-71; and: *Interlibrary Loan/Document Delivery and Customer Satisfaction: Strategies for Redesigning Services* (ed: Pat L. Weaver-Meyers, Wilbur A. Stolt, and Yem S. Fong) The Haworth Press, Inc., 1996, pp. 55-71. Single or multiple copies of this article are available from The Haworth Document Delivery Service [1-800-342-9678, 9:00 a.m. - 5:00 p.m. (EST). E-mail address: getinfo@haworth.com].

55

today. The best evidence for this is found in Thomas Waldhart's review article "Performance Evaluation of Interlibrary Loan in the United States: A Review of Research." In his review, Waldhart outlines four measures commonly used to evaluate interlibrary loan performance: (1) Satisfaction rate (sometimes called success rate or fill rate), (2) Speed of supply (also referred to as response time, turnaround time, or satisfaction time), (3) Cost or efficiency, (4) User satisfaction or user inconvenience.[1] Of these four measures, the last has received the least attention in the published literature, and most of the studies that do exist have been conducted in the United Kingdom.[2] User satisfaction was identified by Waldhart in 1985 as an area in need of additional published research despite the otherwise large body of literature dealing with interlibrary loan performance.

The paucity of user satisfaction studies in interlibrary loan is still noticeable in the mid-1990s. Moreover, the extant literature is limited to data that is primarily descriptive in nature. An exception to this is the study done by Francoise Hebert, who conducted a survey of ILL users in large public libraries in Canada. Her research pointed to "a mismatch between library measures of quality for interlibrary loan, which are based on fill rate and turnaround time, and customer measures of quality, which are based on different criteria."[3] To date, the only published study of ILL user satisfaction in U.S. libraries is that written by Perrault and Arseneau.[4] Their study of ILL service at Louisiana State University examined descriptive data and was limited to one institution. Ten years after the publication of Waldhart's review, the need for more research in the area of ILL user satisfaction is still apparent.

This report compares the results of a 1995 ILL user satisfaction survey conducted among the Greater Midwest Regional Library Consortium (GMRLC) members with those results specific to Iowa State University (ISU) and University of Arkansas (AFU). Policies and procedures at these institutions are described and compared throughout the analysis to determine how different service strategies may affect customer satisfaction.

METHODOLOGY

In April 1994, ten members of the Greater Midwest Research Library Consortium (GMRLC) distributed a survey instrument to users of their respective interlibrary borrowing services (see Appendix, Figure A.1). Each library was instructed to reproduce two hundred copies of the questionnaire and enclose one form with every third borrowing request received in the office, regardless of whether the material was a copy or a book loan, or whether the patron had already received a questionnaire for a previous request. The intent was to have the user evaluate each transaction, rather than the interlibrary borrowing service in general.

Before attaching the questionnaire to the requested material, interlibrary loan staff filled out the following information: method of request placement, method of delivery, date requested, type of notification, and requestor's status (faculty, graduate student, undergraduate, etc.).

Patrons were asked to fill in the date they actually received the item and estimate how many books or articles they had requested in the past year. In addition, they were asked to respond to thirteen questions regarding ILL service by assigning a Likert-type scale from 1 to 5, with 1 indicating strong agreement and 5 strong disagreement. If users had any comments they wanted to make, a section was also provided.

Users were asked to return the form to the Interlibrary Loan office in person or by mail. A return address was placed on each survey instrument, along with postage, if the patron's address was off campus. Two months were allowed for the return of all survey forms. When the deadline had elapsed, all forms were sent to the project coordinator at the University of Oklahoma.

SAS statistical software was utilized to analyze the data for each institution and for the group as a whole. Pearson Product Moment correlations, statistics of central tendency and multiple regressions were all used in comparisons of the services at ISU and AFU.

Interlibrary Borrowing and Document Delivery at Iowa State

Rapid growth in interlibrary borrowing and document delivery appears to be the norm among research libraries in the United States, and the situation at Iowa State University (ISU) is no exception. The last three years have witnessed exceptional growth in the volume of borrowing activity. In FY92 a total of 6,499 borrowing requests were filled. This grew to 7,529 in FY93, a 16 percent increase. The following year there was a 10 percent growth to 8,279 filled requests. In FY95 the situation exploded, growing to 11,172. Never before had the total number of filled requests at the ISU Library been in five figures. The 35 percent increase in a single year brought with it a real challenge to the ILL borrowing staff and coincided with the subsidization of borrowing fees by the Iowa State University Library.

Subsidized borrowing, or the payment of ILL borrowing fees by the host library rather than the end user, is a recent development at Iowa State University. Before July 1994 all fees charged by suppliers (hereafter called charges) were passed on to the ILL patron. Since that time, however, all charges up to $20 per request have been paid by the library from collection funds. Any amount over $20 must be paid by the end-user. In FY95, the first full year of subsidized borrowing, the ISU library spent $16,256.06 to obtain documents and book loans for its patrons. Of this total, $10,405.75 (64 percent) was paid to other libraries, $4,703.76 (29 percent) was paid to commercial suppliers such as Ebscodoc, UMI, and CARL Uncover, and $1,146.55 (7 percent) was paid to the Copyright Clearance Center (CCC) for copyright royalties. Clearly, the ISU borrowing operation makes heavier use of other libraries than it does commercial suppliers. Dividing the total charges paid in FY95 ($16,256.06) by the total number of filled requests (11,172), results in an average charge of $1.46 per request.

As outlined above, there was a total growth rate of 72 percent in filled requests from FY92 to FY95 at Iowa State University. Despite this significant increase in business, it appears that service has not suffered. In fact, it would appear that it has actually improved. One measure of ILL service quality is turnaround time. Since March 1992, six samples of turnaround time have been taken of the ILL borrowing service at ISU. The first four samples were measured in terms of calendar days from the date ordered by the ISU library patron to the date the item (photocopied document or book loan) arrived in the ILL office. The initial sample of 153 requests placed in March 1992 showed an overall average of 24 days. The next two samples demonstrated a consistent and steady drop in turnaround time. In August 1992 it averaged 13 days for 132 requests and in November 1992 it averaged 12 days for 152 requests. The fourth sample, in April 1993, bucked the trend and increased the time to 17 days in a sample of 100 requests. Beginning with the fifth sample in October 1993, turnaround time was calculated differently: from the date ordered by the ILL office to the date received in the office. The overall average time was 11 days for 201 requests. The final sample of February 1994 showed an overall average of just nine delivery days on 319 requests. In this two-year period, delivery time had therefore been cut by an impressive 63 percent.

Many changes have been put into place at ISU to improve ILL borrowing service, especially as it relates to turnaround time. Some of these changes include the installation of ARIEL text digitizing technology, streamlined work procedures, extensive use of union list information, the use of SaveIt for work flow management, and a new expedited level of borrowing service. Since July 1993, the ISU library has offered a two-tiered level of ILL service for its borrowing clientele: Priority and regular. ILL patrons are told that regular service will take anywhere from one to three weeks to arrive, and there is normally no charge. There is no limit to the number of regular requests a user can make. If ILL users need an item in less than a week, they are directed to the priority service. There is a minimum charge of $5 to the patron for each priority request, and there is a limit of one per person per day. Full-time staff work individually with the patron to negotiate the delivery time and cost of all priority requests. The priority service has proven quite popular; since its inception, an average of 26 such requests have been filled per month.

Currently, ISU's borrowing service is limited to faculty, staff, students, and extramural borrowers (individuals with an ISU library card). Users are required to place requests by filling out paper forms. These forms may be mailed in, but it is recommended that they be submitted in person. Plans are underway to offer patron access to electronic ILL borrowing forms, preferably on the World Wide Web (WWW). Because the options for placing ILL borrowing requests are limited, it is deemed important to have the office open on the weekends and evenings. Thus, during the time school is in session, the ILL office is open a total of 65 hours per week at ISU.

Staffing is a key element in the provision of ILL service. The borrowing service at ISU is staffed by 1.67 FTE's of student labor, almost one FTE of a faculty librarian position, and almost 4 FTE's of paraprofessionals, called merit staff at ISU.

It is important to note that the ISU borrowing service has two specialized services beyond obtaining book loans and photocopied documents. One is the on-demand purchase of NTIS reports. If a patron wants an NTIS report and it is available at or below a predetermined cost, the library will purchase the item through the ILL operation, place the material in Microforms when it arrives and then notify the patron. The ILL office also purchases personal copies of theses and dissertations for library patrons from UMI.

Interlibrary Borrowing and Document Delivery at the University of Arkansas, Fayetteville

The University of Arkansas, Fayetteville, is the main university campus in the state with a current enrollment of 14,850 students. This campus supports twenty-four doctoral degree and seventy master's degree programs, in addition to a broad-based undergraduate curriculum. The University Libraries are comprised of the main library, Mullins, and several branch and departmental libraries. The library mission includes a statement pledging support of graduate studies and faculty research. The Interlibrary Loan Borrowing Unit, vital to this support, is staffed by four FTE paraprofessionals, one FTE hourly, and 20-35 workstudy student hours per week.

In FY94, a three-year pilot began in the University Libraries that directly addressed graduate studies and faculty research support. The pilot, partially funded from graduate fees, explored the introduction of a new service (SuperService), coordinated through Reference. Beginning with disciplines in the sciences, the Reference SuperService Coordinator began training graduate students and their graduate faculty in specific search techniques using FirstSearch, as well as discipline-specific indices in electronic form and paper. Interlibrary Loan assigned one full-time technician the primary responsibility for searching and sending all interlibrary loan requests submitted through SuperService.

Two related events preceeding and during the SuperService pilot reinforced interlibrary loan's commitment to support graduate studies and faculty research. University Libraries conducted an initial serials review in 1990, resulting in the cancellation of 1,150 titles, many of which were cheaper subscriptions or titles held in fiche. A second, more stringent, serials review followed in 1995. This further reduced serial title holdings by 675 titles. After each review and cancellation, some new titles were added, but not at the same rate as the cancellations. At the conclusion of the second review, library administration met with the faculty to discuss a philosophical shift from ownership to access for certain serial titles. Administration pledged forty-eight hour ILL turnaround, based on previous interlibrary loan performance, for Rush SuperService requests.

Interlibrary Loan's commitment included priority treatment of all Super-Service requests, with top priority given to those requests specified as rush. Additionally, the staff resolved to seek the fastest source of supply for these requests, with timeliness taking precedence over cost. A maximum cost for ILL material was not set, but a negotiable figure of $25 per request was used. Our goal was rapid service for graduate faculty and graduate students, with all charges paid for from a designated SuperService account.

The year before SuperService was implemented, the Borrowing Unit's average turnaround time for requests was 21 days. During the first year of the pilot, standards were implemented for both the ILL bibliographic searchers and the processor. The searcher had a two day standard for entry of requests. The processor's standards allowed for no more than two days to elapse from receipt of the material until the time the material was processed and available for the patron.

In the second pilot year, those standards remained in place, but both the searchers and the processor accepted new goals. Searchers strove to have *every* request searched and sent within two hours of receipt. The processor's goal was to have every day's receipts processed and on the interlibrary loan hold shelf for patron pick-up by the end of the business day.

The searchers met their goal 70 percent of the time, and the processor achieved similar success.

During FY95 Arkansas' Interlibrary Loan Borrowing Unit filled 12,228 items, with 68 percent requested through SuperService. The pilot's first two years' statistics revealed that while interlibrary loan borrowing increased only two percent, SuperService requests increased 229 percent. While the GMRLC study was underway, the AFU borrowing unit completed a separate study of delivery speed. This study was limited to requests made from other GMRLC libraries and commercial document suppliers for photocopies in April 1995. The average delivery speed for the GMRLC lenders was 9.5 days with a range of 1-25 days (date sent to date received in ILL office). The four commercial document suppliers had a range of 1-37 days with an average delivery speed of 2.2 days. So, for a price, an average of 7.3 days could be eliminated from the delivery speed for photocopies.

This information must be considered within the larger framework of AFU's ILL operation. The borrowing unit experienced rapid growth from FY93 with 6,737 filled requests to FY95 with 12,228 requests filled. The 82 percent growth paralleled a dramatic decrease in turnaround time for receipt of requested materials, moving from an average of 21 days to eight days. The rapid growth is attributable to the advent of SuperService and improved library technology, such as new online public catalog (OPAC), and increasing availability of end-user electronic databases. At the same time, the Borrowing Unit changed its philosophy about requesting procedures for all interlibrary loan requests. Now, for each serial request, the searcher verifies holdings using the OCLC union list function. If a potential lender does not list holdings, that library becomes a lender of last resort.

The Reference SuperService Coordinator and the Head of Interlibrary Loan chose to use vendors more heavily during the three-year pilot in order to gain information on vendor performance. The improved delivery speed for all interlibrary loan requests does come at a price. Arkansas' new interlibrary loan philosophy meant that not all special agreements were fully utilized if potential lenders do not union list their serial holdings. As a result, AFU was free to obtain items from non-reciprocal libraries or commercial document suppliers, such as UMI, TGA, BRI, and CARL Uncover. In FY93, before this change, monies paid out to other institutions totaled $6,373, with an average charge of $.95 per request. Two years later, that expense jumped to $25,807 yielding an average charge of $2.11 per request.

Results

Analysis of the 1995 GMRLC customer satisfaction survey results for Iowa State University and the University of Arkansas provide interesting comparative insights for interlibrary loan departments concerned with patron satisfaction. Institutions must consider their user population and library philosophy in relationship to the survey results.

Figure 1 compares the means of responses to the likert-type scale questions on the survey form (see Appendix Figure A.1) for ISU, AFU and all GMRLC survey participants. Questions three through fifteen asked the

FIGURE 1. Means of Response to GMRLC Satisfaction Survey

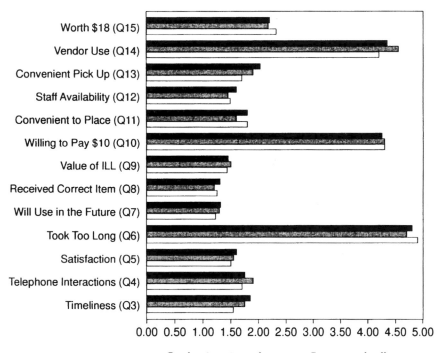

Scale: 1 = strongly agree   5 = strongly disagree

participants to respond with their opinion. Except for questions six, ten, and fourteen, a lower number is desirable for the questions represented in Figure 1. These ask patrons about their perception of how well interlibrary loan has served them focusing on satisfaction, availability, convenience, and value. The University of Arkansas and Iowa State, as well as the aggregate GMRLC scores, show patron responses to be positive.

Question six states that interlibrary loan takes too long for date-sensitive requests. The average response was greater than four, revealing that most patrons disagree. Question ten asks if patrons would pay for a guaranteed faster service. Again, most respondents disagreed. In three years, Iowa State had dramatically cut turnaround time, and the University of Arkansas, through SuperService, now offers rapid turnaround at no cost to qualified patrons, perhaps offsetting any compelling reason for patrons to respond more positively to this query. Question fourteen asked patrons about current vendor use. Neither Arkansas nor Iowa as yet offers subsidized, unmediated vendor access. The means for Arkansas, Iowa, and all GMRLC institutions are not significantly different.

One area where differences are dramatic, delivery speed, is shown in Figure 2. The average turnaround time for Iowa State, Arkansas, and all ten participating GMRLC libraries, ranges from eight days to 19. Within all GMRLC institutions the delivery time of requested materials ranged from zero to 313 days. The average delivery time from the date ordered by the patron to the date received by the patron was 8.4 days for Arkansas, 15.4 days for Iowa State, and 16.3 days for all libraries. (Iowa State factored out one request that took 313 days which was believed to be a foreign dissertation purchased by the Center for Research Libraries.)

Figure 3 shows the average number of requests each patron estimated they had requested in the past year, another area in which the two institutions differed dramatically. Iowa shows a lower average number of 15.69

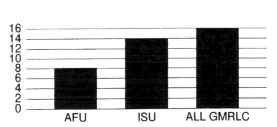

FIGURE 2. Delivery (Q1)
Delivery Speed

FIGURE 3
Requests (Q2)

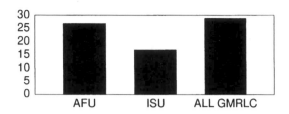

■ Estimated Number of Requests by Patron

requests per person with a range from 1 to 175 requests per person. Arkansas shows a higher average of 26, with a narrower range of 1 to 100. This difference may be attributed to varying institutional fee structures.

Tables D.2 and D.8 in the Appendix provide the Pearson coefficient of correlation for the responses by each institution's patrons.[5] Assuming the focus is patron satisfaction, looking at the correlation of all other questions to satisfaction (Q5), reveals additional comparative information on Iowa and Arkansas. Iowa's customer satisfaction has a significant positive correlation with timeliness, telephone interactions, future use, value, convenience, staff availability, convenient pick up, and investment worth. There was a significant negative correlation with material taking too long to reach the patron. Arkansas showed similar positive correlations with three exceptions. Arkansas showed no significant correlation between satisfaction and investment worth; however, Arkansas had two additional positive, significant correlations between satisfaction and delivery speed and satisfaction and receipt of the correct item.

Tables 1 and 2 report regression analysis results for Arkansas, Iowa, and all GMRLC institutions in which satisfaction is the dependent variable. In the regression, the variance for satisfaction is most strongly attributable to timeliness for Arkansas. For Iowa, the variance for satisfaction is also most attributable to timeliness. The following remaining variables contribute, in descending order of importance, to the variance for Arkansas ILL patrons: correct item, convenience, doesn't take too long, delivery speed, pick up convenient, and staff availability. The remainder of the variance accounted for in Iowa's patron satisfaction is, in descending order, future use, doesn't take too long, convenience, correct item, speed, and telephone interaction.

This information raises some questions. For example, is it convenient to

TABLE 1

AFU

Regression Analysis

Dependent Variable = Patron Satisfaction

Variable	Partial R2	C(p)	F	Probability
Timeliness	0.6183	26.5883	97.1947	0.0001
Correct Item	0.0578	15.7751	10.5326	0.0019
Convenient to Request	0.0704	2.1659	16.1190	0.0002
Delivery Too Long	0.0151	0.8292	3.6001	0.0628
Delivery Speed	0.0113	0.3205	2.7919	0.1003
Pickup Convenient	0.0061	0.9578	1.5309	0.2212
Staff Availability	0.0032	2.2495	0.7928	0.3772

n = 62

No other variable met the .5 significance level for entry into the model.

TABLE 2

ISU

Regression Analysis

Dependent Variable = Patron Satisfaction

Variable	Partial R2	C(p)	F	Probability
Timeliness	0.4809	10.0589	56.5045	0.0001
Future Use	0.0559	4.6206	7.2427	0.0092
Delivery Too Long	0.0318	2.3894	4.3499	0.0413
Convenient to Request	0.0234	1.2822	3.3200	0.0736
Correct Item	0.0178	0.9150	2.5991	0.1125
Delivery Speed	0.0096	1.6407	1.4092	0.2402
Telephone Interaction	0.0069	2.7235	1.0145	0.3182

n = 63

No other variable met the .5 significance level for entry into the model.

place an interlibrary loan request? What procedure is in place to guarantee the correct item is received? How do we guarantee a correct item if it is in a language we don't read? Are we mindful of patron deadlines? What patron service attitudes are evident when working with a patron in person or over the phone?

Although Arkansas has significant positive correlations with telephone interactions, future use, and value, none were strong enough contribute to the prediction of patron satisfaction. At ISU, staff availability, convenient pick up, and investment worth all had significant positive correlations, yet no predictive value for customer satisfaction. On the other hand, two items that showed no significant correlation for Iowa, delivery speed and receipt of the correct item, are predictive for patron satisfaction at Arkansas.

To be sure, there are some similarities between the data at the University of Arkansas and Iowa State University. But there are most certainly a number of differences too. Perhaps some of the differences, such as delivery time, can be ascribed to the operational procedures in place at each library. Other differences may also be a reflection of different operations, or reflect a different ILL customer base. It is quite possible that the needs of ILL users in Iowa and Arkansas are as dissimilar as the ILL operations.

DISCUSSION

If user satisfaction is the Holy Grail of Interlibrary Loan activities, then it would appear that the ILL staff at the University of Arkansas and Iowa State University satisfy the needs of their users quite well. With average satisfaction scores of 1.3544 for Arkansas and 1.4000 for Iowa State on a scale of 1 to 5 (with 1 being strong satisfaction), it would appear that the customers have a good opinion of the service they received on the individual requests they were asked to evaluate. For all ten institutions involved in the study, the mean for user satisfaction was 1.4563. This suggests that GMRLC ILL users were also satisfied with the service received during the study period and that the users at Iowa State and Arkansas specifically were somewhat more satisfied than the group as a whole.

It should come as no surprise that users at the University of Arkansas were more satisfied with the service received than those at Iowa State or all 10 institutions in the study, for Arkansas had the lowest turnaround time of all the ILL operations in the study: 8.3896 days (as calculated from the time between the date ordered by the patron and the date the patron received the material). Although Iowa State was less than the overall study mean of 16.3250 days, its average turnaround of 15.4000 days was still almost twice the average at the University of Arkansas, though satisfaction levels were nearly as high as those at AFU. Clearly, these responses make it important to scrutinize differences in the borrowing operations at both institutions.

One of the most obvious differences is the level of priority, or "rush," handling of borrowing requests at the two institutions. Both Iowa State and the University of Arkansas offer a two-tiered borrowing service: regular service and an expedited, or "priority," service. The great difference between the two libraries is the proportion of overall business that is processed on an expedited basis. The University of Arkansas, which levies no charge to qualified registered SuperService patrons, processed 68 percent of its borrowing requests in FY95 on a priority basis through its SuperService. Iowa State, on the other hand, which charges the end user a minimum of $5 per priority request (with a limit of one per person per day), processed just 3 percent of the total filled requests on a priority basis. The overall filled volume for the two schools was somewhat similar: the University of Arkansas filled 12,228 borrowing requests in FY95, while Iowa State filled 11,172. Clearly, the level of urgency in processing borrowing requests at the University of Arkansas is not matched at Iowa State University.

Policy and procedural differences are fundamental to the level of expedited borrowing at these two libraries, but funding also plays a role. It is difficult to draw comparisons between Iowa State and the University of Arkansas since each has different accounting procedures and available financial information. The University of Arkansas ILL staff work on the premise that they will find the best source available to guarantee rapid supply of the needed material, paying for commercial suppliers when necessary. Iowa State, on the other hand, has a finite amount of funds available to purchase documents and borrow books and relies more upon library suppliers. This difference in philosophy is not only apparent in widely variant turnaround times (15.4 days at Iowa State and 8.4 days at Arkansas, representing a 83 percent difference), but also in the different amounts paid per filled request ($1.46 at Iowa State and $2.11 at Arkansas, representing a 45 percent difference).

The debate concerning the use of library suppliers vs. commercial suppliers for ILL borrowing continues to rage despite the majority of published reports that state commercial suppliers are actually slower than other libraries.[6] For instance, Iowa State University's published study of commercial suppliers approached via OCLC concluded that using other libraries with special delivery agreements resulted in faster turnaround times than those achieved by the six commercial document suppliers studied.[7] Internal studies at the University of Arkansas, however, report just the opposite: the four commercial suppliers utilized were faster than other GMRLC libraries that heavily utilize ARIEL, fax, and Federal Express delivery. However, none of these differences create any apparent disparity in patrons' perceptions of timeliness; until the data is analyzed by regression analysis.

The regression analysis data shows that at AFU, where delivery speed was the fastest, timeliness was predictive of satisfaction about 62 percent of the time (see Table 1). At ISU (Table 2), timeliness was predictive of about 48 percent of the variance in the model for prediction of patron satisfaction and at all 10 institutions together .5070 of the variance for satisfaction was timeliness. Actual speed in the regression model was rated fifth for AFU (.0113) and sixth at ISU (.0096). Even more interesting is that for all 10 institutions, delivery speed did not even meet the test for statistical significance. The differences between Iowa State University and the University of Arkansas in policies, supplier choice, funding and their respective turnaround times are quite demonstrable. What is not so demonstrable is any difference in the ultimate satisfaction of the two libraries' ILL patrons. The University of Arkansas scored better than Iowa State on this question, but was the resultant difference significant enough to justify the apparently greater expenditures that accompanied this effort? The question of cost-benefit is a central issue in interlibrary loan today and needs further inquiry. Much is known about ILL costs, but the question still remains, what is the benefit derived from varying levels of investment? Is the pursuit of ever lower turnaround times necessary in the face of evidence that somewhat slower times may suffice for the user?

The disparity between actual turnaround time and the user's perception of turnaround time was an important finding of this study. At Iowa State, for instance, the highest correlation with patron satisfaction was timeliness as perceived by the end user (.76920). There was no statistically significant correlation between user satisfaction and actual delivery speed. Similarly, the University of Arkansas also had a high correlation between user satisfaction and timeliness (.82909), but a low correlation between actual delivery speed and user satisfaction (.22904). Such data suggests a gap between timeliness as perceived by the user and timeliness as determined by actual ILL turnaround time. It would appear that ILL users are much more forgiving than one might anticipate. It would also appear that more attention should be paid to the opinions of the end user than to traditional measures of turnaround time. This finding has been corroborated by ILL users in Great Britain[8] and is similar to that of Francoise Hebert, who found "that participants in this study whose requests was filled used different criteria than fill rate and turnaround time for evaluating the quality of interlibrary loan services. . . . "[9] Perrault and Arseneau also concluded: "the findings of this survey do not bear out the generally held impression that fast turnaround time is a universal demand from the user."[10]

After timeliness, there was no consistent pattern of variables that correlated well with user satisfaction at Iowa State, the University of Arkansas, and the 10 GMRLC libraries as a whole. For instance, the second ranked variable at Iowa State was patron's willingness to use ILL service in the future. At Arkansas, the second ranked variable was the correct item was received. For the whole group, the second most important variable was again future use. One might conclude that patrons in general are most concerned with timeliness as they view it, and there is a great deal of variability in other factors that affect their opinions of ILL service at different institutions.

The data produced by this study, combined with previous research on user satisfaction with interlibrary loan, suggests a distinct gap between users' perceptions of this service and the perceptions of ILL practitioners about the needs of their users. At the very least, it appears interlibrary loan operations in general, and those at the University of Arkansas and Iowa State University in particular, would benefit by devoting more time to assessing the needs of their users, and spending less time measuring and documenting turnaround times. This reflects a shift away from the procedural dimensions of interlibrary loan and toward a greater concern for the personal dimensions.

Both the University of Arkansas and Iowa State University view the continued provision of a flexible, perhaps tiered, approach to ILL as an important component of public service. Both libraries fully intend to continue to offer their SuperService and priority service, respectively. The level to which these expedited delivery options can be supported, however, is dependent upon the administrative and financial support available at each institution. The limits placed upon priority service at Iowa State, for instance ($5 minimum fee to the user and limit of one per day), will be reviewed as a result of this survey, but any liberalization will probably be dependent upon additional staffing. Similarly, at the University of Arkansas continued funding is a prerequisite for the continuation of SuperService at the level it is currently being offered.

Continuing to subsidize ILL borrowing service is deemed of central importance to both libraries. Iowa State University ILL staff would like to adopt the more flexible funding model in place at the University of Arkansas. Efforts are now underway to secure additional funding for those requests that exceed the $20.00 maximum cost. It is hoped that the Head of Resource Sharing will be able to individually renegotiate the maxcost to a higher amount, such as $50.00. Arkansas is considering a second pilot targeting one university research program for subsidized, unmediated vendor access. This pilot will, in part, address the importance Arkansas patrons attributed in the survey to the areas of timeliness, convenient to request, delivery speed, and convenient pick up.

One of the most important issues to be resolved for both libraries is the appropriateness of the ILL suppliers being used. Arkansas, with its impressive turnaround time, has established an impressive standard of achievement. Iowa State's users are also quite satisfied. Is this "satisfaction differential" attributable to a better turnaround time? Apparently not, since it is the user's perception of timeliness that is most important.

Iowa State's interlibrary loan staff are comfortable with the level of user satisfaction considering the current funding and staffing that have been made available. Notwithstanding turnaround time data, the survey findings were not sufficiently compelling to cause a wholesale shift away from the practice of obtaining most materials from other libraries rather than commercial suppliers. This is partially due to the higher charges incurred, but also because the extant literature does not support such a change. Iowa State feels that a shift toward commercial suppliers should be accompanied by a shift toward unmediated, or systems mediated, document delivery such as that offered by UnCover2.[11]

Overall, Arkansas' Borrowing Unit is pleased with the patron satisfaction level. The data reinforces the unit's emphasis on quality control checks that occur both in searching for the correct bibliographic record, as well as the final accuracy check conducted, when the material is received by the unit processor. One area that bears further investigation is the correlation of satisfaction and user charges, perhaps differentiating between user groups such as faculty and graduate students. The high satisfaction rating at AFU may indeed be partially connected to lack of immediate patron charges if the patron is using SuperService. Additionally, further studies on patron perception of timeliness will be undertaken at Arkansas.

The balance between cost and service quality in interlibrary loan is not at all clear. This is understandable, especially considering that traditional measures of ILL quality do not correlate well with user satisfaction. Also, the interlibrary loan cost studies available today are for the most part measures of the average cost of an ILL transaction. There needs to be a shift in the direction of this research toward cost/benefit analysis. When this kind of data becomes available, ILL operations such as those at Iowa State University and the University of Arkansas will surely be able to move toward the future with more confidence.

NOTES

1. Thomas J. Waldhart, "Performance Evaluation of Interlibrary Loan in the United States: A Review of Research." *Library and Information Science Research* 7 (February, 1985): 313-331.

2. See Diana Barr and Jean Farmer, "Waiting for Inter-Library Loans." *BLL Review* 5 (1977): 8-12 and B. Houghton and C. Prosser, "A Survey of Opinions of British Library, Lending Division Users in Special Libraries on the Effects of Non-Immediate Access to Journals." *Aslib Proceedings* 26 (1974) :354-366.

3. Hebert, Francoise, "Service Quality: An Unobtrusive Investigation of Interlibrary Loan in Large Public Libraries in Canada." *Library and Information Science Research* 16 (Winter, 1994): 3-21.

4. Perrault, Anna H. and Arseneau, Marjo. "User Satisfaction and Interlibrary Loan Service: A Study at Louisiana State University." RQ 35, no. 1 (Fall 1995): 90-100.

5. Keep in mind that a coefficient of 0 shows that no relationship exists and a coefficient of 1 demonstrates a perfect relationship, whether negative or positive. A positive value indicates a tendency for high values of one variable to be associated with high values of the other variable. A negative value indicates an inverse relationship, that high values of one variable are associated with low value of the other variable.

6. See Kathleen Kurosman and Barbara Ammerman Durniak, "Document Delivery: A Comparison of Commercial Document Suppliers and Interlibrary Loan Services," *College & Research Libraries* 55 (March, 1994): 129-139 and Connie Miller and Patricia Tegler, "An Analysis of Interlibrary Loan and Commercial Document Supply Performance." *Library Quarterly* 58 (October, 1988): 352-366.

7. Wayne Pedersen and David Gregory, "Interlibrary Loan and Commercial Document Supply: Finding the Right Fit." *Journal of Academic Librarianship* (November, 1994): 263-271.

8. Barr and Farmer, p. 11.

9. Hebert, p. 15.

10. Perrault and Arseneau, p. 97.

11. Minna Sellers and Joan Beam, "Subsidizing Unmediated Document Delivery: Current Models and a Case Study." *Journal of Academic Librarianship* (November, 1995): 459-466.

Changing Workloads and Productivity in Interlibrary Loan

Nancy E. Paine
John Ward

SUMMARY. As interlibrary loan departments process a rapidly increasing number of transactions annually while staffing levels rise slowly, interlibrary loan procedures and decision-making have grown more complex and staff training has become more important. This survey of GMRLC and ARL libraries compares the transaction to staff ratio in ILL borrowing and lending with a similar survey completed six years ago. Average transaction to staff ratios can serve as benchmarks to evaluate ILL operations. Data show an increase in transaction to staff ratio since 1989 and a negative correlation between transaction to staff ratio and lending fill rate. Factors affecting productivity, such as automation and work flow, are related to staffing levels. Libraries defined as effective or non-effective by fill rate are compared. *[Article copies available from The Haworth Document Delivery Service: 1-800-342-9678. E-mail address: getinfo@haworth.com]*

Recently I heard an interlibrary loan librarian say: "How many requests we process is important; how well we do is irrelevant." While that may not be true in all libraries, most librarians would agree that productivity

---

Nancy E. Paine is Head of Inter-Library Service at the University of Texas at Austin.

John Ward is Lending Assistant in Inter-Library Service at the University of Texas at Austin.

[Haworth co-indexing entry note]: "Changing Workloads and Productivity in Interlibrary Loan." Paine, Nancy E., and John Ward. Co-published simultaneously in *Journal of Library Administration* (The Haworth Press, Inc.) Vol. 23, No. 1/2, 1996, pp. 73-93; and: *Interlibrary Loan/Document Delivery and Customer Satisfaction: Strategies for Redesigning Services* (ed: Pat L. Weaver-Meyers, Wilbur A. Stolt, and Yem S. Fong) The Haworth Press, Inc., 1996, pp. 73-93. Single or multiple copies of this article are available from The Haworth Document Delivery Service [1-800-342-9678, 9:00 a.m. - 5:00 p.m. (EST). E-mail address: getinfo@haworth.com].

73

has become an important issue as budgets dwindle, ILL requests increase, and staffing levels remain static. Automation has changed traditional interlibrary loan operations, increasing productivity, complexity, and the sophistication of daily routines. Electronically based technologies currently coexist with manual procedures, offering patrons as well as staff more choices, while often increasing decision-making and workload for ILL staff.

CHANGES IN ILL

When the access approach to collection development was introduced and adopted by many academic libraries several years ago, libraries committed to obtaining documents "just in time" for their patrons instead of maintaining "just in case" on-site collections. The recently revised National Interlibrary Loan Code affirms that "interlibrary borrowing is an integral element of collection development . . . not an ancillary option."[1] Even so libraries do not always support interlibrary loan at a satisfactory level and "library staff is expected to do more and more with no additional personnel.[2] One obvious effect of the move from ownership to access is the rapidly escalating number of ILL transactions, increasing both borrowing and lending workload. For fiscal year 1993-94, ARL reported that borrowing had more than doubled since 1986, and lending had increased more than 50 percent.[3]

Libraries no longer rely solely on other libraries for materials but increasingly purchase documents from commercial document delivery services. Vendors offer a wide variety of cost structures and delivery options to choose from, requiring continuous cost-benefit analysis to ensure most effective use of available resources.

Automation has become an integral part of ILL. Most orders are placed electronically from the requesting library to the supplier, primarily through bibliographic utilities such as OCLC or RLIN. In many libraries, local patrons can submit requests electronically to the ILL office. Transmission of scanned documents via the Internet is commonplace. Libraries often use software to manage statistics, copyright compliance, invoicing, and other record keeping functions. Electronic databases assist patrons in identifying needed materials not owned locally, thus increasing the demand for ILL. Databases also help staff verify incorrect and incomplete citations. The Internet offers easy access to the on-line catalogs of libraries worldwide, providing both patrons and ILL staff opportunities to verify and locate needed materials.

While automation reduces the time formerly spent on many tedious manual tasks and brings information from supplier to patron more quickly, it also introduces new procedures and changes old routines for ILL staff. Examples are: installing and maintaining computer systems and programs, troubleshooting when a system malfunctions, downloading borrowing requests, scanning documents, and searching databases.

The interaction between staffing, productivity, service quality, and workload determine whether organizational goals will be satisfactorily met in the interlibrary loan operation. These factors will be discussed in turn.

STAFFING

New technologies and increasing complexity in ILL work flow require higher levels of staff and more training. ILL is experiencing some of the same changes faced earlier by technical services with the introduction of automation. Martin comments that:

> Despite managerial expectation that ILL can be clericalized, it is becoming clear that more and more sophistication and training is needed to determine priorities, unravel bibliographic snarls, and choose between mechanisms, in order to respond to user need. . . . Paradoxically, technological improvements have brought with them new problems and new sources of conflict even while they have helped solve other problems.[4]

Library assistants have become a second level of professionals to supervise operational units such as interlibrary loan offices, and cross-training is becoming standard. "The ILL work flow is far less segmented than previously because of such systems as OCLC/ILL. All the staff must be conversant with nearly all aspects of a system."[5] Observers at the University of British Columbia noted that clerical activities decreased and bibliographic verification duties were transferred to paraprofessionals when automation was introduced to ILL. In addition staff spent less time away from the ILL office and more time answering in-person patron queries.[6]

Despite the increasing volume and complexity of ILL transactions, a recent survey of ARL libraries indicated that neither the number of full-time equivalent staff in ILL nor the mix of professional, classified, and student staff changed significantly between 1987 and 1992. The median FTE staff added was less than one person, increasing the median total staff from 6.8 to 7.63.[7] (See Table I.)

TABLE I. Median Levels of ILL Staff 1987-1992*

	1987	1991	1992
Professional	1.0	1.0	1.0
Classification	4.0	4.6	4.7
Student	1.2	1.5	1.8
Total	6.8	7.60	7.63

*Source: Dearie, 5,

The difficulty of maintaining ILL staff commensurate with workload is understandable as library administrators grow increasingly concerned with allocating scarce financial resources to various library departments. An ARL cost study completed in 1992 found that 77 percent of the cost of ILL represented staff costs. The average staff cost per borrowing request was $14.22; the average staff cost per lending request was $8.40. Professional staff were more often used for borrowing than lending,[8] while student staff contributed more frequently to lending costs.[9] In addition to providing bibliographic verification, professionals were involved in helping patrons with research needs and in "deciding location choice by evaluating consortial agreements, costs, turnaround time."[10]

LaGuardia found a wide range in ILL staffing levels in a survey of 100 ARL libraries, and concluded that what was regarded as sufficient staff in one library might not be sufficient in another.[11] Workload which includes factors such as volume of transactions, level of automation, and activities performed is often used to allocate an appropriate level and size of staff. The relationship between workload and staffing affects productivity and service quality.

PRODUCTIVITY AND SERVICE QUALITY

When ILL staff process more requests per person, productivity rises. Williams defines productivity as output divided by input:

> Productivity is a concept that expresses the relationship between the quantity of goods and services produced—output—and the quantity of labor, capital, land, energy and other resources that produced it—input . . . . The most commonly used measure of productivity is the relationship between output and input of labor time, called output per hour. This measure, however, ignores use of other input resources, such as capital and equipment.[12]

Further he cautions that to be meaningful, a measure of productivity should be judged in conjunction with goal setting.[13] For example, an ILL department handling a high volume of requests (output) with a small staff (input) will show a high transaction to staff ratio and may appear highly productive. Yet the department might fill only a small percentage of requests received, have a long turnaround time and/or make frequent errors. The high level of productivity (output per staff member) means nothing if the department is not meeting institutional goals or achieving a reasonable level of performance.

Patron satisfaction, fill rate, and turnaround time are excellent measures of service quality in ILL. Measuring service quality and correlating it with productivity is difficult because of the number of variables involved.

Weaver-Meyers did not find a positive or negative correlation between fill rate (output) and efficiency (transaction to staff ratio). Lending fill rate, defined as a measure of effectiveness, may be significantly affected by non-staff-related variables such as large non-circulating collections, incomplete journal runs, inadequate in-house bibliographic resources, and receipt of unverified requests.[14] Weaver-Meyers concluded cautiously that "lower fill rates were not a direct indicator of an overworked office staff in this study."[15] Another survey found it was common for ILL units to process only part of the requests received, either on a first-come or selective basis, when there are too many incoming requests for staff to handle.[16] This practice would have a negative effect on both fill rate and turnaround time.

In a study of ILL turnaround time at Northwestern, Hert found that document characteristics and fulfillment group affected turnaround while staffing levels did not.[17] Since the sample consisted only of requests processed at Northwestern, it is possible that staffing levels did not affect turnaround time because they did not change significantly for this library during the study.

Determining the optimal level of productivity depends not only on desired service quality goals but also on workload, including the level of automation and availability of equipment. Training and the relative expertise of employees may also affect the optimal staffing level. A level of productivity or transaction to staff ratio that produces an efficient service provider in one library may yield an operation that provides substandard service with overworked staff in another. Although no survey can define an optimal level of staffing for all interlibrary loan operations, transaction to staff ratios can serve as guides. Libraries below the average can seek ways to streamline procedures, while libraries above average can examine service quality to determine if institutional goals are being met.

TRANSACTION TO STAFF RATIO

The Texas State Library uses the transaction to staff ratio as a measure of productivity in the ten major resource centers in TexNet, the ILL network of Texas public libraries. Data collected annually by TexNet show that the transaction to staff ratio is increasing. For fiscal year 1988, an average 6969 transactions were processed per ILL staff member in TexNet libraries. By 1995, this had jumped to 10,317.[18] Since ILL transactions in public libraries are different from those in academic libraries (requests are primarily for books, considered easier to locate, and include referrals from many small public libraries), direct comparisons with academic libraries are not necessarily appropriate. Nonetheless, the steadily rising transaction to staff ratio in Texas public libraries is indicative of a trend that may be expected in ARL libraries.

In 1989, Weaver-Meyers surveyed ARL libraries to compare staffing and workload in interlibrary loan, using the transaction to staff ratio as a measure of efficiency or productivity. Information was gathered on full-time equivalent staff and ILL requests processed and filled for seventy-six ARL libraries. The mean number of transactions processed per lending staff member was 5905; per borrowing staff member, 2439 transactions.[19]

Weaver-Meyers selected fill rate as a measure of effectiveness because information was readily available. A sixty-one percent fill rate for lending and an 84 percent fill rate for borrowing were chosen as minimal levels of effectiveness,[20] based on average fill rates for libraries studied. The transaction to staff ratio was used as a measure of efficiency. Weaver-Meyers notes that:

> . . . while some of the libraries processed an abnormally large number of requests, those libraries were not necessarily the most efficient in that they did not process the most requests with the least staff. Also, those libraries that were the least busy were not always the most effective in that they did not always have the highest fill rates.[21]

Transaction to staff ratios for the 38 libraries meeting the base level of effectiveness were computed. But the authors concluded that the study "did not clearly establish criteria which would unequivocally demonstrate that a particular library has an unreasonable workload. . . . "[22] The data did show that effective libraries used more professionals and fewer students,[23] probably resulting in a higher cost per transaction.

Even though the transaction to staff ratio did not correlate with fill rate in this study, transaction to staff ratios have continued to be useful for many ILL librarians in their effort to measure staffing levels and seek additional staff commensurate with their volume of activity. The data are now more than six years old, and ILL staffing levels in relation to requests processed have changed as collection development philosophies, budgets, and automation levels have changed.

STAFFING LEVELS

The present study was mailed to 108 ARL libraries and four other libraries that participate in the Greater Midwest Research Library Consortium (GMRLC). Forty-one usable responses (36.6 percent) were returned, including 15 from the 17 GMRLC member libraries. Data analysis compared the total sample of 41 responses, GMRLC libraries as a group, and non-GMRLC libraries as a group. Since most of the comparisons did not show measurable differences, only data for the whole sample have been presented. Comments have been made on exceptions.

The goal of the present survey was to obtain data comparable to the 1988 study by Weaver-Meyers—specifically, borrowing and lending FTE staff by rank and borrowing and lending requests processed and filled. Additional questions were included to determine which phases of the ILL process were handled in ILL and what new technologies had been adopted. Finally respondents were asked to share their perspectives on the increasing or decreasing need for staff.

Table II gives staffing and workload data from 1995. Nine libraries (21.95 percent) had no librarians in ILL. Lending averaged one FTE staff member more than borrowing, a difference which was not reflected in comparison of medians. Lending processed 2.5 times as many requests as borrowing with 1.22 times the staff. This confirms the assumption made by Weaver-Meyers that borrowing requires at least twice as many staff as lending to process a given number of transactions.

Comparison of 1995 median staffing levels (Table II) to those found by Dearie in 1987, 1991, and 1992 (Table I) shows only a slight upward change in 1995 (less than .5 FTE), with approximately the same FTE staff additions occurring at the classified and student levels. Table III compares 1995 staffing levels to those found in 1989 by Weaver-Meyers. Lending staff showed a small increase in student staff hours, while the borrowing staff showed increases at both classified and student levels. While more staff has been added to borrowing than to lending, volume of requests in borrowing has also increased more. More importantly staffing is not increasing in proportion to the volume of transactions.

Seventy percent of the responding libraries indicated staff had been

TABLE II. 1995 Staff FTE, Transaction to Staff Ratio, and Volume of Activity

	High	Mean	Median	Low
Lending Staff				
Professional	1.00	.26	.20	0.00
Classified	23.77	2.90	2.00	0.00
Student	7.20	1.93	1.50	0.00
Total	26.23	5.10	3.90	.60
Borrowing Staff				
Professional	1.25	.40	.50	0.00
Classified	5.00	2.64	2.80	.50
Student	3.00	1.10	1.00	0.00
Total	7.75	4.17	3.87	.40
Borrowing and Lending				
Professional	1.50	.69	1.00	0.00
Classified	25.57	5.54	5.00	0.00
Student	9.18	3.03	2.30	0.00
Total	28.45	9.26	8.00	1.00
Lending Activity				
Requests Processed	108,176	38,006	35,795	3,176
Requests Filled	67,752	20,405	18,559	835
Fill Rate	87.7%	53.7%	51.6%	23.0%
TSR	24,929	7454	8293	970
Borrowing Activity				
Requests Processed	60,000	15,286	12,314	588
Requests Filled	50,000	12,934	11,172	530
Fill Rate	97.7%	85.0%	86.3%	65.1%
TSR	14,118	3670	3165	1470

TABLE III. Median Borrowing Lending FTE Staff
1989* and 1995

	1989	1995	1989	1995
Lending Staff				
Professional	.3	.2	5.11%	9%
Classified	2.0	2.0	56.97%	61%
Student	1.0	1.4	37.93%	30%
Borrowing Staff				
Professional	.50	.5	10.31%	18%
Classified	1.75	2.8	63.31%	64%
Student	.50	1.0	26.38%	18%

*Source: For 1989 data Weaver-Meyers, 2.

added in the last five years, averaging 1.25 FTE for those libraries adding staff. More classified staff were added (60.2 percent) than student staff (33.0 percent) and professional staff (8.8 percent). Only 29.27 percent of the responding libraries used lending fee revenue for additional staff, and no libraries used revenue from borrowing fees for staff. Libraries using lending fees for staff had a lower average transaction to staff ratio (5706) than libraries that did not use lending fees for staff (9117). This suggests greater flexibility in meeting staffing needs when lending fees fund staff hours. As volume and consequently income increase, staff can be added to meet demand.

As in Weaver-Meyers' survey, the transaction to staff ratio was computed as an indicator of efficiency or productivity. GMRLC libraries had a higher average number of transactions per lending staff member (9184) and lower average number per borrowing staff member (3127) than other ARL libraries (8285 lending, 4071 borrowing). This suggests that GMRLC libraries may give a higher overall priority to borrowing over lending than other ARL libraries.

Table IV compares Weaver-Meyers' findings with those of the current survey. Comparison of the mean transaction to staff ratios found in 1995 to those found in 1989 shows an increase of 1549 transactions per FTE in lending (26.23 percent) and an increase of 1231 transactions in borrowing (50.47 percent). In the last five years, the number of requests processed per FTE staff in borrowing has increased more than in lending. This may

TABLE IV. Borrowing and Lending Transaction to Staff Ratios in 1989* and 1995

	Lending	SD	Borrowing	SD
1989 Mean	5,905	2,715	2,439	1,163
1995 Mean	7,454	4,124	3,670	2,334
1989 Median	5,429		2,130	
1995 Median	8,293		3,165	
1989 High	14,000		7,371	
1995 High	24,929		14,118	
1989 Low	1,119		97	
1995 Low	970		1,470	

Source: For 1989 data, Weaver-Meyers, 2.

be because operational changes such as the use of commercial document delivery services, improved verification tools, electronic patron request forms, and increased use of automation have had a greater effect on borrowing than lending in the past five years. Or it may simply be that resources were given first to borrowing operations to ensure provision of service to local patrons, and now lending operations are catching up.

EFFECTIVENESS

Fill rates for borrowing and lending changed little in the past five years. Weaver-Meyers found the median fill rate for lending was 58 percent, for borrowing 84 percent. The present survey found median fill rates were 51.6 percent and 86.3 percent respectively. Weaver-Meyers suggested that the effect of time pressure placed on lending staff using bibliographic utilities such as OCLC may mean that staff "give priority inadvertently to lending requests at the expense of borrowing."[24] The present study shows borrowing fill rates have risen and lending fill rates dropped, suggesting that ILL operations are placing higher priority on borrowing requests as resources diminish.

As in the earlier survey, fill rate, as a measure of service quality or effectiveness, was correlated with transaction to staff ratio. Although in 1989 there were no positive or negative correlations between fill rates and transaction to staff ratios in borrowing or lending, a negative correlation of -0.419 was found for lending in the 1995 survey. No comparable correlation was found for borrowing. (See Table V.) The direction of the relationship indicates that the lower the transaction to staff ratio, the better the fill rate for lending. A correlation was found at the higher 1995 transaction to staff ratio that was not present at the lower transaction to staff ratio in 1989. This suggests the possibility of an optimal productivity level or transaction to staff ratio, beyond which further increase yields decreasing service quality.

Based on minimum fill rates, effective and non-effective libraries were identified. (See Table VI.) As in the earlier survey, a lending fill rate of 58 percent and a borrowing fill rate of 84 percent were used as minimum levels of effectiveness. Sixteen borrowing libraries were defined as non-effective, while twenty-five were defined as effective. Twenty-eight lending libraries were defined as non-effective, while thirteen were defined as effective. While only 32 percent of responding libraries were effective lenders, 61 percent were effective borrowers.

Non-effective lenders had a higher lending transaction to staff ratio (9080) than effective lenders (5627). The same relationship is true for

TABLE V. Pearson Correlations

	r	r^2 Common Variance	Statistically Significant at .01 level
Borrowing Fill Rate with TSR	−0.193	0.040	
Lending Fill Rate with TSR	−0.419	0.180	x
Borrowing Fill Rate and Requests Processed	−0.040	0.002	
Lending Fill Rate and Requests Processed	0.280	0.080	
Lending TSR and Borrowing TSR	0.090	0.008	
Lending Fill Rate and Borrowing Fill Rate	0.130	0.017	
Lending FTE Professionals and Fill Rate	0.181	0.030	
Lending FTE Classified and Fill Rate	0.320	0.100	
Lending FTE Student and Fill Rate	0.184	0.030	
Borrowing FTE Professionals and Fill Rate	0.138	0.020	
Borrowing FTE Classified and Fill Rate	−0.008	0.0001	
Borrowing FTE Student and Fill Rate	−0.080	0.010	
Lending FTE Professionals and Requests Processed	0.145	0.020	
Lending FTE Classified and Requests Processed	0.259	0.070	
Lending FTE Student and Requests Processed	0.752	0.570	x
Borrowing FTE Professionals and Requests Processed	−0.109	0.010	
Borrowing FTE Classified and Requests Processed	0.347	0.120	
Borrowing FTE Student and Requests Processed	0.465	0.220	x

effective and non-effective borrowers. Effective borrowers had a lower transaction to staff ratio (3177) than non-effective borrowers (4418).

Effective lenders had a smaller proportion of student staff than non-effective lenders. Effective borrowers had more professional staff than non-effective borrowers. As in the 1989 survey, effective lenders had more professional staff than the average for all libraries. Effective lenders had more staff than the average for all libraries and more staff than non-effective lenders. Staffing averages for effective borrowers approximate the mean for the total sample and do not differ substantially for non-effective borrowers. The proportion of professional staff in effective lenders and borrowers has declined since 1989.

Although asked to provide information on turnaround time, many respondents did not provide data, and when they did, responses were often rough estimates. Correlating this information with staffing levels was not feasible.

Although this study did not analyze the reasons that requests were

TABLE VI. Comparison of Effective and Non-Effective Libraries

	Effective 1995	Non-Effective 1995	Effective 1989*
Lending			
Mean TSR	5627	9080	
% Professional	4.89%	5.32%	15%
% Classified	59.45%	54.68%	62%
% Student	35.67%	40.0%	23%
% Making Copies	69.23%	39.29%	
% Mailing Copies	76.92%	71.43%	
% Invoicing	84.62%	85.71%	
% Fees for Staff	30.77%	28.57%	
Borrowing			
Mean TSR	3177	4418	
% Professional	11.58%	8.55%	19%
% Classified	62.07%	65.13%	62%
% Student	26.35%	26.33%	19%

*Source: For 1989 data, Weaver-Meyers, 7.

unfilled by an ILL operation, doing so might highlight decreased service quality related to insufficient staff. For example, requests not found as cited suggest staffing levels insufficient for adequate verification in the borrowing library while requests not filled because maxcost was exceeded do not. Lending requests not found on the shelf (too few shelvers) suggest insufficient staff in supporting areas of the library. Insufficient staffing may yield requests rejected for time limitations, such as requests not processed in lending because the OCLC symbol was not listed twice or because too many requests were received that day and requests returned because a per person limit on borrowing requests was exceeded. Requests unfilled for any of these reasons are a service quality issue directly related to staffing levels. Whether or not a library chooses higher productivity as a priority goal with possible resulting decreased service quality depends on the library's goals and budget.

WORKLOAD: ACTIVITIES, INNOVATIONS, AND AUTOMATION IN ILL

The main functions for ILL units are to receive and verify requests, order materials for patrons, and oversee loans to other libraries. Additionally there are supporting tasks that may be done in ILL or other departments in the library. The literature of ILL as well as practical experience offer numerous ideas for saving staff time and improving service. To understand how innovations or performance/non-performance of supporting tasks affected productivity, the transaction to staff ratios for ILL operations using/not using innovations or doing/not doing supporting functions were compared. Table VII indicates the results.

One third of the survey respondents packaged more than 25 percent of their loans for mailing; approximately 50 percent made photocopies for lending, although 75 percent mailed the copies. Forty-four percent both made and mailed copies. Weaver-Meyers found that wrapping and photocopying reduced the ability of lending staff to process as many requests, but noted that the reduction was less than 150 transactions per FTE annually.[25] The current study found lending operations that made photocopies processed 3500 fewer transactions per FTE annually than lending operations that did not make copies. However, lending operations defined as effective (fill rate greater than or equal to 58 percent) were more likely than those defined as non-effective to make photocopies. In his evaluation of six RLG libraries, Smith concludes that the "biggest obstacle observed to more efficient handling of interlending requests [was] the absence of any post at operational level which appeared to have overall responsibility for the entire interlending operation from receipt to final dispatch."[26] Whether ILL or some other library department has responsibility for copying may be a productivity versus service quality issue, regardless what department has the copying responsibility, copying still uses staff time.

Eighty-five percent of the ILL units surveyed were involved in accounts receivable. Invoicing loans was handled by 60.98 percent, invoicing copies by 73.17 percent, receiving payments by 51.22 percent, and following up on unpaid invoices by 58.54 percent. More than half of the respondents were using OCLC's ILL Fee Management system for transferring payments. Libraries engaged in the preparation of lending invoices had a lower transaction to staff ratio than libraries not preparing invoices by 2474 transactions. This relationship changed in direction when libraries used IFM. IFM libraries were more productive by 2229 transactions per staff FTE.

Borrowing staff are often advised to search union list holdings for serial requests before ordering on OCLC. The current survey found that just under half of the responding libraries were union listed, and many of those union lists were not updated. While using union lists improves the success rate for borrowing staff, it may also impede load leveling as union listed lenders are likely to be selected first. In addition, lending operations of

TABLE VII. Specific ILL Tasks and Innovations: Comparison of Productivity Levels

Percent ILL Units Doing Tasks/Using Innovations

	Yes	No
Lending Efficiency		
Percent on a Union List	47.5	52.5
Fill Rate	64.5	61.2
TSR Lending	5719	8779
Percent Wrapping Packages	31.7	68.3
TSR Lending	6133	8241
Percent Making Copies	48.8	51.2
TSR Lending	6063	9589
Percent Mailing Copies	73.2	26.8
TSR Lending	6972	9412
Percent Making and Mailing Copies	43.9	56.1
TSR Lending	5959	9525
Percent Involved in Invoicing	85.4	14.6
TSR Lending	7205	9679
Percent Using ARIEL	82.9	17.1
TSR Lending	7440	7604
Percent Using IFM	56.1	43.9
TSR Lending	8733	6504
Percent Using Record Keeping Software	72.5	27.5
TSR Lending	7236	8157
Percent Using Lending Fees for Staff	29.27	30.73
TSR Lending	5706	9117
Borrowing Efficiency		
Percent Using Databases to Verify	95.1	4.9
TSR Borrowing	3727	2783
Percent Using Full-Text	26.83	73.17
TSR Borrowing	3812	3630
Percent Offering Electronic Requests	65.9	34.1
TSR Borrowing	3774	3487
Percent Using Automated Circulation	14.6	85.4
TSR Borrowing	3657	3684
Percent Using Record Keeping Software	72.5	27.5
TSR Borrowing	3725	3551

libraries not union listed often have lower fill rates. This study found the mean fill rate was 64.5 percent for union listed collections versus 61.2 percent for non-union listed holdings. There was a higher transaction to staff ratio in operations not union listed. Non-union listed libraries need more lending staff to process the volume of requests received. However, the number of requests for issues not owned is high, and processing those requests should be quick if not fruitful. This survey found that when union list information was unavailable, the lending transaction to staff ratio was 3060 requests higher per FTE staff annually than when union list information was available.

An area of great interest to libraries is commercial document delivery, an alternative many libraries are funding as they adopt the "just in time" model. Ninety three percent of the responding libraries used commercial document delivery services as part of the borrowing process, with about 40 percent using commercial services routinely. This was considerably higher for GMRLC libraries, with 57.14 percent using document delivery routinely in contrast to 33.33 percent for non-GMRLC libraries. However, of the 29 responses received to the question "Does use of commercial document delivery save staff time?" 62.1 percent of the libraries responding agreed that use of document delivery services did not save staff time. Considering the expenses of commercial vendors and the fact that staff represents the greatest portion of the ILL cost, cost-benefit analysis of commercial document delivery appears useful. The use and cost of commercial services may support institutional goals in libraries that give higher priority to rapid turnaround time or in libraries that have significant weaknesses in their collections.

Generally, respondents indicated increased automation of tasks. Ninety-five percent of the respondents used some electronic verification tools for borrowing requests, 85.36 percent used on-line databases, 65.85 percent used CD ROM databases, 58.5 percent used other libraries' on line catalogs, and 39.0 percent used other Internet sources. Some libraries (26.8 percent) used full-text databases to retrieve documents for patrons rather than obtaining them through ILL or commercial document delivery sources. Libraries using full-text databases were slightly more productive than libraries not using full-text.

Traditionally ILL operations maintain large files and keep extensive statistics. Software such as SAVEIT, Patron Request System, and AVISO have made record keeping easier; and 72.5 percent of responding libraries used record keeping software. However, more than 80 percent of these operations maintained duplicate manual files for some computerized functions, suggesting that ILL managers do not believe automated systems are sufficiently dependable to give up manual ones at this time. Interestingly, lenders using record keeping software were less productive than lenders not using record keeping software, although the relationship is reversed for borrowers.

Books borrowed from other libraries were charged on the borrowing library's automated circulation system by 14.63 percent of the ILL units.

Several options are available for patrons to submit ILL borrowing requests electronically, and 65.85 percent of the surveyed libraries used one or more of these options. More than half of the respondents allowed patrons to use local e-mail and/or FirstSearch to send requests; two libraries had ILL forms on the on-line catalog, six had forms on the Internet or World Wide Web, and three used Eureka (RLIN). Most libraries using an electronic request form offered patrons more than one electronic option. However, for the most part, patrons have not accepted these alternatives with enthusiasm. Only one library reported receiving more than half its incoming borrowing requests electronically, and more than half of the libraries reported receiving less than 25 percent of their borrowing requests electronically. The advantages of electronic requesting are obvious—no illegible handwriting needs to be deciphered, no requests may be submitted without addresses or cost information, patrons may transmit requests from home or office workstations. However, there are some potential problems: requests lost in cyberspace, more places to retrieve incoming requests, less convenient format for ILL use, and increased volume of requests prompted by ease of requesting. Also, it is still often necessary to convert electronic requests to paper format for record keeping.

Almost half of the respondents accepted ILL lending requests from other libraries via Internet, although this was often restricted to foreign libraries only. This option carries many of the advantages and disadvantages of electronic borrowing requests.

Innovations may increase the workload of some ILL units, depending on traditional organizational and work flow patterns. For example, only half the responding ILL units made photocopies for lending while 91.2 percent of ILL units using ARIEL were responsible for scanning and transmitting documents via ARIEL. ARIEL, the document transmission system marketed by the Research Libraries Group, transmits scanned documents via the Internet almost as quickly as fax but without telecommunications costs. Most administrators and ILL managers assume that use of ARIEL is a service quality goal that reduces document delivery time and postage costs. It is often suggested that ARIEL and conventional postal delivery are an even trade-off in staff time. However, lending operations not responsible for making photocopies must either scan photocopies (rather than scan directly from journals) made by another unit or they must add the task of copying/scanning to their work routine. So for some ILL operations, use of ARIEL is not the simple trade-off of scanning and transmitting instead of copying and mailing but an added responsibility. Some libraries used ARIEL minimally, transmitting documents only to specific reciprocal libraries or on a staff availability basis. Only 64.7 percent of respondents that had ARIEL used it to routinely send documents.

In the past, slow scanning speed was a limitation of ARIEL frequently mentioned by ILL managers. Although this limitation can be virtually eliminated by using a faster, more expensive scanner, only a quarter of the responding ARIEL libraries used the faster scanner. Half of the responding libraries photocopied all documents to be transmitted via ARIEL. Only 55.8 percent had document sheet feeders, a labor-saving device that permits unattended scanning of photocopies. Scanning photocopies rather than original journal pages is a compromise that costs more in paper and toner but saves staff time particularly with the slower scanners, making selection of ARIEL equipment and pre-copying important financial decisions. Eight of the libraries (23.5 percent) using ARIEL had more than one ARIEL workstation, but only three of the eight owned the faster scanner.

COMMENTS ON TRAINING AND NEED FOR STAFF

Eighty-five percent of the respondents agreed that staff training was more complex in today's automated world, and almost half agreed better trained staff was needed. Almost 70 percent said they needed more staff because the volume of ILL requests had increased. More than one-third said they needed more staff because of the innovations taking place in ILL, 14 percent said staffing needs had decreased because of innovations, and 17 percent said procedural innovations had not affected staffing needs.

ILL managers were invited to add comments. Several mentioned the need to become more efficient to maximize staff resources. Another noted a decline in face-to-face patron communication in favor of electronic communication. One commented: "Pressures on staff have grown in recent years because of the very significant increase in the number of requests, particularly in borrowing; and because new services have been introduced." Another wrote: "Innovations have helped us keep pace, but the growing demand has increased staff needs." One wrote: "Workload increases have absorbed any 'savings' of staff time acquired via automating in office processes." The benefits of retaining both classified and student staff were not overlooked. Staff longevity provides "a core of highly trained and motivated employees." Another manager noted that limited office space assigned to ILL precluded ability to add staff. Also mentioned was the necessity for professional staff to work on clerical tasks along with classified and student staff. This is a choice that is often necessary to get the work done but is not cost effective for the library. Some managers indicated that new technology had not so much saved as absorbed staff time. Another noted that students were increasingly assigned to non-clerical ILL tasks, even such responsibilities as bibliographic verification and ordering.

CONCLUSION

The survey reinforces experiential evidence that ILL operations are processing not only more requests but more requests per staff member than they were five years ago. ILL is gaining in importance as libraries turn to "just in time" access rather than "just in case" collection to meet patron information needs. In this environment, which seems destined to continue in the coming years, professional staff are necessary to balance the multiplicity of factors that determine whether cost and service goals acceptable to patrons, administrators, and ILL professionals will be met.

Many factors can be mentioned that might increase ILL productivity, including higher ranking and better trained staff, increased use of document delivery services, more equipment, more efficient record keeping, more patron input into the ILL process, and elimination of highly labor-intensive tasks such as extensive bibliographic verification of hard-to-locate items. Many of these factors require automating manual processes and/or additional equipment and funds. Although it is possible that assigning some ILL tasks to other units (e.g., making copies, preparing invoices, charging borrowed materials) might reduce ILL workload and increase productivity, the more likely result is decreased service quality and time delays as well as reduced efficiency and higher staff cost for the library as a whole.

While high productivity as measured by transaction to staff ratio would initially seem a preferred goal, there may be disadvantages to higher productivity. Too few staff handling too many requests can lead to poor service, as measured not only by lower fill rates, but by slower turnaround time and inaccuracy as well. Low morale and stress lead to staff turnover and added expense when new staff must be hired and trained. Under any given set of conditions, an optimal level of productivity must be sought. ILL managers and library administrators can alter work routines, add new technology, and increase staff to find the desired balance of productivity and service quality.

ILL is in a state of transition. New ways of doing traditional ILL tasks proliferate and improve month by month, and year by year, bringing greater potential for increased productivity. ILL department heads are evaluating these innovations, determining whether they are affordable, integrating them into existing work flow patterns, and training staff to use and accept them. If new ways of doing old tasks seem to take more staff hours, it may be time to analyze work flow and change traditional organizational patterns to promote maximum efficiency by effective use of innovations.

The complex and difficult choices ahead for ILL managers and library administrators make it clear that no single combination of efficiency measures can be recommended for every library, just as there can be no fixed productivity level. In combination, transaction to staff ratios, average fill rates, and turnaround times can be excellent guides to evaluate an ILL operation. Patron needs, available resources and budgets, service quality standards, and library goals must also be factored into the equation. One thing is certain: ILL and libraries are changing rapidly. Libraries willing to adopt new methods of operation will benefit by increased efficiency and cost savings.

NOTES

1. "National Interlibrary Loan Code," *RQ 33* (Summer 1994): 477.

2. Donald E. Riggs, "Managing Academic Libraries with Fewer Resources," *Journal for Higher Education Management* 8 (Summer/Fall 1992): 34, 38.

3. *ARL Statistics: 1993-94* (Washington, DC: Association of Research Libraries, 1995), 9.

4. Noelene P. Martin, "Information Transfer, Scholarly Communication, and Interlibrary Loan: Priorities, Conflicts, and Organizational Imperatives," in *Research Access Through New Technology,* ed. by Mary E. Jackson (New York: AMS Press, 1989), 6.

5. Rod Henshaw, "Library to Library," *Wilson Library Bulletin* 60 (April 1986): 44-45.

6. Anne B. Piternick, "ILL Meets Technology," *Canadian Library Journal* 41 (October 1985): 269.

7. Tammy Nickelson Dearie and Virginia Steel, *Interlibrary Loan Trends: Staffing and Organization, SPEC Kit 187* (Washington, DC: Association of Research Libraries, 1992): 5.

8. Marilyn M. Roche, *ARL/RLG Interlibrary Loan Cost Study* (Washington, DC: Association of Research Libraries, June 1993): 19.

9. Ibid., 38, and Dearie, flyer.

10. Roche, 19.

11. Cheryl LaGuardia, and Connie V. Dowell, "The Structure of Resource Sharing in Academic Libraries," *RQ 30* (Spring 1991): 372.

12. Robin V. Williams, "Productivity Measurements in Special Libraries," *Special Libraries* 79 (Spring 1988): 102.

13. Pat Weaver-Meyers, Shelly Clement, and Carolyn Mahin, *Interlibrary Loan in Academic and Research Libraries: Workload and Staffing* (Washington, DC: Office of Management Services, Association of Research Libraries, 1989), 103.

14. Ibid., 10.

15. Ibid., 5.

16. Lois C. Gilmer, Interlibrary Loan: *Theory and Management* (Englewood, CO: Libraries Unlimited, 1994), 105.

17. Carol Anne Hert, "Predictors of Interlibrary Loan Turnaround Times," *LISR: Library and Information Science Research* 9 (July-September, 1987): 224-225.

18. Rebecca Linton, "Summary of Interlibrary Loan Performance and Costs for FY 1994," (Austin, Texas: Texas State Library, 1995), photocopied.

19. Weaver-Meyers, 4.

20. Ibid., 3.

21. Ibid., 3.

22. Ibid., 5

23. Ibid., 7.

24. Ibid., 11.

25. Ibid., 9.

26. Malcolm D. Smith, *A Project to Improve Inter-Library Loans Services Within the Research Libraries Group: Report of Consultant* (London: British Library Lending Division, May 1984), 17 and 77.

BIBLIOGRAPHY

ARL Statistics: 1993-94. Washington, DC: Association of Research Libraries, 1995.

de Bruijn, Erik. "The Effect of Automation on Job Duties, Classification, Staffing Patterns, and Labor Costs in the UBC Library's Cataloguing Divisions: a Comparison of 1973 and 1986." Vancouver: University of British Columbia, December 10, 1986. ERIC, ED 301207.

Dearie, Tammy Nickelson and Virginia Steel. *Interlibrary Loan Trends: Staffing and Organization. SPEC Kit 187*. Washington, DC: Association of Research Libraries, 1992.

Gilmer, Lois C. *Interlibrary Loan: Theory and Management*. Englewood, CO: Libraries Unlimited, 1994.

Henshaw, Rod. "Library to Library." *Wilson Library Bulletin* 60 (April 1986): pp. 44-45.

Hert, Carol Anne. "Predictors of Interlibrary Loan Turnaround Times." *LISR: Library and Information Science Research* 9 (July-September, 1987): 213-234.

LaGuardia, Cheryl and Connie V. Dowell. "The Structure of Resource Sharing in Academic Libraries." *RQ 30* (Spring 1991): 370-374.

Linton, Rebecca. "Summary of Interlibrary Loan Performance and Costs for FY 1994." Austin, Texas: Texas State Library, 1995. Photocopied.

Martin, Noelene P. "Information Transfer, Scholarly Communication, and Interlibrary Loan: Priorities, Conflicts, and Organizational Imperatives." *Research Access Through New Technology.* Edited by Mary E. Jackson. New York: AMS Press, 1989.

Molyneux, Robert. "Staffing Patterns and Library Growth in ARL Libraries, 1962/63 to 1983/84." *Journal of Academic Librarianship* 12 (November 1986): 292-297.

"National Interlibrary Loan Code." *RQ 33* (Summer 1994): 477-479.

Piternick, Anne B. "ILL Meets Technology." *Canadian Library Journal* 41 (October 1985): 267-273.

Riggs, Donald E. "Managing Academic Libraries with Fewer Resources." *Journal for Higher Education Management* 8 (Summer/Fall 1992): 27-34.

Roche, Marilyn M. *ARL/RLG Interlibrary Loan Cost Study.* Washington, DC: Association of Research Libraries, June 1993.

Smith, Malcolm D. *A Project to Improve Inter-Library Loans Services Within the Research Libraries Group: Report of Consultant.* London: British Library Lending Division, May 1984.

Waldart, Thomas J., and Thomas P. Marcum. "Productivity Measurement in Academic Libraries." *Advances in Librarianship* 6 (1976): 53-78.

Weaver-Meyers, Pat, Shelly Clement and Carolyn Mahin. *Interlibrary Loan in Academic and Research Libraries: Workload and Staffing.* Washington, DC: Office of Management Services, Association of Research Libraries, 1989.

Williams, Robin V. "Productivity Measurements in Special Libraries." *Special Libraries* 79 (Spring 1988): 101-114.

Interlibrary Loan Management Software:
A Comparative Analysis
of SAVEIT, AVISO and PRS

Yem S. Fong
Penny Donaldson
Enid Teeter

SUMMARY. Recent advancements in technological distribution and connectivity, and rising interlibrary borrowing and lending volume find many libraries seeking electronic solutions. As interlibrary loan offices increasingly eliminate paper files, the role of interlibrary loan software assumes greater and greater importance. This article provides a comparative analysis of three products: SAVEIT, AVISO and PRS (Patron Request System), and assesses how these systems meet interlibrary loan management needs and the changing Internet environment. *[Article copies available from The Haworth Document Delivery Service: 1-800-342-9678. E-mail address: getinfo@haworth.com]*

INTRODUCTION

As interlibrary loan (ILL) and document delivery (DD) have evolved in recent years, the promise of an integrated interlibrary loan management

---

Yem S. Fong is Assistant Professor and Head of Information Delivery Services, University of Colorado at Boulder.

Penny Donaldson is Head of Interlibrary Loan, University of Kansas.

Enid Teeter is Head of Interlibrary Loan, University of Wyoming.

The authors wish to acknowledge the assistance of Tom Delaney, Head of Interlibrary Loan, Colorado State University, and Dudley Emmert, Library Technician, Interlibrary Loan, University of Colorado at Boulder.

[Haworth co-indexing entry note]: "Interlibrary Loan Management Software: A Comparative Analysis of SAVEIT, AVISO and PRS." Fong, Yem S., Penny Donaldson, and Enid Teeter. Co-published simultaneously in *Journal of Library Administration* (The Haworth Press, Inc.) Vol. 23, No. 1/2, 1996, pp. 95-124; and: *Interlibrary Loan/Document Delivery and Customer Satisfaction: Strategies for Redesigning Services* (ed: Pat L. Weaver-Meyers, Wilbur A. Stolt, and Yem S. Fong) The Haworth Press, Inc., 1996, pp. 95-124. Single or multiple copies of this article are available from The Haworth Document Delivery Service [1-800-342-9678, 9:00 a.m. - 5:00 p.m. (EST). E-mail address: getinfo@haworth.com].

95

system has loomed large on the horizon. Spurred by the efforts of the Association of Research Libraries (ARL) North American Interlibrary Loan and Document Delivery (NAILDD) Project, much attention has been focused on software development that seeks to fulfill the gamut of interlibrary loan/document delivery(ILL/DD) needs.[1] From the perspective of interlibrary loan librarians, these ILL/DD needs include local patron request updating and management, financial tracking, copyright reporting, collection development data, transfer of data from union databases, integration with local or regional databases and with e-mail request systems. A tall order indeed. Many software programs designed to provide automated control of interlibrary borrowing and lending have occurred with regularity in the past decade. Some have started as home grown, locally written programs. Others are commercially available. A number of these have survived with continued product support and enhancements. Among members of the Greater Midwest Research Libraries Consortium (GMRLC) ILL software in use varies from in-house systems to beta testing of AVISO. Realizing that ILL software contributes significantly to redesigning interlibrary loan, this article will focus on a comparison of three products, currently being used or considered by members of GMRLC: SAVEIT, AVISO and the Patron Request System (PRS). SAVEIT is the software of choice for a large number of libraries nationally, while the new kid on the block is AVISO. PRS is a university-supported product designed specifically to manage borrowing operations.

To a degree, the utilities, OCLC, RLIN and WLN provide basic borrowing and lending statistics. However, this has been insufficient for most high volume departments. Interlibrary loan software has frequently developed in response to a library's specific need for data such as collection management reports, internal ILL record keeping and statistical tracking. As ILL/DD offices face increasing challenges to improve turnaround time, utilize document delivery vendors, and work with gateways to full text sources such as OCLC's First Search, the requirements for management software continue to evolve. The development of an ideal system, as described by Jackson and Baker in the famous 1992 ARL white paper,[2] capable of meeting most interlibrary loan specifications, may be just around the corner.

ILL SOFTWARE

A review of the literature within the last five years indicates that the interlibrary loan software that has been most successful are those developed by ILL staff or by computer programmers working closely with ILL librarians. Some of these have been built using a database management system on a pc such as dBase III Plus. Various locally programmed systems are reportedly functioning well to meet interlibrary loan and collection development purposes. The Briscoe Library at the University of Texas Health Science Center utilizes a VAX 8700 minicomputer to download from both OCLC and Docline.[3] Michigan State University designed a system using R:base software with the intent of focusing on a limited set of borrowing functions while maintaining the potential for future development.[4] Other pc based ILL programs include: Texas Tech's Data Management System for ILL written in dBase III Plus; I'LLFile and Tracker that strips selected fields from OCLC ILL work forms then imports the data into database or spreadsheet programs; Consortium Loan Service (CLS), developed by George Mason University for the Washington Research Library Consortium, which is a pc based system using Turbo Pascal that interfaces with NOTIS; plus various programs developed using CLIPPER, Q&A, FoxPro.[5]

Medical libraries have also been quick to develop pc database applications. QuickDOC is an ILL management software specifically designed to function with DOCLINE, the ILL subsystem of the National Library of Medicine. It has become a standard for many one-person medical libraries.

Interlibrary Loan subsystems that are part of a library's or consortium's integrated online database are increasingly becoming the norm. In Minnesota the PALS system offers an ILL subsystem that supports resource sharing activities of libraries in the MINITEX region and allows transmission of request between libraries in Minnesota, North Dakota and South Dakota. This subsystem links requests to users through circulation records and offers easy access to status checks on ILL requests. Notification is electronic through these records. Authors Chapman and Smith note that recordkeeping, statistics, and copyright files are quickly available through the subsystem.[7] Commercial library vendors, such as Innovative Interfaces, are also beginning to develop and beta test ILL subsystems that will interface with OCLC and provide statistical and management data.

GMRLC

GMRLC is a resource sharing consortium of 18 libraries. (See Appendix Table A.1.) According to statistics provided by a sample of 10 of the members, the volume of both borrowing and lending by GMRLC libraries has risen each year between 1990 and 1995. This activity mirrors reports by ARL of a 99 percent increase in ILL borrowing and a 50 percent increase in lending between 1986 and 1994 among major research libraries.[8] In order to meet this growth GMRLC libraries are very involved in utilizing technological enhancements, including ILL software, that will both improve services and manage ILL workflow efficiently.

In a poll of GMRLC libraries, half are currently using SAVEIT in some way (see Table 1). Another four own the program but are not currently using it for institutional reasons. Colorado State is a beta site for AVISO, testing both borrowing and lending functions. The University of Wyoming and the University of Colorado have tested AVISO using demonstration diskettes of version 5.0. The University of Colorado is actively using PRS for borrowing. Many of the libraries using commercial ILL software supplement the information produced with manual statistics, spreadsheets and even other databases. Some of the GMRLC libraries are also currently testing the Prism Interlibrary Loan Reports (PILLR) system produced by OCLC that provides a wide range of in-depth data. This survey of GMRLC members indicates that many institutions are in transition, either discontinuing software they had been using or beta testing new products. This again mirrors national trends where libraries are investigating how different software packages can be adapted locally to provide the maximum benefit.

In this climate of greater connectivity, ILL software must interact with electronic request and delivery mechanisms, interface with OCLC and other utilities, accept requests from local and remote databases and do all this without re-keying information. To the authors, it is evident that most current software has not yet arrived at this point, but that at least one of the products reviewed is progressing towards that goal. As a result, the authors focus on those characteristics of ILL management software that would be useful to libraries in differing stages of transition regarding technology and automating ILL functions. Evaluation criteria were developed that would speak to the potential for future connectivity, as well as criteria that focused on replacing manual sorting and counting procedures. These fell into the broad categories of: comprehensiveness, reports, accounting, request management, technical requirements, technical support and costs. Most of these categories do not require explanation. However, the term comprehensiveness is used to encompass the wide-ranging scope of possibilities for ILL software that will capture data from multiple sources and import it into a local system where the request can be tracked and data manipulated. We hope that this comparative review of three software programs will provide some ground work for those libraries trying to decide what to do about ILL software.

SAVEIT

SAVEIT allows users to store records of OCLC interlibrary loan transactions in a database on their workstation's hard drive. These workstations

TABLE 1. GRMLC Libraries Current ILL Software Use

INSTITUTION	SAVEIT	OTHER
Baylor	Owns a copy	Does manual tracking of paper files but not using it.
Colorado St.		Beta site for AVISO, had been using manual files.
Iowa St.	Borrowing	
Kansas State	Yes	
Linda Hall	Used in 1994 Not using 1995*	OCLC statistics (lending).
Oklahoma St.	Used 2.5 years Not this FY**	Currently manual.
Southern Illinois		Developing prototype.
Texas A & M	Yes (Bor & Lend)	Some manual backup.
Texas Tech		Local system developed in 1987 by Amy Chang.
U. of Arkansas	Own but not in active use.	Symphony / Borrowing, some manual stats & OCLC statistics.
U. of Colorado (Boulder)		PRS for borrowing, Excel & Quatro Pro, OCLC. statistics, some manual.
U. of Kansas	Yes–LAN (Borrowing & Lending)	Spreadsheets in Excel & Quatro Pro, OCLC.
U. of Missouri (Columbia)	Borrowing	Monthly statistics in Lotus.
U. of Nebraska (Lincoln)	Yes	Supplemented by other database & spreadsheets.
U. of New Mexico		OCLC statistics, Excel, Fox Pro (for copyright & collection develop.).
U. of Oklahoma	Yes	
U. of Texas (Austin)	Yes, but not all functions	Excel (Invoices-switching to Filemaker). OCLC statistics, manual cards for copyright.
U. of Wyoming	Yes	

*Linda Hall used SAVEIT in 1994, but their lending rate tripled in 1995. They felt like the manual input of so many their requests took too much time to continue using the program.
**Oklahoma State was using SAVEIT on the same computer as OCLC which caused a file conflict. After 2.5 years of use, they abandoned the program this fiscal year. Attempts are still being make to install it on a separate workstation.

may also be networked on a LAN. Most of the electronic record creation is integrated into the OCLC workflow as OCLC records are being sent, received and updated, so there is very little extra time spent on creating SAVEIT records. Future versions of SAVEIT will capture records of RLIN, WLN and DOCLINE. SAVEIT permits the user to manually create records of non-OCLC transactions so that records on all ILL activity can be stored in the database for inclusion in statistics and reports. SAVEIT can print a complete ALA form from any database record.

SAVEIT was initially developed in the Interlibrary Loan Department of Case Western Reserve University between 1985 and 1988 by Patrick Brumbaugh, then head of the department, and Rick Gillaspy, a computer engineering major and student assistant in the Library. Following installation of an OCLC M300 and Micro Enhancer software, it became apparent that the M300 was under-utilized when confined to the upload/download features of the Micro Enhancer and the on-line activities of OCLC. The combination of hard disk storage space and the SaveScreen feature of the OCLC software offered the possibility of capturing permanent copies of ILL records before they disappeared from the ILL Subsystem. Once the records were captured on the workstation's hard disk, database management software could be used to manipulate the data and produce a far greater amount of information about ILL activity than that provided by the OCLC monthly statistics. Dbase III Plus was selected. Later, when over 100 different dBase programs had been written to manipulate the ILL data, the dBase compiler Clipper was used to create a free-standing program.

When the success of the project became apparent it was marketed by the Library and was quickly purchased by more than 60 other libraries. In 1990 the developers formed their own company, Interlibrary Software and Services, Inc., to continue development and marketing of SAVEIT. They have since released two expanded versions: Version 1.5 in 1991 and Version 2 in 1993. A new release, Version 3, is being prepared for 1996. SAVEIT is now used by over 400 libraries in 46 states and the District of Columbia. Its users include academic, corporate, government and public libraries.

STRENGTHS OF SAVEIT

- SAVEIT supports both borrowing and lending and creates database records from OCLC by using OCLC's SaveScreen feature. It interfaces with the OCLC Micro Enhancer and allows updating to move either from OCLC to SAVEIT or the reverse, depending on the workflow arrangement of the ILL department. Depending on how much information is downloaded from OCLC, records can be tracked for current and on-going status.

- Items are added to the library/address file during conversion of OCLC lending requests, during creation of non-OCLC records, during updating and manually. The secondary screen contains policy information such as charges and length of loans. A handy feature allows the user to assign five group names to each library. Reports can be run by these groupings. Other data are the billing address and a notes field. If kept up, a lot of information is provided on these screens.
- In the borrowing records, SAVEIT keeps track of invoices that will be received from lending libraries if the library/address file indicates there will be a charge. If invoice information is entered, SAVEIT can verify the transaction when the invoice is received and can keep track of payments. For lending, if your library/address file indicates that you charge a particular library for a transaction, an invoice can be printed (or one invoice for multiple transactions in a specified time frame can be generated). A record for indicating charges and receiving payments is then automatically created. This record can be used to verify transactions for expected checks. The record can be edited to record the receipt of a check which then becomes a permanent record of the payment and cost of the transaction. Previous records of both borrowing and lending billing and payment activity may be archived to a disk and retrieved when needed.
- SAVEIT has both a single-user and multi-user format. Networking the multi-user format allows many staff members access to SAVEIT simultaneously. Security is controlled by a server software sign-on and a batch file on the hard drive of each workstation.
- As the databases grow, records may be archived.

LIMITATIONS OF SAVEIT

- SAVEIT does not capture records from other utilities such as RLIN, DOCLINE and WLN (promised Version 3), nor does it capture records from document suppliers not on a utility (planned for the future, but not Version 3). The software does not interface with a local OPAC or supply a local patron database. There is no Internet transmission or messaging. The name and address of a library may convert in a garbled form from OCLC (because of the way it is entered on OCLC, not because SAVEIT scrambles it) and need considerable editing. Interlibrary Services and Software intends to issue a separate address directory to take care of this.

- The databases are a record of a transaction, but there is no provision for circulation of borrowing items. SAVEIT needs to develop a way to indicate a renewal situation. This section should be optional for those who do not use an automated system to check out ILL materials. There is no ability to notify patrons either by print or e-mail. Borrowing may print a notice to the patron of overdue materials, but the address of the patron does not print out on the form. Only the name, department and status are printed.

- While most of the reports provide a lot of useful information, many do require a long time to run and tie up a single use workstation. In the Collection Manager's Report, to sort by call number requires that you enter the call number manually as they do not drop in from the OCLC record. The titles are truncated, which causes confusion for some bibliographers. The journal citations do not include the volume, number or pages (promised as future fix). In the Copyright Compliance Report, a way to keep track of royalty payments would be very helpful. The Invoice Report by library symbol is a good idea. Some libraries send monthly statements giving a record of an account. When the grouping of invoices function is used, only those invoices not paid are included. SAVEIT does not have a field to enter an invoice number, nor does it automatically generate a unique invoice number (Version 3). Other reports that would be useful include the ability to keep a separate record for each library's charge account in lending and separate departmental accounts in borrowing. Reports cannot be customized, but must be chosen from limited fields; however, reports can be sent to a disk file and divided using a text editor.

- The system allows fields to be filled in, but will not search on many of those fields. Searchable fields for borrowing are ILL number, title, patron, request date and call number. For lending the searchable fields are ILL number, request date, title and call number. The borrowing code is only searchable in the borrowing database and not lending. The author field is not searchable in either borrowing or lending and would be especially useful in borrowing. Boolean searching is not available.

- Editing borrowing requests is menu driven, making it cumbersome to correct. A better editing ability such as OCLC's command line method is necessary. In spite of a whole array of "no" types, there is no provision for owning a serial title but lacking that issue. Using NOT (not owned) connotes that the title is not owned.

- There are many positive aspects to working in a LAN environment, but sharing a library database can prove difficult. Sometimes the borrowing and lending units of a library have different addresses, creating overwrites. The borrowing notes field is limited and there is no lending notes field. Indexing requires considerable time.

EVALUATION OF SAVEIT

Comprehensiveness

1. User friendliness—Choosing items from the menu is a good concept, but it is not always readily apparent what is meant by the choice (indexed value, for example). Going through the many layers can be a lengthy process. It is not always readily apparent where to find what you are looking for, however the manual is indexed.

   Training students and staff—Rote training such as updating records can be learned in a short time. Longer tasks such as running reports and archiving take more training time. Workshops are occasionally available for training.
2. Supports both borrowing and lending.
3. Creates database records.
   Converts from OCLC (uses OCLC's SaveScreen feature).
   Interfaces with OCLC Micro Enhancer.
   Non-OCLC records created manually.
   (Will not convert from RLIN or WLN until version 3 in 1996.)
   Will not interface with local OPAC.
4. No Internet transmission or messaging.
5. ALA forms may be created manually.
6. Has an address book for new libraries (created from OCLC's BILL TO line).
7. Patron database—no, cannot create from OPAC.

Reports

1. Degree of customization—limited ability to define report options. Only those choices on the menu are available.
2. Copyright—tracks and reports.
   Title list of CCG journals ordered—yes, tells how many times CCG titles ordered.

Title list of violations–can be set to print only those ordered 5 times or more.
Reports by month and year.

Warning of possible violations–can be set to print when title hits four or five orders; printed weekly and checked List of copyright cleared/paid items–only CCG's print on the copyright report. You would have to run a report of Document Delivery vendors by code to get list of items from them. Copyright Clearance Center items impossible to sort out.
Limitations–Titles are truncated. Journal entries do not give volume, number or pages.

Copyright Compliance Report–can print full or summary report. For a title to appear on the Copyright Compliance Report, you must decide the "number of repeats for copyright list" in System Defaults and whether or not you want it to count pending records. The full Copyright Compliance List prints bibliographic records of each request counted, including ILL number, OCLC number, request date and patron data. The summary report prints each journal title and the number of times each title was requested.

3. Collection Management Report-
   By department, title, call number.
   By copies, loans or both within defined time frame on printer or disk.

4. Patron Statistics-
   By patron, department or status. (Either specific or all data in each category.)
   Subtotaled by loans and photocopies and display the percentage of requests filled.
   Options–average turnaround time and total cost.
   Reports can be statistics only or include bibliographic profiles of each transaction.

5. Statistical Reports-
   Borrowing and Lending activity can be defined within a specified date range.
   Full statistics report–can be sent to printer, screen or disk file; may include bibliographic information.
   Borrowing or Lending–number of requests sent, number filled (subtotals for loans and photocopies) and the percentage of requests filled.

Options–average turnaround time and total cost; borrowing only–fill rate; lending only–will specify "no" types if "no" type categories are being filled in.

Screen displays only–useful for displaying information such as number of photocopies received or number of loans supplied.

6. Overdue Notices-

Overdue Borrowing–notice to patrons of items that you have borrowed for them that are now overdue.

Overdue Lending–notice to other libraries of items that you have loaned to them that are now overdue.

Accounting

1. Invoices–Lending, two formats:

Single invoices (which create the accounting database).

Invoices for a library symbol (charges will be listed only for records that already exist in the accounting database). Range of dates may be specified.

Checks Received For Lending Requests.

Lists all payments that have been received on a specified date.

Overdue Checks–notice to other libraries of charge for lending transactions that have not yet been paid.

2. Borrowing–Invoices Received:

Keeps track of invoices that will be received from lending libraries if the LIBS (library/address files) record indicates there will be a charge. If invoice information is entered, SAVEIT can verify the transaction when the invoice is received and can keep track of payments. (Useful if department keeps track of invoices. May be ignored if invoices go directly to an accounting department.) If an invoice record is created in borrowing, you may indicate patron charges either as a cash payment or debit account (such as departmental). Departmental Charges–for borrowing–lists debits when patrons pay through department accounts.

Overdue Payments–notice to patrons of charges for borrowing transactions that have not yet been paid.

Additional reports:

Deposit accounts–In lending, deposit accounts may be created for vendors. Reports are run by submit date and combine the libraries. You cannot run a report on the activity for one library.

New Deposit Account Charges–Will update lending charges in deposit accounts.

Previous Deposit Account Charges–Will review lending charges in deposit accounts by submit date (drawback).

Aged Account Reporting–Previous records of both borrowing and lending billing and payment activity may be archived to a disk and retrieved when needed.

Generate monthly statements–May be printed for individual items or collectively for a given library during a specified time period. If you choose to print the activity for one library for a monthly period, only the individual invoices not paid will show up. The printout is labeled an invoice rather than a statement.

Request Management

1. Tracking requests–Current and on-going status–When records are ordered on OCLC and downloaded into SAVEIT, the status is "pending." "In process" and "shipped" status can be moved from OCLC, but it is easier to just wait and update "received" on SAVEIT and not try to update each record daily. "Received" records are then uploaded into OCLC's Micro Enhancer where they wait to be updated "returned." The operator can also update on OCLC and move the information to SAVEIT.

   Circulation of loans–overdue items–notices can be printed.
   Returns are updated as such.
   Notification messages–does not print paper or e-mail notices.

Technical Requirements

1. Equipment Specifications: IBM-PC or 100 percent IBM-compatible PC. It is not necessary to run SAVEIT on an OCLC terminal. Requires 530K of available memory to install; 570K of available memory to run, or higher memory (a megabyte or more of memory). SAVEIT can address higher memory, which prevents crashes that can occur when conventional memory is monopolized by other software.

   A hard disk with 20-40 megabytes available (for smaller libraries) or 40-80 megabytes (for larger libraries). The number of records

SAVEIT can manage is limited only by the available hard disk space. Approximately 10 megabytes are needed to store and manage 5000 records. SAVEIT supports most dot matrix printers that can receive system commands to switch between normal and compressed print while printing. SAVEIT will also support some laser printers.

2. Software requirements–SAVEIT version 2 must be run under DOS 3.3 or higher. SAVEIT is compatible with the OCLC Passport Software for PRISM-ILL. It is not necessary to use the OCLC Micro Enhancer Plus in order for SAVEIT to interface with OCLC, but using it will greatly expedite Updating operations.
3. Network capability–SAVEIT has both single-user and multi-user format.
4. Archiving/backup functions–Borrowing and lending records are archived to two places simultaneously: a diskette, and an archive database. The archive database may be purged and archived records stored on disks. Records in the hard disk archives are included in all reports and statistics. Backup may be to disks or tapes.
5. Data security/password protection–Security is controlled by a software server sign-on and a batch file on the hard drive of each workstation.

Technical Support

1. Vendor maintenance–Provides enhancements, upgrades.
2. User support–Pat Brumbaugh monitors the SAVEIT L list and replies regularly to questions. Interlibrary Software and Services supplies an 800 number where messages may be left if no one is there and they also have an e-mail address. Workshops are also occasionally conducted in various libraries.
3. Upgrades–1990 Version 1.
   1991 Version 1.5; 1993 Version 2.
   1996 Version 3 (projected).
4. Documentation–Manuals are supplied. Information is provided on SAVEIT-L listserv.

Cost

$525 for the single-user format.
$650 for the multi-user format.
(Plus $4.00 shipping/handling in each case.)

ANALYSIS OF SAVEIT

Interlibrary Services and Software, Inc. is very receptive to suggestions and continues to work on upgrades. Version 3 promises that the lender field will be divided into three fields representing libraries to which the request has not yet been routed, libraries that have refused the request and the library that supplied the request (if any). The status field will be extended and all fields that are currently sub-fields, such as Copyright Compliance, Max Cost, Dept, Status, etc., will become fields. Other enhancements promised for Version 3 include the use of the ISSN number for generating reports for the Copyright Clearance Center. When the data exists in the on-line record, the format of SAVEIT will include ISBN numbers, Series Notes and Uniform Titles. Statistics and reports will be expanded, as will the use of SAVEIT-generated requests (previously called "non-OCLC requests"). There will also be Mouse and Windows support. Version 3 will be marketed in separate modules for converting RLIN, OCLC, WLN, etc.

In spite of the limitations, SAVEIT serves a very useful function in the management of interlibrary loan records. Many of the current functions would take much more time to do manually. Because it supports both borrowing and lending, many libraries choose to convert borrowing workflow first and bring up lending later. Staff can be easily trained to do routine daily tasks such as updating. Some other functions take longer to learn, such as running reports. Since these sections of the program are not used frequently, the learning retention takes longer. When using the software, choosing items from a menu is a good concept, but it is not always readily apparent what is meant by the choice (indexed value, for example). At the University of Kansas (KU), staff who do not work with other software rate the ease-of-use higher than those who are familiar with other software.

At KU, SAVEIT has allowed us to shuffle less paper files when checking on patron requests, but did not eliminate our paper circulation file. It makes copyright compliance easier. In lending, we appreciate the ability to send overdue notices. However, in order for any of the databases to work properly, the information must be kept accurate and up-to-date. The need to customize reports and the time it takes to run reports is a drawback of SAVEIT. In a high volume ILL department time is crucial. The fact that the system also requires a great deal of time-consuming indexing in order to maintain the database also affects workflow, dictating that certain functions take place at non-peak times.

AVISO

AVISO was originally created by Dave Binkley of Simon Fraser University Library in Vancouver, British Columbia. Mr. Binkley wrote the program to manage ILL accounting functions. He later went on to enhance it with batch e-mail and other functions. In 1990, Dave Binkley decided to sell his software after demonstrating it at the Canadian Library Association Conference. In the Spring of 1993, Information Systems Management Corporation (ISM) purchased the software. ISM was recently acquired by IBM Canada. ISM Library Information Services is a computer-based service organization for libraries and the information industry. The Research Libraries Group (RLG) of the United States joined forces in adapting AVISO to U.S. standards. Under the guidelines of the North American Interlibrary Loan and Document Delivery (NAILDD) project, programmers continue to work on refining a sophisticated yet user-friendly system. Version 5.1 was released in January of 1996.

AVISO is a menu driven system. It manages the entire ILL process from patron request through overdue notice. It accepts records from OCLC, RLIN, WLN and various local systems. A request is first created in AVISO, then, via a pathway to a utility, such as OCLC, AVISO connects into the ILL subsystem so that OCLC can be searched, the request can be transmitted on OCLC, then the OCLC records are essentially captured into AVISO. AVISO subsequently is used to track the request and interface with the OCLC Micro Enhancer to update items to received, returned, etc. The OCLC data is attached to the patron information, eliminating the need for paper files. AVISO supports both the borrowing and lending workflows of ILL using savescreen functionality without the need to download to diskette as is true of other software packages. ALA request forms may be entered into AVISO to simplify statistics collection. It is also capable of generating an ALA borrowing request to be sent to another library. AVISO has a comprehensive report generation mechanism that includes user options and customization features. Statistics for the complete ILL operation can be generated from the AVISO software.

AVISO supports Internet messaging using the ISO protocols. Requests and messages can be sent over the Internet. This increases the efficiency of staff and reduces the delivery time of messages to other libraries and local patrons. For instance, if a borrowing request is unfilled, staff can pull the request up on AVISO, attach a message and send it via the Internet to the patron. This eliminates the time to write a letter explaining the unfilled status, typing the citation into the letter and addressing an envelope.

AVISO creates a patron database and a library database. The patron database includes address information as well as phone numbers and e-mail addresses. The preferred method of delivery is also included. The patron database can also be set up to include statistical categories for the patron, maximum number of orders the patron is allowed to order, upper limit in charges and a purge date for inactive patrons. The Library database includes a code for each library, address fields, e-mail address, preferred method of delivery and information on charges to be paid. Each library can be identified with categories for statistical gathering.

STRENGTHS OF AVISO

- Services both the borrowing and lending workflows of ILL.
- Provides easy access to current information regarding any patron request entered into the system—retrieves lists of requests by patron name.
- Interfaces with utilities—requests created in AVISO are directly uploaded into the utility where searching and transmitting occur. AVISO records track status of requests by interfacing with micro enhancing software such as OCLC's Micro Enhancer.
- Automates the receiving process using MicroEnhancer functionality interfaced with AVISO.
- Utilizes the Internet for messaging to help control library costs. With the Internet, ILL staff can communicate library-to-library or library-to-patron via e-mail. No need to re-key citations into e-mail for patron notification.
- Provides copyright compliance tracking.
- Provides the ability to customize collection management and statistical reports to the meet local needs.

LIMITATIONS OF AVISO

- The Library database must be created manually. AVISO does not provide an existing database. It would take many hours to key in this information.
- There are not yet currently any United States Libraries that are using AVISO. Consequently, there is no one to contact who has a similar working setup to confer with.
- The complexity of the system may require considerable attention to properly implement.

EVALUATION OF AVISO

Comprehensiveness

1. User friendliness—AVISO is menu driven. The menu choices seem to be clearly stated. It is easy to navigate in the program. It would not take a large amount of time to train staff for using the program. There will be some time spent to ensure that the program is properly installed with a lot of the connections made appropriately (communications package and AVISO interconnectivity).
2. Supports both borrowing and lending.
3. Creates database records.
4. Interfaces directly to OCLC, RLIN, WLN. According to AVISO documentation, it can capture ILL requests generated from an OPAC.
5. Has Micro Enhancer interface.
6. Supports the ISO Interlibrary Loan Protocol for the international exchange of ILL data in machine-readable form.
7. Allows the addition of ALA requests through a manual process.
8. AVISO creates an address book of libraries/vendors.
9. The patron database can be as detailed as you like. There are fields for address, e-mail address, phone numbers, etc. Does not interface with OPAC patron records.

Reports

1. Customized—AVISO offers user defined, custom options for reports. There are fifteen different types of reports available and all can be defined by specific dates. Includes: Department, Patron Status, Cancellation, Journal Title, etc.
2. Can be specified by date.
3. Copyright tracking and reporting—developed under NAILDD recommendations. AVISO provides a set of compliance flags that are customizable. Reports can be created by compliance flag or item type. Title list of CCG journals can be printed.
   Title list of violations can be printed. You would need to compare to previous list to check for copyright fees being paid.
4. Collection Development Report—can be run by title, department, call number, date ranges.
   Patron reports—patron history, department, status, average turn-around.
5. Statistical Reports—gives breakdown of lending and borrowing activity within specified dates. By number, percentage of requests

filled; calculates average turnaround. Analyzes borrowing and/or lending with any other library or group of libraries.

6. Overdue notices generated–borrowing and lending.
7. Notification–e-mail messages can be sent to patrons without re-keying citation information.
   Types of notification–item received, unfilled, ready for pick-up. Can also be printed for mail.

Accounting

1. Lending–AVISO doesn't track payments, report on overdue payments or handle deposit accounts. (Expects to develop in the future.)
2. Borrowing–can indicate that an order was invoiced, system flags as invoiced, and can enter payment information.
3. Deposit Accounts–can set up account types for patrons or libraries to indicate deposit account status but AVISO does not track payments.
4. There are four reports that include cost information–Net Activity, Invoices, Account Number, Library Charges.

Request Management

1. Tracks status of request–action on requests captured via Micro Enhancer, then updates AVISO records.
2. Circulation of loans–Can print overdue notices. (Authors are uncertain as to circulation functions.)
3. AVISO can be set up to produce a Circulation Slip, i.e., call number, due date, restrictions on use that can be used as a book band for items borrowed.
4. Will also produce a lending send-out slip which includes borrower's mailing address, but does not print this to labels.

Technical Requirements

1. Equipment Specifications:
   AVISO will run on an IBM PC or a compatible PC with a 386 processor or higher processor. A minimum of 4 MB of RAM, including at least 500 K free conventional memory. Hard disk with 5 MB available for software and the initial database, plus additional space for orders and reports.
2. Software:
   DOS Version 5.0 or higher.

Backup or compression software.

Passport and Micro Enhancer for OCLC.

Communications software package for data capture and messaging.
3. Network Platforms:
AVISO runs on Novell Netware (3.11 or 4.01), Windows NT and Banyan Vines. 1996 Upgrade Version 5.1.

Technical Support

1. ISM has a toll-free number for their Help Desk. There is an AVISO support coordinator who fields questions. Installation support is free for the first 60 days after receiving AVISO and continued support can be purchased for $475 annually or $55 per call. On-site visits can be arranged and are priced separately. There is an AVISO list-serv where questions can be asked.

Costs

Stand alone version costs $2500.
Network version starts at $3000.
Prices go down as the number of copies or workstation setups increases.

ANALYSIS OF AVISO

AVISO is impressive due to the complexity and flexibility of the program. The electronic messaging component of the program really makes the program efficient. That portion of the program will be worth a lot as libraries utilize e-mail request systems more fully.

The input of data into the program is relatively easy. Records can be imported from OCLC, RLIN, WLN and various local programs or manually entered. The procedures to manipulate the data are straightforward. The program is menu driven and easily followed. The tracking ability of the program is excellent. A request can be checked or updated in a few key strokes. Patron requests for status checks are easily handled.

The report function is thorough. There are prepared report styles available for twelve different reports. If those do not meet your needs, it is possible to export the specific database needed into a commercial database package and create your own reports.

The patron and library database can be as extensive as you desire. The required fields are minimal. The optional fields are where you will see an advantage. This is what allows libraries to work more efficiently. The e-mail addresses, billing charges and statistical categories for each type of patron and library are inserted.

According to AVISO marketing information available at the American Libraries Association MidWinter Meeting, January 1996, "Patrons can initiate an ILL request either through a supported local system (OPAC) or through a World Wide Web page that is integrated with AVISO." The same literature also notes that AVISO allows for data capture from online and CD-ROM union catalog services. The authors were unable to verify this prior to press.

The cost of AVISO is high, although within the last year the prices have been coming down. Hardware requirements are not difficult to meet.

Overall, AVISO would serve libraries well as their ILL management program. It is comprehensive yet flexible enough to meet the increasing needs to collect data for libraries. The program is well on its way to playing a major role in the ILL management software arena.

PATRON REQUEST SYSTEM

The Patron Request System (PRS) was developed by Brigham Young University (BYU) as a way of creating patron status reports for interlibrary borrowing. In 1985 BYU began experimenting with spreadsheets to collect data but quickly discovered that this was an inefficient way to generate ILL reports. They then hired a student programmer to develop a database which eventually led them to the campus computer systems office. After working closely with the campus department they discovered that the program they designed with the systems staff would require extensive funding, $30,000 to program. Ultimately the BYU ILL department decided to utilize student programming support. The program is currently written in Pascal with the intention of being available in a network version. Over the years BYU has continued to enhance its product, adding new reporting features as the need arose. Several large libraries who are also heavy borrowers use PRS. In addition to BYU, the University of Colorado at Boulder, Denver Public Library, Auraria Library of the University of Colorado, Denver and the University of California at Berkeley use PRS.

PRS is a menu driven program. It automates the processing of patron requests by creating a system record for each request received in borrowing. This is accomplished via an initial entry function that allows the system to assign a PRS number to each request entered. As the request moves through the workflow and receives action, i.e., ordered, received, etc., the corresponding PRS record is updated by entering data into PRS or via the OCLC Micro Enhancer. Ultimately each record tracks the history of action upon that request.

Patron files form the database for PRS. Reports and statistics are generated from the information stored in patron records. PRS interfaces with OCLC by using OCLC Save Screen functionality. After initial entry, the request is researched and ordered. If a request is made via OCLC, a copy of the OCLC workform is saved onto a disk and ultimately imported into PRS. ALA workforms can be created and printed by PRS as well. PRS takes the data from the OCLC workform or the ALA workform and updates its records. At that point, when PRS is queried about any request, the screen shows the title, the date the request was ordered, where it was ordered from, how it was ordered (OCLC, ALA, Letter, etc.), and the status of the order, i.e., canceled, in process, shipped, received, or returned.

Once an item is received in the office, the PRS record is updated to 'received,' and in the process, circulation records are created and labels are printed. PRS also batches 'received' and 'returned' messages to a disk which is in turn used to update OCLC records via the MicroEnhancer.

STRENGTHS OF PRS

- Provides easy access to current information regarding any patron request entered into the system retrieves lists of requests by patron name.
- Is searchable by patron name, PRS number, two 'Title' fields, lender, and a variety of other fields.
- Imports/exports–updates records with OCLC SaveScreen data and RLIN Typed data.
- Automates the receiving process–as items are received and returned on PRS this information is captured to a Micro Enhancer disk that is used to update OCLC records.
- Provides a number of collection management reports–19 different reports that include activity reports, turnaround time, patron reports by type, department, etc., lending library reports by fill rate and turnaround time, call number report, and copyright report.
- Prints labels that are attached to specific transactions–patron request form, article or band for the front of a book, patron notification form, etc.
- Affordable, low cost initial investment, $500.00.

LIMITATIONS OF PRS

- PRS currently operates on a single workstation and is not yet available in a network version although as of this writing BYU is planning to produce that enhancement in 1996. (The enhancement will be a Windows-based version written in DELPHI, and fully networkable.)
- PRS is for use only by borrowing units so lending transactions and reports must use different software, spreadsheets or must be manually counted and sorted. (BYU is in the final stages of completing a software package for Lending called 'Lending Log,' which is currently being used by the University of Utah and BYU. Demo disks are available.)
- Labels printed from PRS include patron information that is in very small type and not always easy to read.
- PRS cannot be searched by OCLC ILL number.
- PRS does not have an archiving function.
- PRS does not have a backup function, so backups need to be made using a different utility (i.e., MS Backup).
- Lacks ability to track payment of borrowing charges.

EVALUATION OF PRS

Comprehensiveness

1. User friendliness—very easy to install and to convert existing paper records. Training is straightforward and fairly intuitive.
2. Supports borrowing. Lending software in development.
3. Creates file-based records. PRS was originally written in PASCAL as a file-oriented database program. The '96 enhancements will be written in DELPHI and the program will be a true database.
4. Converts from OCLC using OCLC's SaveScreen feature.
5. Interfaces with OCLC Micro Enhancer.
6. Can create non-OCLC records; i.e., ALA forms.
7. Converts from RLIN.
8. Will not interface with local OPAC.
9. No Internet transmission or messaging.
10. Patron database must be created separately.

Reports

1. PRS is not user-customizable, though the programmers at BYU will make simple modifications.

2. Reports include: Status of patron requests listed by patron name and current status, i.e., received, returned, etc.
   Use by Patron.
   Patron Department Listing.
   Patron Status Ratios—by patron type and percentage of use.
   Patron Charges.
3. Borrowing Activity—Requests Logged In, Total Orders Placed, Orders Per Request, Requests Canceled, Materials Received, Materials Received by Patron Category.
   Turnaround time by format: Average First Order Lapse, Average Between Order Lapse, Average Times.
   Ordered (before being filled), Average Fill Lapse (from In Process date to Receive date).
   Requests by Call Numbers.
4. CCG Copyright Report by Title
5. Fill Rate Report by Lending Library.
6. Turnaround Time Report by Lending Library.
7. Overdue Notices.

Accounting

PRS can be configured to compute and print (on labels) default costs for items, or specific costs can be printed at the time the item is received. PRS can also assign account numbers to specific patrons. PRS does not track payment of bills, nor does it produce invoices or statements.

Request Management

1. Tracks current status information, i.e., ordered, shipped, canceled, etc., for any request by retrieving chronological lists of a patron's requests. Individual requests may also be displayed and include journal or book title; article title or publication information; vol, date, issue and pages; lender string.
2. After items are updated to received on PRS, labels are printed that can be placed on book wrappers or articles and to a patron notification form.

Technical Requirements

IBM PC, XT, AT, PS/2. or 100 percent compatible computer.

DOS Version 2.2 or higher.

512K of free memory.

Hard drive (with at least five megabyte free space).

Technical Support

BYU usually has a programmer on hand who can field any questions or problems. CU Boulder's experience has been that questions and problems are handled quickly and effectively.

Cost

Costs $500.00, including software, a user's manual, instructions for installing and converting to the program, and suggestions for implementing the program into the interlibrary loan borrowing routines. Discounts are available for those who attend PRS demonstrations or request a demo disk.

ANALYSIS OF PRS

The University of Colorado at Boulder chose PRS specifically to enable the office to move from paper files and manual processes to using ILL software. In its investigation of software, CU initially hoped that AVISO would provide the comprehensive package that Jackson and Baker allude to in their ARL paper. CU worked with one of the first demonstration diskette versions of AVISO and early in the process managed to crash the program and test records. This early version did not offer Micro Enhancer downloading and uploading and seemed to involve a level of complexity that the ILL staff was hesitant to assume.

CU's experience with converting printed patron files to PRS has proven to be a fairly straightforward process. BYU provided immediate telephone support during installation and implementation. BYU also did minor customization of the software for CU's needs.

While PRS is not comprehensive it provided a much-needed function in the ILL office's transition from paper files and manual processes to automated functionality, utilizing OCLC features and integrating with OCLC. It is evident that BYU plans to support its product with enhancements that will include a Windows version, network applications and a lending module.

SAVEIT, AVISO, AND PRS: A COMPARATIVE ANALYSIS

According to Jackson and Baker, "A comprehensive local interlibrary loan management system would allow for the electronic management of all requests, from initiation to final counting."[9] Functions they describe as ideal include:

1. From a patron's unsuccessful search of the local online catalog, provides electronic prompting for a search of library-determined bibliographic utilities and document suppliers.
2. Connects to bibliographic utility or document supplier for the search and captures the critical information, either for direct submission of the request (with verification of the patron's status from the local system, lender choice made according to the library's predetermined criteria, and billing and statistical information recorded appropriately) or for review by local resource sharing staff before submission.
3. Uses patron data already captured in the library's patron files.
4. Captures in the local patron record the information on items borrowed which need to be returned and provides overdue notice and fined functions by the local circulation system.
5. Provides the option of communicating with patrons and other libraries electronically or via print.
6. Provides the opportunity to enter requests into the system which do not originate from an electronic source and to handle and track those requests.[10]

How do SAVEIT, AVISO, PRS meet these requirements?

From examining these three software products it is quickly apparent that none of them come close to fulfilling this wish list (see Table 2). While both SAVEIT and AVISO approach the internal management of ILL processes with the intent of being comprehensive systems, there are still elements missing from both systems. If the goal of ILL software is to eliminate paper and reduce re-keying of information, all three products still have much development to do.

AVISO's strength in utilizing the ISO protocol for messaging is an important feature and an advantage it has over other ILL software. It is perhaps the most comprehensive software in terms of automating ILL processes and in its ability to integrate with the utilities and use utility functions such as the OCLC Micro Enhancer. It also accepts ILL requests via an OPAC or the Web. The degree of complexity in the program can be a plus or a minus depending on a local library's ability to deal with technology requirements. AVISO requires a great deal of time and energy initially setting up so that the program runs seamlessly as staff use it on a day to day basis. AVISO does not interface with a local OPAC to utilize patron records, or to use OPAC bibliographic records for patron initiated

TABLE 2. Interlibrary Loan Management Software

	SAVEIT	AVISO	PRS
COMPREHENSIVENESS			
User Friendliness (Scale of 1-10)	5	6	10
Supports Borrowing	Yes	Yes	Yes
Supports Lending	Yes	Yes	No
Creates Database Records	Yes	Yes	Yes
Interface to OCLC, RLIN, etc.	Yes	Yes	Yes
Connects Directly	No	Yes	No
Via SaveScreen	Yes	No	Yes
MicroEnhancer Interface	Yes	Yes	Yes
OPAC (Local) Interface	No	Yes	No
Internet Messaging (E-mail)	No	Yes	No
ALA Forms	Yes	Yes	Yes
Address Database	Yes	Yes	Yes
Patron Database	No	Yes	Yes
REPORTS			
Customized	Limited	Yes	Limited
Can be limited by Date?	Yes	Yes	Yes
CCG Titles	Yes	Yes	Yes
Copyright Violation Report	Yes	Yes	Yes
Copyright Violation Warnings	No	Yes	No
Copyright Cleared / Paid Report	No	?	Yes
Collection Development (T/C*)	T/C	T/C	T/C
Borrower Statistics	Yes	Yes	Yes
Turn-Around Times	Yes	Yes	Yes
Fill Rate	Yes	Yes	Yes
Patron Statistics (P/D/S**)	P/D/S	P/D/S	P/D/S
Lender Statistics	Yes	Yes	N/A
Turn-Around Times	Yes	Yes	N/A
Fill Rate	Yes	Yes	N/A
By Type / Specific Library / Region	Yes	No	N/A
Overdue Notices (B/L***)	B/L Yes	B/L Yes	Borrower / Yes
2nd Overdue Notices	No	No	Borrower / Yes
Delivery Notices	No	Yes	Yes
ACCOUNTING			
Prepares Bills for Lender	Yes	Yes	N/A
Tracks Payment	Yes	No	N/A
Dunning Notices	Yes	No	N/A
Deposit Accounts	Yes	No	N/A
Tracks Invoices for Borrower	Yes	Yes	No

Tracks Paid Invoices	Yes	Yes	No
Prepares Bills (P/D****)	Grouped	Yes	No
Tracks (P/D****) Payments	Grouped	No	No
Dunning Notices	No	No	No
Deposit Accounts	No	Yes	Yes
Generates Monthly Statements	Yes	Yes	No

REQUEST MANAGEMENT

Tracks Current Status of Requests	Yes	Yes	Yes
Tracks Circulation of Items	No	Yes	Yes
Prepares Labels for Lending	No	No	N/A
Prepares Labels for Borrowing	No	No	Yes

TECHNICAL NEEDS

Compatability (IBM / Macintosh, etc.)	IBM	IBM	IBM
Installation Memory Requirements	530k	5mb	512k
Minimum Memory to Run	570k	4mb	5mb
Optimal Memory to Run	507k+	4mb+	5mb+
Operating System Requirements	DOS 3.3+	DOS 5.0+	DOS 2.2+
Network Capability	Yes	Yes	No
Archiving Functions	Yes	Yes	No
Backup Functions	Yes	Yes	No
Security / Password Functions	Yes	No	No

TECHNICAL SUPPORT

Vendor Maintenance	Some	Yes	Yes
User Support From Vendor	Yes	Yes	Yes
User Support—Other (Listserve, etc.?)	Yes	Listserve	No
Documentation	Yes	Yes	Yes
Latest Upgrade	2	5.1	1995

COST

Initial Purchase	$525-$600	$2.5k-$3.0k	$325-$500
Upgrades	Approx $100	W / Contract	N/A

* Reports by Title / Call Number?
** By Patron / Department/Status?
*** For Borrowing / Lending?
**** By Patron / Department?

ILL. While AVISO has a high degree of sophistication, it should be capable of pulling data from local OPACs. It does offer extensive reports and user defined options. Overall, it appears to have the most potential for reaching the ideals described earlier. As libraries in the United States begin to fully test its capabilities the true measure of its worth will be more evident.

It is clear that SAVEIT has provided a very important contribution and set a standard in ILL software. It has laid some very important ground work in developing software applications for internal ILL processes. Like AVISO, SAVEIT does not interface with local online catalogs nor does it link to local patron files, or circulation system. Unlike AVISO, there is no mechanism for sending either a printed notice to a patron or generating an e-mail message. The next version of SAVEIT will add utilities, RLIN, WLN and DOCLINE, that records can be captured from, but still will fall short of the connectivity that interlibrary loan is moving towards. The producers of SAVEIT appear to be responsive to the ILL community's software needs. Many users are currently running the multi-user format under Windows, and awaiting a new version that will provide increased functionality.

PRS is not yet at the point of either SAVEIT or AVISO since it currently only supports borrowing functions. For libraries seeking to take the first step in the automation of ILL, PRS is user friendly and affordable. PRS is most effective when it is used in conjunction with an e-mail request system, and OCLC features, such as ILL Prism Transfer, Custom Holdings, ILL Fee Management. The combined end product approaches comprehensive local management of borrowing functions. Like the other software PRS falls short in its ability to interface locally with OPACs. However, PRS does offer the potential for moving into a more sophisticated program since the database of files that reside in PRS can ultimately be exported. The proposed upgrades will do much to bring PRS up to the speed with SAVEIT.

CONCLUSIONS

Since 1992 libraries have upped the ante to vendors in seeking competitive ILL software products that will offer more and more functionality. This comparison of three current software packages shows how far the ILL community has come in finding software to meet internal record keeping needs and reduce paper. It also points out that there is still a distance to go. On one end of the spectrum, PRS is low cost, low maintenance and easy to install and implement. On the other end, AVISO is a greater dollar investment and time and energy commitment. Its flexibility and comprehensiveness are significant, especially its use of the International Standards Organization, ISO Interlibrary Loan Protocol for the international exchange of ILL data in machine-readable form. Another point in its favor is that product development has occurred under the guidance of the NAILDD Project.

For many years librarians have focused on the utilities, especially OCLC, with the hopes that given a large captive audience, it would be economically feasible to offer additional ILL statistical and record keeping options. OCLC's PILLR project may provide the impetus to move further in that direction. In the meantime efforts on the part of the NAILDD project to determine ILL electronic standards are yet another step towards the possibility of ILL software that captures data between disparate systems. In this environment of transition and change, the need for comprehensive software becomes increasingly paramount as borrowing and lending rise.

SOFTWARE VENDORS

SAVEIT
Patrick Brumbaugh
Interlibrary Software and Services, Inc.
P.O. Box 12237
Research Triangle Park, NC 27709-2237
SAVEIT@ILSS.com
1-800-572-4252

AVISO
ISM Library Services
3300 Bloor Street West
16th Floor, West Tower
Etobicoke, Ontario
Canada M8X 2X2
1-800-684-8184

PRS
Kathy Hansen, Head, Interlibrary Loan
Harold B. Lee Library
Brigham Young University
P.O. Box 26800
Provo, Utah 84602-6800
(801)378-6344

NOTES

1. For information on NAILDD see: Mary Jackson, "The Future of Resource Sharing: The Role of the Association of Research Libraries," *Journal of Library Administration*, 21 no. 1/2 (1995):193-202.
2. "Maximizing Access, Minimizing Costs: A First Step Toward the Information Access Future," prepared by Shirley K. Baker and Mary E. Jackson for the ARL Committee on Access to Information Resources. November 1992.

3. Elizabeth Anne Comeaux and Susan Wilcox, "Automating Interlibrary Loan Statistics," *Technical Services Quarterly*, 8 no. 3 (1991):35-57.

4. Leah Black, "Managing Interlibrary Loan Borrowing Records with R:base," *OCLC Micro* (April/June, 1991):25-28.

5. Carolyn S. Thompson, "The Use of Q&A in Interlibrary Loan," *Journal of Interlibrary Loan, Document Delivery & Information Supply*, 5 no. 1(1994):61-66; Amy Chang, "A Database Management System for Interlibrary Loan," *Information Technology and Libraries* 9(June 1990):135-143; Michael Sarro, "Using ILLFILE for Record-Keeping of OCLC ILL Loan Requests," *Journal of Interlibrary Loan & Information Supply*, 3 no. 4 (1993):34-37; Clyde W. Grotophorst, "CLS: An ILL Management System for User-Generated Requests," *Library Software Review* (September-October 1991):320-321; Jim Nolte, "I'LLFILE and TRACKER: Interlibrary Loan Software for Detailed OCLC Interlibrary Loan Records," *Library Software Review* (November-December 1990): 370-371.

6. Penny Klein and Nancy S. Hewison, "QuickDOC: An Interlibrary Loan Department in a Microcomputer," *Medical Reference Services Quarterly*, 10(2):11-33, 1991.

7. Shari Chapman and Mary Kay Smith, "Sidebar 4: How PALS Interlibrary Loan Impacts an Interlibrary Loan Department," *Library Hi Tech* 45, 12(1):23-24, 1994.

8. Association of Research Libraries, *ARL Statistics 1993-94* (Washington, DC: ARL, 1995), 8.

9. Shirley K. Baker and Mary E. Jackson, "Maximizing Access, Minimizing Costs: A first step toward the Information Access Future," 11.

10. Ibid.

How Much Are Customers Willing to Pay for Interlibrary Loan Service?

Molly Murphy
Yang Lin

SUMMARY. An analysis of user requests for interlibrary loan materials revealed that about five percent of the total requests placed at the University of Oklahoma required lending fees. The authors review costs and the users' willingness to pay those costs to draw conclusions about the best policy for cost recovery. *[Article copies available from The Haworth Document Delivery Service: 1-800-342-9678. E-mail address: getinfo@haworth.com]*

INTRODUCTION

A substantial body of literature exists about charging users for library services. Philosophical, ethical, legal, political and economic rationales have been presented in discussions on this topic.[1] Using phrases currently in vogue, one might ask about the "political correctness" of charging fees for library services or question the collective "social consciousness" of

Molly Murphy is the Interlibrary Loan Office Manager at the University of Oklahoma.

Yang Lin is a doctoral student in communications at the University of Oklahoma.

The authors wish to acknowledge the contributions of Kay Womack, Head of Reference at the University of Oklahoma.

[Haworth co-indexing entry note]: "How Much Are Customers Willing to Pay for Interlibrary Loan Service?" Murphy, Molly, and Yang Lin. Co-published simultaneously in *Journal of Library Administration* (The Haworth Press, Inc.) Vol. 23, No. 1/2, 1996, pp. 125-139; and: *Interlibrary Loan/Document Delivery and Customer Satisfaction: Strategies for Redesigning Services* (ed: Pat L. Weaver-Meyers, Wilbur A. Stolt, and Yem S. Fong) The Haworth Press, Inc., 1996, pp. 125-139. Single or multiple copies of this article are available from The Haworth Document Delivery Service [1-800-342-9678, 9:00 a.m. - 5:00 p.m. (EST). E-mail address: getinfo@haworth.com].

125

any library that levies fees on its clientele. The question becomes especially problematic for libraries which receive public funding. The controversy arises because a hallmark of service in publicly funded American libraries has been to provide "free service." Users of library services have been led to believe that the services they receive should not cost anything, providing an unrealistic view of the actual cost of library services. Yet, as Budd, Zink and Voyles have noted, "all library services cost, not all are priced."[2] Turock furthers the point, "Information has always had a cost—no matter what the format. The question is: Who should pay?"[3]

In examining customer service and interlibrary loan policies in 1994, the University of Oklahoma Interlibrary loan (ILL) staff questioned whether their customers should pay. At that time, loan fees assessed by the lending libraries were passed along to ILL customers. In October of 1994, the library administration made a decision to absorb costs, and evaluate the effect of that effort. During the evaluation period from October 1994 to June 1995, ILL requests for which lending fees were absorbed were examined. Patrons' comments about willingness to pay were compared with the actual lending fees the library absorbed. This study reports the conclusions reached about those comments and the effect of the policy change on office procedures.

FREE VERSUS FEE–LITERATURE REVIEW

The National Commission on Libraries and Information Science lists numerous services such as photocopying, audiovisual equipment, reserve notification, and rental of art prints, typewriters, films, and sound recordings, to name a few, for which libraries charge.[4] In recent years much of the free versus fee debate, however, has focused on two library services: online database search services and interlibrary loan. Factors influencing this discussion are the four elements which Mitchell and Walters have identified as "shaping the contemporary library environment." Those four factors are: (1) increase in amount of information published; (2) expansion of technological access to that information; (3) growing demand for physical access commensurate with bibliographic access; and (4) libraries' reduced buying power.[5]

As the amount of available information increases and the variety of ways in which that information can be acquired or accessed expands, libraries with decreasing purchasing power face difficult choices. The expansion of technological access to information exacerbates the situation as users request an increase in available electronic resources and as more delivery options become available. To augment inadequate budgets, some libraries have established user fees for online database searches and interlibrary loan. A summary of the arguments for and against charging such fees seems warranted.

The 1986 report of the National Commission of Libraries and Information Science lists 17 anti-fee arguments and 16 pro-fee arguments providing a comprehensive litany of the discussion found in the literature.[6] Those arguments are summarized below.

Anti-Fee Arguments

1. Library services are a public good and free access is a fundamental right for each citizen in a democratic society.
2. The American tradition of free library services is damaged by charging fees.
3. Fees are illegal in some state legislation supporting library service.
4. Fees are discriminatory in that an individual's access to information will be based on ability to pay rather than on need.
5. Fees represent a form of double taxation.
6. Libraries will shift emphasis from nonrevenue producing services to those that generate revenue, even if the nonrevenue services are vital to a part of society that cannot afford the fee.
7. Fees will have the long-term effect of reducing public support for libraries.
8. Revenues received from library fees may be returned to the general revenue fund and used for nonlibrary purposes.
9. Fees charged have been set by tradition and habit and not from an analysis of market demands or costs.
10. It is difficult to define special services and basic services and to distinguish between them.
11. Private and public sector markets are separate and should remain separate.
12. The cost of administering and collecting fees outweighs the financial benefits of fees.
13. Most users have little need for fee-based online services.
14. If the service cannot be provided without a fee, the service should not be provided.
15. Improvements within library management and delivery of services would diminish the need for fees.
16. There is considerable staff resistance to fees.
17. Charging for a service subjects libraries to liability risks because of the responsibilities implicit in providing a service for a fee.

Pro-Fee Arguments

1. Charging fees increases recognition of the value and importance of library services.
2. Fees encourage efficient use of public resources.
3. Fees promote service levels based on need and demand.
4. Fees encourage management improvements.
5. Fees limit waste and over consumption.
6. Fees enhance investment in ongoing maintenance and repair of public facilities.
7. Fees encourage a better understanding of the financial limitations of the local government.
8. Premium service should be provided only to those willing to pay a premium.
9. The tradition of charging for services is part of American culture.
10. Fees control growth of and lower demand for service.
11. Escalating service costs make user fees a necessity.
12. Most library users can afford to pay a fee.
13. Without fees, public and academic libraries could not serve the larger community or nonresidents.
14. Fees cover only a small portion of the total cost of service provision.
15. Fees for most services are simple and inexpensive to collect.
16. Local policy may require libraries to charge for services.

The Anti-fee arguments most relevant to interlibrary loan include the view that fees are discriminatory and a form of double taxation. It is also argued that the cost of administering and collecting fees outweighs the financial benefits because users may have insufficient funds to pay for materials they really need. Users who pay taxes which support a publicly funded library budget may feel they have already paid for the right to free interlibrary loan service, or that the library is not using their taxes appropriately to purchase materials which meet their needs.

The Pro-fee arguments relevant to interlibrary loan suggest that fees encourage efficient use of public resources, limit waste and overconsumption, control growth of and lower demand for service, and cover only a small portion of the total cost. For example, interlibrary loan departments typically receive requests for some materials available in the local collection. This means these requestors have not learned to accurately use the online catalog, other bibliographic tools, or to ask for reference assistance. Charging for interlibrary loan, it is argued, encourages requestors to look harder for alternative resources in the local collection and reserve interlibrary loan for essential items which are not held. Another point made by proponents of fees states that fees rarely include the cost of staff salaries, electronic access to bibliographic databases used in interlibrary loan operations, or equipment maintenance.

Kennedy states, "Academic and public library services are not really free to the user; they are paid for by tuition, taxes and contributions. Likewise, conducting loans or filling photocopy requests is not really free to the ILL unit. There is widespread recognition that significant overhead (indirect cost) exists. The issue is not really fee vs. free but how the costs are distributed. Most library users still do not pay directly for ILL requests."[7]

COST OF INTERLIBRARY LOAN

Landes indicates, "The major issue confronting libraries today is how to cope with the financial and workload ramifications of providing expanding access to materials through ILL."[8] User fees are one method discussed for financing interlibrary loan.

As early as 1922 the idea of charging a lending fee for interlibrary loan requests was presented to the College and Reference Section of the American Library Association.[9] In 1933, the University of Nebraska reported it had instituted interlibrary loan service charges.[10] Sweetland and Weingand, citing the 1972 Palmour Study, date the modern concern with ILL charges to the early 1970s.[11] A recent ARL study of interlibrary loan trends noted, "One of the most widely discussed topics among ILL librarians and managers is that of ILL fee structure."[12]

The current increase in charges by lending libraries has been well-documented. Jackson noted an increase in the number of libraries charging for the loan of materials. She says, "While charging for photocopies was widely practiced and accepted, a charge for a loan request was the exception in 1980. The 1983 study of ILL in ARL libraries documented that twice as many libraries were charging for ILL as those responding to a similar survey in 1976. By 1989, the number of charging libraries had exploded."[13]

Budd and Jackson both describe why a lending library frequently levies a charge for loaning materials. They describe wide variation in how lending fees are paid. Reasons given for charging other libraries include: to reduce the volume, to recoup a portion of the costs, to generate enough income to cover borrowing charges, or to "'return the favor'" to libraries that charge.[14] The rationale for charging other institutions used by most ARL libraries responding to the 1992 interlibrary loan study was to recoup some of the costs (77 percent) and to discourage excessive requests (37 percent). Only 11 percent expected to recoup all of the costs associated with ILL lending.[15]

Borrowing libraries, on the other hand, may absorb the fees or charge them back to the individuals requesting the material.[16] Policy may depend more on historical precedent than on the actual borrowing fees involved.[17] Of the ARL libraries responding to the 1992 ILL survey, 18 percent passed all charges to the user; 24 percent partially subsidized the charges; and 48 percent paid all fees and did not charge users. The average amount of subsidy was $12.89.[18]

The 1972 Palmour Study reported $7.61 as the average borrowing cost and $4.67 as the average lending cost, bringing the total average cost of an item received through interlibrary loan to $12.28.[19] In 1992 these costs had risen to an average of $18.62 for borrowing and $10.93 for lending.[20] This represents an increase of 144 percent in the twenty intervening years.

USERS' WILLINGNESS TO PAY

As these discussions show, overall costs for providing interlibrary loan services have steadily risen. With this increase, the question arises as to how to pay for interlibrary loan services. Martin writes, "Financing the current interlibrary loan system is a patchwork of subsidies, fees, user charges, cost recoveries, institutional support, and mutual acceptance of free exchange."[21] As Nielsen has pointed out, "A key question is whether ILL costs can or should be passed onto users, or absorbed into the library's budget."[22] If users are charged interlibrary loan fees, are they willing and able to pay them, and if so, how much are they willing to pay? What effect does the fee have on users' ability to acquire materials not available in their local library?

Studies regarding the impact of interlibrary loan fees on users and on their willingness to pay have been conducted. University of Tennessee faculty and graduate students surveyed in 1974 were, on average, willing to pay a maximum of five dollars to obtain a book on loan for research and 10 to 20 cents per page for journal articles.[23] In summarizing three studies of interlibrary loan activity, Katz concluded the number of requests dropped when a fee was initiated, but gradually began to rise again especially if the turnaround time was faster.[24] Everett found that fees affect relatively few requests to borrow material through interlibrary loan. In his nine-month survey of interlibrary loan transactions at Colgate University, less than 5 percent of approximately 1,900 filled ILL requests involved fees, with an average charge of $5.11. When the fees were distributed over all 1900 filled requests the charge was less than 25 cents per request.[25]

Kinnucan randomly surveyed faculty and graduate students at Ohio State University, Ohio University and Wright State University and found that most were willing to pay up to $6.00 to receive a desired article through interlibrary loan or up to $4.00 to receive the article from a commercial document delivery service. Timeliness of delivery was much less important than the price.[26] Obtaining material, regardless of either speed or cost, ranked highest with both faculty and graduate students at Louisiana State University; cost was of more concern to graduate students than to faculty.[27]

While more research is needed on users' willingness to pay for interlibrary loan requests and the effect of fees on interlibrary loan traffic, these studies seem to suggest that users are willing to pay a nominal amount to acquire information and that the overall effect of charging is minimal. The following study compares customers' willingness to pay the actual lending fees assessed on a particular transaction, adding further to our understanding of how realistic users' perceptions are about ILL costs and document delivery fees.

METHODS

To compare the charges the library had to absorb for requested material with the amount users were willing to pay, only those submitted interlibrary loan requests for which the library had to absorb a charge were analyzed. During the study period, October 1994 through August 1995, a total of 648 requests required a lending fee. These requests made up about five percent of the total borrowing requests filled during the study period. The requests, made on cards or on electronic request forms, were analyzed by requestor's status, requestor's academic department, type of materials requested, amount the requestor was willing to pay, and the cost of obtaining the item (this cost is limited only to the actual lending fees assessed by non-reciprocal lenders or commercial vendors). Despite the decision to absorb costs for the evaluation period, when a user asked about costs at the Reference Desk (where interlibrary loan requests are submitted), the following policy was used to answer the inquiry:

> Although every effort is made to obtain Interlibrary Loan materials free of charge, some items, (especially photocopies) cost. In most cases, you will be responsible for any costs incurred. Therefore, it is necessary that you indicate the maximum charge you are willing to pay. Few items can be acquired for less than $6.00. Items that cannot be acquired for free will be canceled if the actual price is greater than

the amount approved on the request form. A blank amount is assumed to be $0.00.[28]

In addition to the analysis of the requests, a small sample of frequent interlibrary loan patrons were interviewed by telephone to determine their opinions regarding interlibrary loan services and costs to users.

RESULTS

Table 1 illustrates that faculty members and graduate students comprise the majority of users for which the library had to pay a fee to obtain requested materials. This distribution is reasonably consistent with that of all interlibrary requests submitted over the three year period represented in column two except that the figure for graduate students, 61.3 percent, is 5.7 percent higher than in the overall graduate borrowing population. It appears that graduate students are somewhat more likely to request materials that cost. Also, the figure for faculty, 26.1 percent, is 6.2 percent lower than the overall faculty borrowing population, suggesting that faculty requests may be less likely to require a lending fee. Undergraduate students comprise a slightly higher percentage of the study group indicating that their requests may be more likely to require payment. Conversely, staff are less likely to order items that require payment, although these last two groups are such a small percentage of the sample group that less confidence can be placed in such a conclusion.

Table 1 also shows that although undergraduate students make up a small percentage of the total requests, they are the most willing to pay.

TABLE 1. Willingness to Pay

By Customer Status

	*Study Group	**Borrower Population	Willing to Pay Partial Costs	Willing to Pay Full Costs
Undergraduates	10.8%	9.0%	73.9%	25.5%
Graduates	61.2%	55.6%	61.3%	27.0%
Faculty	26.1%	32.4%	46.7%	60.3%
Staff	1.9%	3.0%	0.0%	0.0%
Total	100.0%	100.0%		

*Total sample size of study group = 648
**3 year average (1990-1993) Total borrower population = 35,904

Among graduates and faculty, 61.3 percent of graduates and 46.7 percent of faculty are willing to pay a fee that partially covers costs. However, among the requests for which users are willing to pay, the amount of money undergraduate students are willing to pay is the least likely to cover the actual cost of obtaining the material. Faculty members' willingness to pay covered the total costs 60.3 percent of the time.

Requests were arranged by requestor's academic discipline and organized by broad subject groupings. Social scientists comprised 40 percent of the study group, scientists and mathematicians 32 percent and humanists and fine artists 23 percent. Requests on which customers failed to identify their discipline made up the remaining five percent. Although unique to this institution, these figures are comparable to the distribution among disciplines in those requests which did not require a lending fee, suggesting fees are evenly distributed among disciplines.

Table 2 is organized by these same broad subject categories and reports the proportion of users by discipline that were willing to pay an amount that covered only a portion of the lending fee required. The second column reflects the percentage of requestors by discipline who designated they were willing to pay an amount sufficient to cover the full lending fees assessed.

It is evident from Table 2 that the majority of customers, regardless of discipline, are not willing to pay enough to cover the cost of lending fees. When they are willing, however, customers in the sciences and mathematics are more willing to pay for the full costs. Customers in the humanities and fine arts disciplines are more willing to pay something, but less willing to pay enough to fully cover lending fees.

Table 3 indicates that for the three major types of materials requested

TABLE 2. Customers' Willingness to Pay vs. Full-Fee Recovery

By Broad-Discipline Category

Department	Willing to Pay Partial Costs	Willing to Pay Full Costs
Social Sciences	63.1%	32.9%
Humanities and Fine Arts	69.1%	31.9%
Sciences and Mathematics	49.7%	38.9%
Other	25.9%	42.9%

Social Sciences includes: social sciences, business, and education.
Humanities includes: humanities, architecture, journalism, and fine arts.
Sciences includes: sciences, math, geoscience, health science, and engineering.
Other includes those surveys which did not indicate a department.

TABLE 3. Customers' Willingness to Pay

By Request Type

	Requests	Willing to Pay Partial Costs	Willing to Pay Full Costs
Article	51.1%	63.1%	31.1%
Book	17.4%	54.9%	25.8%
Thesis	19.0%	61.0%	38.7%
Other	12.5%	38.1%	58.3%
Total	100.0%		

(periodical articles, books, and theses), the percentages of the requests for which users are willing to pay partial costs are relatively close, varying from 54.9 percent to 63.1 percent. The percentages of the requests fully covered by the customers' willingness to pay is 38.7 percent for theses, 31.1 percent for articles, and 25.8 percent for books. Interestingly, for the uncommon requests (these include patents, videos, newspapers, etc.), patrons were willing to pay the full costs for 58.3 percent of these items.

Table 4 groups the actual dollars customers said they were willing to pay into four ranges and compares these percentages to the real cost of lending fees. Not surprisingly, customers are least willing to pay the largest amounts. At the same time, a large percentage of requests, 48.1 percent, cost more than $10.00.

Additional analysis revealed that of the 648 requests for which the library paid lending fees, the average (mean) amount paid was $9.83 while the average (mean) users were willing to pay was $3.87, approximately 39 percent of the actual average cost. The most any customer was willing to pay was $50.00; $70.00 the maximum actually paid to acquire an item. In comparison, Thornton and Fong found that users were willing to pay for document delivery only 50 percent of the time; the remaining 50 percent were willing to pay only $5.00 or less.[29]

IMPACT OF SUSPENDING CHARGES
ON ILL REQUEST PROCESSING

When comparing figures on what patrons said they were willing to pay versus what items actually cost, patrons' willingness to pay consistently fell well below the actual costs incurred. Since only 19.4 percent of the patrons (126 out of 648) were willing to pay enough to cover the actual

TABLE 4. Customer's Willingness to Pay Actual Lending Fee Costs

By Dollar Amount

Amount	Actual Cost	Willingness To Pay
Less than $0.99	0.5%	44.3%
$1.00-$4.99	13.4%	17.7%
$5.00-$9.99	38.0%	21.3%
More than $10.00	48.1%	16.7%
Total	100.0%	100.0%

costs, a discussion of the impact of collecting fees on procedures is in order.

When the cost pass-through policy was in effect, the "shortfall" between willingness to pay and actual costs caused a series of additional procedures to be added to the normal processing. Prior to our change of policy, the interlibrary loan staff attempted to contact patrons in such cases to establish whether they were willing to pay the additional cost. First, the borrowing technician would establish, usually by searching OCLC and RLIN, the range of costs for that item. A letter was then sent to the patron informing them of the potential costs and requesting a reply from them as to their willingness to pay that amount. When and if this reply arrived, the technician reinitiated the request. This whole procedure–determining cost, notifying patrons, waiting for responses, reordering items–often added weeks to the borrowing process.

In the majority of cases, patrons either did not respond to the notices informing them that their requests would cost more than their initial willingness to pay, or they responded that they were not willing or able to pay the price. The net effect in both instances is that patrons were denied material they clearly wanted. Even in the cases where extra costs were paid, the effect of those delays went beyond mere patron inconvenience. Patrons often request at one time many items on a particular topic of interest. When some of these items were delayed due to our previous policy concerning cost, it negatively impacted their ability to evaluate *all* of their requested material in a comprehensive manner.

The change in policy improved turnaround for the 522 requests that only partially covered fees. Also, graduate students, shown by Perrault and Arseneau to be most sensitive to costs, may be the biggest beneficiary of cost absorption, since Table 2 indicates graduate students are most likely to request items that cost.[30] By increasing the range of material available to patrons (regardless of their willingness to pay), and the speed at which it can be provided, the library improves its ability to facilitate and service the university community's educational and research efforts.

By absorbing costs, the library also eliminates a situation in which patrons are forced to make a decision about the relative importance of a given request just because it happens to cost. In the telephone follow-up, patrons frequently said their willingness to pay was based on how important an item is to their research and on their perception (often inaccurate) of how difficult it is to obtain. The library's decision to absorb costs releases the patron from having to make a decision about relative importance, without knowing the specific content of the item or the level of difficulty involved in obtaining it. The potential for dissatisfaction is reduced because patrons are not paying for items they may decide upon reading not to be worth the cost incurred.

Beyond the impact that this policy change has had on the patrons of the library, the automatic absorption of costs has resulted in greater efficiency in the work of the interlibrary loan staff (in addition to increasing the fillrate). Approximately 3.5 percent of all items requested through interlibrary loan had a cost that exceeded the patron's willingness to pay; all of these required the steps described above. In addition to the savings in labor, the elimination of this category of requests streamlined the often complicated borrowing process. Given that in the past approximately 90 percent of those contacted did not respond to the notice or did not want to pay those costs, much of the work involved in handling requests for which there was a cost became wasted effort.

In this study, the library absorbed lending fees for 648, or about five percent of the total requests for that period. By absorbing the costs for all cases, as well as the remaining 75.9 percent, the library spent a total of $4,502. This translates into $.33 for each of the 13,250 requests filled during 1994-95 compared to the $.25 per request Everett found in the Colgate study in 1986.[31]

CONCLUSIONS

The following conclusions summarize those points most compelling in the data collected.

- The findings of other studies which show graduate students are more concerned about costs and this study's results which indicate graduates are more likely to request material that costs and less likely to be willing to pay, suggests that pass-through charging may genuinely discriminate against graduate users.

- Given patrons' generally poor notion of the cost of items for which there is a fee, their unwillingness to pay a sufficient amount to cover actual costs, the small percentage of requests for which the library is charged, and the increased processing time that results, it is inefficient and counterproductive to pass-through loan fees to patrons.
- Pass-through charges or flat fees for unusual items such as patents, newspapers, videotapes, films, etc., might be more acceptable to customers and may be more easily identified during submission, thereby reducing the additional procedures pass-through charges often require.
- Pass-through costs do not discriminate disproportionately by subject discipline of the requestor.
- Considering the small percentage of total requests that require lending fees and the average current ILL costs found in other cost studies, the cost of lending fees amounts to less than $.33 per filled $18.62 request or only two percent of the total cost to borrow. Such a small percentage of the cost suggests that pass-through charges are not an effective way to reduce ILL costs.
- Libraries seeking cost recovery would more democratically serve and more efficiently serve their constituency if flat charges levied on all requests or on all potential customers were used.

Interlibrary loan and other document delivery services are now essential and growing components of good library service. The patchwork of charges and reciprocal policies that have developed historically need to be examined. Although simple solutions to complex problems can be problematic, simplifying fees for ILL services may be an appropriate solution at this time.

NOTES

1. Miriam A. Drake, *User Fees: A Practical Perspective* (Littleton, CO: Libraries Unlimited, Inc., 1991); Harry M. Kibirige, *The Information Dilemma: A Critical Analysis of Information Pricing and the Fees Controversy* (Westport, CT: Greenwood Pr., 1983). *(New Directions in Librarianship, no. 4)*; "Fees for Library Service: Current Practice & Future Policy," *Collection Building* 8, 1 (1986): 2-61; John M. Budd, "It's Not the Principle, It's the Money of the Thing," *Journal of Academic Librarianship* 15, 4 (September 1989): 218-222; Pete Giacoma, *The Fee or Free Decision: Legal, Economic, Political and Ethical Perspectives for Public Libraries* (New York, NY: Neal-Schuman Publishers, Inc.), 1989; Brian Neilsen, "Allocating Costs, Thinking about Values: The Fee-or-Free Debate Revisited," *Journal of Academic Librarianship* 15, 4 (September 1989): 211-217.

2. John M. Budd, Steven D. Zink, and Jeanne Voyles, "'How Much Will it Cost?' Predictable Pricing of ILL Services: An Investigation and a Proposal," *RQ* 31, 1 (Fall 1991): 70.

3. Betty J. Turock, "Fees: A Hot Potato" in *The Bottom Line Reader: A Financial Handbook for Librarians,* ed. Betty-Carol Sellen and Betty J. Turock (New York, NY: Neal-Schuman Publishers, 1990), 136.

4. "Role of Fees in Supporting Library and Information Services in Public and Academic Libraries (1985)," *The Bowker Annual of Library & Book Trade Information,* 31st ed., comp. and ed. Filomena Simora (New York, NY: R. R. Bowker Co., 1986), 103; National Commission on Libraries and Information Science, "Role of Fees in Supporting Library and Information Services in Public and Academic Libraries," *Collection Building,* 8, 1 (1986): 11.

5. Eleanor Mitchell and Sheila A. Walters, *Document Delivery Services: Issues and Answers* (Medford, NJ: Learned Information, Inc., 1995), 1.

6. "Role of Fees in Supporting Library and Information Services in Public and Academic Libraries (1985)," *The Bowker Annual of Library & Book Trade Information,* 31st ed., comp. and ed. Filomena Simora (New York, NY: R. R. Bowker Co., 1986), 98-100; National Commission on Libraries and Information Science, "Role of Fees in Supporting Library and Information Services in Public and Academic Libraries," *Collection Building,* 8, 1 (1986): 9-10.

7. Sue Kennedy, "The Role of Commercial Document Delivery Services in Interlibrary Loan, *Research Access through New Technology,* ed. Mary E. Jackson (New York, NY: AMS Pr., 1989), 75.

8. Sonja Landes, "Interlibrary Loan Issues in Academic Libraries," *Journal of Interlibrary Loan, Document Delivery & Information Supply* 4, 2 (1993): 36.

9. "College and Reference Section," *Library Journal* 47 (August 1922): *661.*

10. "Service Charge on Inter-Library Loans," *Library Journal* 58 (December 1, 1933): 661.

11. James H. Sweetland and Darlene E. Weingand, "Interlibrary Loan Transaction Fees in a Major Research Library: They Don't Stop the Borrowers," *Library and Information Science Research,* 12 (1990): 88.

12. Association of Research Libraries, "Interlibrary Loan Trends: Making Access a Reality," *SPEC Flyer* 184 (May 1992): 1.

13. Mary E. Jackson, "Library to Library: Trends in Resource Sharing," *Wilson Library Bulletin* 64, 8 (April 1990): 55.

14. John M. Budd, "It's Not the Principle, It's the Money of the Thing," *Journal of Academic Librarianship* 15, 4 (September 1989): 219; Mary E. Jackson, "Library to Library: Fitting the Bill," 95.

15. Association of Research Libraries, "Interlibrary Loan Trends: Making Access a Reality," *SPEC Kit 184* (May 1992): 7.

16. John M. Budd, "It's Not the Principle, It's the Money of the Thing," 219; Mary E. Jackson, "Library to Library: To Charge or Not to Charge," 94.

17. Ibid.

18. Association of Research Libraries, "Interlibrary Loan Trends: Making Access a Reality," *SPEC Kit 184* (May 1992): 7.

19. Vernon E. Palmour, Edward C. Bryant, Nancy W. Caldwell, and Lucy M. Gray, *A Study of the Characteristics, Costs and Magnitude of Interlibrary Loans in Academic Libraries* (Westport, CT: Greenwood Publishing Co., 1972): 22, 24.

20. Marilyn M. Roche, *ARL/RLG Interlibrary Loan Cost Study: A Joint Effort by the Association of Research Libraries and the Research Libraries Group* (Washington, DC: Association of Research Libraries, 1993): 4.

21. Noelene P. Martin, "Information Transfer, Scholarly Communication, and Interlibrary Loan: Priorities, Conflicts and Organizational Imperatives" in *Research Access through New Technology, ed. Mary E. Jackson,* New York, NY.

22. Brian Neilsen, "Allocating Costs, Thinking about Values: The Fee-or-Free Debate Revisited," *Journal of Academic Librarianship* 15, 4 (September 1989): 213.

23. Danuta A. Nitecki, "Interlibrary Services: Report on a Study Measuring User Awareness and Satisfaction," *Tennessee Librarian* 28, 2 (Summer 1976): 88-89.

24. William A. Katz, *Introduction to Reference Work, v. II: Reference Services and Reference Processes*, 3d. ed. (New York, NY: McGraw-Hill, 1978): 229.

25. David Everett, "Interlibrary Loan Fees: A Different Perspective," *Journal of Academic Librarianship* 12 no. 4 (September 1986): 232.

26. Mark T. Kinnucan, "Demand for Document Delivery and Interlibrary Loan in Academic settings," *Library and Information Science Research* 15(1993): 355-374.

27. Anna H. Perrault and Marjo Arseneau, "User Satisfaction and Interlibrary Loan Service: A Study at Louisiana State University," *RQ* 35 no.1 (Fall 1995): 90-100.

28. University of Oklahoma Libraries, *Interlibrary Loan Policy* (Norman, OK: University of Oklahoma, 1994).

29. Glenda A. Thornton and Yem Fong, "Exploring Document Delivery Options: A Pilot Study of the University of Colorado System," *Technical Services Quarterly* 12 no. 2 (1994): 1-12.

30. Anna H. Perrault and Marjo Arseneau, "User Satisfaction and Interlibrary Loan Service: A Study at Louisiana State University."

31. David Everett, "Interlibrary Loan Fees: A Different Perspective," 232.

ZAP: An Electronic Request System. Planning, Development and Adaptation in a Network Environment

Tom Delaney

SUMMARY. Colorado State University began to experiment with a patron initiated E-mail request system in 1990. This initial project was the first step in moving the Interlibrary Loan Department into an enhanced electronic environment. Since then, the program has grown in scope and has been adopted for use by other libraries in the state. This paper describes the evolution of ZAP from its early design stages to the successful development of network applications. *[Article copies available from The Haworth Document Delivery Service: 1-800-342-9678. E-mail address: getinfo@haworth.com]*

INTRODUCTION

Seldom do long-range plans, such as those developed to create the Ohiolink system, grow rapidly into a complete and coordinated set of procedures. The success of Ohiolink is the result of long-range planning and careful design. On the other hand, while operating on a relatively small scale and with more modest goals, each subsystem that composes the 'ZAP' project was sequentially developed for use solely by Colorado

---

Tom Delaney is Head of Interlibrary Loan, Colorado State University, Fort Collins, CO 80523.

[Haworth co-indexing entry note]: "ZAP: An Electronic Request System. Planning, Development and Adaptation in a Network Environment." Delaney, Tom. Co-published simultaneously in *Journal of Library Administration* (The Haworth Press, Inc.) Vol. 23, No. 1/2, 1996, pp. 141-153; and: *Interlibrary Loan/Document Delivery and Customer Satisfaction: Strategies for Redesigning Services* (ed: Pat L. Weaver-Meyers, Wilbur A. Stolt, and Yem S. Fong) The Haworth Press, Inc., 1996, pp. 141-153. Single or multiple copies of this article are available from The Haworth Document Delivery Service [1-800-342-9678, 9:00 a.m. - 5:00 p.m. (EST). E-mail address: getinfo@haworth.com].

141

State University. Only when Colorado State had the complete system in place, did the Interlibrary Loan department begin to grasp some previously unforeseen potential.

Those of us who have logged onto a mainframe and seen nothing but a "$" prompt and wondered "well, what now?" know that menu driven systems and graphical interfaces today have changed information access. Access to many types of services, previously limited to experienced staff, is now common for library users. At the time that the original "Electronic Remote Requesting Program at Colorado State University" was under development in 1990, use of computer networks was limited primarily to the academic and larger corporate environments. In the past two or three years, however, the necessary technology for networked access among a wider audience has become available. Both price and relative ease-of-use have made this accessibility appealing.

In 1990, Colorado State University (CSU) began to develop ZAP, a software program to allow users to make ILL requests through the Internet. In the ensuing five years, the initial program has grown into a system composed of libraries from across the state, linking those libraries through an RISC/6000 computer housed at CSU. Through this computer, the ILL departments at these libraries are linked to their patrons, to each other, and to OCLC.

PHASE ONE: DESIGN AND DEVELOPMENT

The process of developing an electronic patron-initiated interlibrary loan request system is really the culmination of a series of graduated, and apparently unrelated ideas. The result is a large complex system that has helped define networked interlibrary loan procedures. The system evolved from one small, local program into a system with many applications throughout the state of Colorado.

INITIAL GOALS

The original design of the electronic requesting and message processing programs called for one small program running on a local mainframe. However, the system was plastic enough to accommodate integrated software on an as-needed basis. The result, which became known as "ZAP," was a system capable of evolving along with other growing system applications.

The experiment at Colorado State was part of a department-wide effort to incorporate technological enhancements into daily work flow. Julie Wessling, former department head and now Associate Dean for Public Services, and Jane Smith, who followed Wessling as department head and is currently Manager of Interlibrary Loan at the University of Northern Colorado, foresaw the value of these user-friendly interfaces to library customers. The growing complexity in software designed for staff, it seemed, enhanced customer access.

Once the challenge to build the system was undertaken, the process rapidly turned into a project to design a basic, solid program accessible to anyone with a minimal amount of computer hardware. An additional goal was to invent a service in anticipation of actual demand and to build in functionality that exceeded short-range goals.

DESIGN ELEMENTS

The developmental team was composed of Wessling, Smith, and undergraduate student programmer, Brian Ashworth (now a member of the CSU Libraries Technical Support team—and still close enough to answer when ILL staff yells "HELP!!!"). The design began by assuming that a good ILL system should include efficient, up-to-date programming, an understanding of ILL fundamentals and an extremely simple, easy-to-use interface. In other words, the bulk of the work would be in the programming and design phase. It was important that the resulting interface did not require any special knowledge, experience, or "intuition" by the user.

The plan called for a "menu-driven, prompted format" as detailed by Jane Smith.[1] A fundamental concept, maintained throughout the process, was to keep the program design plastic. Think big, but begin with only what you know you can support, and leave room for future developments for both the end-user and the ILL department. All of the programming for the first phase and subsequent phases was done by undergraduate programmers. While they were inexperienced at creating end-user software, they did have a grasp of the way data needed to be arranged and organized to fit into the ILL work flow. There was no way of knowing that the result of this process would be the development of programs and functions that would be applied at ILL offices statewide.

As the program emerged, new technologies became available to libraries. The designers were adept enough to incorporate new developments as they appeared. For example, as the library's LAN was dramatically expanded in 1990-91, the designers of the program built an interface to allow ILL staff to receive requests in the more familiar DOS environment, although the program itself ran on a campus-wide system.[2] This dynamic developmental approach combined with the programmer's knowledge of ILL processes, insured success.

A second design characteristic that underlies the adaptability of the system was that the program was designed as a technological look ahead at potential demand. The "look-ahead" approach to engineering the program provided opportunity to build in functionality that exceeded short-range goals. Having an electronic system was a convenience, but Smith, Ashworth, and the rest of the designers decided that a complete program would anticipate demand and build in convenience for most users. They decided to have each user only enter personal profile information once— that data was stored and attached to each subsequent request, even on multiple log in sessions. For the ease of the user, and for the convenience of consistent information for the staff who would receive the requests, the system would prompt only for ID number to begin each session. If the patron had made previous requests, they would see their patron profile and accept the information with one keystroke; if they needed to make changes, they could follow a menu-driven set of prompts. Thus for those rare occasions when a user had, for example, changed telephone numbers, they would re-key only the new data, and not the entire profile. The bulk of users who had not changed any personal information could simply accept the data and enter their request. This enhancement stored the data on the mainframe, but the text files occupied only minimal disk space. The designers realized that all user profiles stored in ASCII text would only take up a few megabytes of disk space; on a mainframe scale this added virtually nothing to the program load. The final functions that the users could access allowed them to request renewals and status checks on-line. Nearly all essential user-related department functions were now accessible on-line.

PROMOTION AND USER RESPONSE

The electronic system went on-line on September 23, 1991 marking a milestone in the ILL department at CSU. In effect, the department was accessible 24 hours a day, seven days a week. The users had a versatile program at their disposal. The program, very well tested both in-house and by campus users, worked as a solid, dependable interface.

The only questions that remained to be answered were: would people use the system, and if so, would they turn into abusers? The biggest argument against accepting electronic requests was that users would sit at a terminal and take advantage of the ease-of-use features and accessibility, thereby driving up the number of requests dramatically. The second argument, related to the first, was that users could potentially make spurious or spontaneous requests and forget them. An increase of requests for materials that sat unused on the shelf was not compatible with the library's limited financial and human resources.

In the first four years of use, these anticipated problems have not occurred. While our statistics did continue to increase, the rate of the increase was not beyond the anticipated demands that our expanding campus population, and the availability of rapid-retrieval electronic databases, would be expected to cause.

The program introduction was accompanied by a great deal of publicity, with information in the library newsletter and the campus newspaper. User interest was high from day one, and at this point, we receive up to 50% of our requests electronically. We think that number will only rise as more of our ILL users find both comfort working in a computing environment, and the necessary hardware.

We had the technological edge on accepting requests by networked computers, but long before the "information superhighway" became a media buzzword denoting rapid access to anything from pulp to Shakespeare, the ILL department saw a tremendous untapped potential for providing a new service to our users on the then-barely known "Internet."

When this process began, it seemed likely that the result of writing a program providing users the opportunity to make requests remotely would be little more than another perk that we could provide. There was no way of knowing what the result of this process would be. However, Jane Smith thought that the potential for development was a worthwhile investment.

The only problem that we have experienced from electronic requesting over the years has been that patrons somehow anticipate that their materials will arrive more quickly if they make their requests electronically! Our patrons have adapted to this over time, and we have gone to great lengths to help them. We have, for example, recently developed a menu-driven E-mail notification system to let our users who have access to E-mail know when their materials have arrived so that they feel more in touch, and see electronic requesting as part of a communication link rather than as the result of an ILL request. Like most of the newer advances in ILL, the program has been designed for simplicity so our work-study students or full time staff can run the menu-driven E-mail program. All addressing, protocols, and parameters are addressed by the program—all we do is enter the patron's last name (even part of the last name will do), or ID number. We then enter a single keystroke to send a generic "your material has arrived" message or we can send a message with a due date, or even a personalized text message.

PHASE 2: IMPLEMENTATION AND ENHANCEMENTS

If ILL had stopped there, that by itself would have been enough! The department had accomplished exactly what it set out to do, and it was successful. However, there was a growing demand for these services, both from the user end, and from staffing. ILL felt that it could offer significant improvements to a largely manual, paper-driven system. Smith, Wessling, and Ashworth had made a contribution to the library and the campus community met with general acclaim.

ILL PRISM Transfer (IPT)

It did not take long for Jane and Brian Ashworth to develop the next project–and it is one that, like electronic requesting, many libraries are already using. The idea was simple. Then, the ILL staff at CSU took all requests, both manual and electronic, and re-keyed them into the OCLC ILL subsystem for searching and sending. The staff wanted to eliminate the tracking and re-keying step by sending the electronic requests directly to OCLC. After all, our users were deriving tremendous benefits from this program. It seemed reasonable to believe that similar benefits might transform office workflow.

From a purely functional standpoint, this idea was simple to define, but complex to develop. When Jane and Brian first approached OCLC with the idea, they were at a loss. At the time, CSU was one of the only places accepting requests via the Internet. As a result, CSU was conceptually ahead of many others in refining this idea.

It took two years to develop what is now known as ILL/PRISM Transfer (IPT)–the reformatting of text files into binary information with data tags to locate the correct information into the appropriate fields. This essentially pulled the E-mail request into a file designated by OCLC as the review file. When it was done, the ILL borrowing staff was amazed. Despite the many rough spots in the process (we crashed the OCLC computer more than once when our program kept looping) the project developed into another useful program that we now take for granted. Thanks to the cooperation of OCLC staff, and to everyone who contributed to the development of PRISM transfer, our patrons create on-line requests and with two keystrokes those requests are in a work form ready to be searched and sent.

DEVELOPING MACROS TO INSERT DATA
INTO OCLC WORK FORMS

When CSU, OCLC, and other participants had completed the PRISM transfer program, there was only one step remaining: to create keystroke macros that would capture the uploaded IPT information from the review file and insert it into an OCLC work form so the borrowing staff would not need to do any re-keying of electronic requests. The goal was to insert the data into a work form and move directly into the search-and-send process (now that the OCLC Custom Holdings program is functional, our borrowing time has been further decreased). When these macros were developed, the number of steps needed to process an ILL electronically was essentially reduced to four: (1) keystroke-macro to insert the bibliographic/citation information into the work form, (2) keystroke-macro to insert the patron's information into the request, (3) search the request and identify potential lenders, (4) keystroke macro to send the request and create a bar coded hard copy for record keeping. This process has been so simplified that we now begin training our student workers to send requests during their first week of work.

At this point, Jane Smith left CSU to become ILL Manager at the University of Northern Colorado, and Brian Ashworth graduated. It seemed that the opportunities for developing innovative electronic systems were over. However, a little luck and the willingness to take some chances resulted in more developments. Another of our ILL work-study students, Greg Eslick, was also a computer science major. Without our realizing it, he had been observing the developmental schemes and the flow of ideas. He had also, on his own initiative, worked closely with Brian Ashworth to understand the functions and design of the programming. When Brian graduated, Greg stepped forward with some ideas that he felt could help ILL to continue development. We could not have been luckier.

PHASE 3: BUILDING A NETWORK

So far, all of the ILL development was done immediately before the "boom" in computer communications that could be readily exploited by the bulk of our users. By the time that Greg came on the scene, the Internet was a TV-news soundbite away, and we were in the middle of a "technological revolution," where many campus users know what we have been waiting for them to find out–that you can do *almost* anything by computer.

Our service is no longer a novelty, but a routine. That's fine–we are not scrambling to catch up–yet!

Since we had discovered the benefits of electronic requesting, there were obviously potential benefits on a much wider scale. Julie Wessling applied for a Library Services and Construction Act Grant (LSCA) in the spring of 1994. The grant was approved to design a statewide network of electronic Interlibrary Loan request programs for any library in the state of Colorado. The actual program could be developed by building upon the already existing program, and expanding the functionality without rewriting program code.

NETWORK APPLICATIONS AND RESULTS

The project was planned so that any library of any size could participate. The minimum requirement was an Internet connection with E-mail capability and a PC. To provide a service to as many libraries, and as many types of libraries as possible, the electronic request program was redesigned allowing libraries to select from a set of options. Those libraries that do not participate in OCLC would receive patron requests directly to their E-mail account, other libraries could use the benefits of PRISM transfer and the OCLC macros to reduce work flow. Eslick expanded the system so that any library could decide how to format screens for specific types of material requests. For example, the academic libraries could accept different prompts to separate "Thesis/Dissertation" requests from "Book" requests, but public libraries could use a smaller menu system without those distinctions.

The development team also offered options for Status Checks, and for some pre-formatted, menu-driven FAQ information files to address common questions. When libraries decided how they wanted their request menu to look, there was a predefined set of prompts for information, tailored according to like needs. Library staff could then process these requests according to whatever internal procedures they chose. Eslick developed another menu system that allows staff to define a library profile, establish the account, and set all parameters–in less than five minutes, and without needing to establish familiarity with UNIX syntax. Two student assistants created the user accounts for participating libraries as they were needed.

To design a program with this degree of complexity, we acquired a dedicated RISC/6000 UNIX computer solely for ILL purposes, and Greg Eslick became the student programmer in charge of development. While the fundamentals of the program design were in place, there was a need to extend the scope of the system to accept log ins and have users directed to specific accounts, route the appropriate requests to ILL/PRISM transfer, attach library information to the file, send the request to the appropriate library's review file, or send them off via E-mail to the correct E-mail address. Storing data in back-up files by site was also part of the program.

These tasks were accomplished by one modifiable coded program to maintain structural and environmental consistency. Otherwise, Greg could have been rewriting code for hundreds of libraries, and the program would never have gotten off the ground.

Now, every library is assigned an account name that corresponds to a specific set of instructions, and users log in without a password. The log in triggers the program for their account, and users are prompted for information. According to how the account is set up, the results are either E-mailed to the requestor's library or sent to OCLC. All of this is transparent to the end-user, and all information is treated uniformly. The ZAP program as it is designed is astonishingly efficient and consistent. From a technical point of view, all of the data from account to account is functionally equivalent. From the user point of view, the sophisticated software environment is completely transparent. Except for a redesigned sign-on screen, the program appears now in 1996 almost exactly as it did in September 23, 1991. The entire system is still fully functional, and using that basic design libraries across Colorado produced more than 20,000 requests. The volume is not taxing to the system, and the upper limit of log ins that define how quickly and efficiently the program functions are defined by the number of physical connections that arrive on campus. So far, we are not even close to placing a measurable load on the system.

As for resource sharing, the electronic request program (referred to as ZAP in the state-system) provides tremendous power and flexibility; giving any participating library the opportunity to exploit a networked computing environment to receive requests.

We were not at all surprised that the result of the ZAP grant was to establish a heavily used program, but we were surprised to see new functions emerge from the basic program without programming changes. For example, within some more geographically isolated areas of the state, small library systems use ZAP not as a patron requesting device, but for small local libraries to send requests to the regional library for searching, uploading to OCLC, or routing through their normal processes. In this way, some regional systems have extended the reach of the central ILL system avoiding ground mail or the expense of telephone requests. Transmission through E-mail is virtually instantaneous, and the computing and searching at any central site can be exploited by individual libraries spread over hundreds of miles. The requests all have a standardized format, and the various fields can be changed so that libraries can request subject searches.

As we learned about the newly applied functions of the program, we would adapt the wording on the menu screens so that the field originally delimited for "Additional Information" was changed to "Subject Search:" when needed. This allowed librarians at the local level to conduct patron searches on specific subject areas through the more sophisticated tools at a central library. This allows librarians to combine multiple, formatted requests, along with subject searches, in one request session. They may request an item for a patron and a subject search on the same or a related topic. The librarian at the receiving end can file them away until ready to work with all of the ILL requests.

For the academic environment, which forms the largest number of ZAP users, individual libraries have separate request "forms" for government documents, theses/dissertations, monographs and periodicals. In addition, the patron is "spared" the necessity of rewriting or reentering redundant information on every request they ever make. Consequently, we usually get the information that we need to conduct a thorough search and locate the correct material. Since we have implemented ZAP at CSU, our successful borrowing rate is an astonishing 94.3 percent. Granted, the extraordinary quality and dedication of the borrowing staff needs to be credited more than any computer program, but we do think that the time-savings created by ZAP plays a role in speeding searching time through many databases, and for giving the staff time to practice and learn the most sophisticated bibliographic searching tools. In addition, since we own the computer account, we can maintain backups of requests if we need them. Usually we have a default purge date of one year for the program to delete files selectively; however, if it were ever necessary, we could reprogram the file naming conventions so that we could hold up to 100,000 requests per location without the possibility of duplication.

ADAPTING TO LIMITATIONS

A major reason for the success of the program is that it interacts with the tools already in place in ILL departments—either OCLC or E-mail. Our original goal was to build a program that fit the work flow rather than making the work flow fit the program. Electronic requesting has not been a trauma to even the most staunchly conservative among us. No new procedures, no new tools are necessary, just a more efficient means of handling the same things that we always do.

Not everything that the ZAP project set out to do was successful–some more sophisticated aspects of the program are still under development or are not practical to consider. One item that most libraries desperately wanted was a screen capture program for writing requests from various databases directly to ZAP; however, it is too complex to develop successfully. A second requested development is some type of statistical maintenance package. A basic package is currently under development; however, it will not provide the types and quantities of information hoped for by various libraries. These plans and ideas give us an opportunity to continue developing our programs and expanding our user base.

NEW DIRECTIONS

Now that the ILL department has spent this much time developing enhancements to the borrowers of ILL, we are also implementing several programs to enhance our service as a lending library. One such program developed by CSU as an outgrowth of electronic requesting is our "call number search" program. Our program, again developed by Brian Ashworth (currently in the Technology Support Department of the Libraries), takes information from the lender's pending file and uses that to search our public access catalog (PAC). The call number, location, and status information is inserted into the :CALL NUMBER: field on each record. When the search is complete, the pending file is then printed, but it appears with information from the PAC inserted, and with a barcode attached.

If an item shows in the PAC as checked out, the request is sorted and printed with a group of items that we cannot fill. Other items are sorted by call number locations throughout the building, and then by call numbers for each of these areas. The lenders then have the opportunity simply to tear off a section of requests (such as "First Floor") and pick up the items. This program has as much potential to save time, paperwork, sorting, filing, etc., as all of the borrowing programs that we have developed so far. The program also scans the request to determine if periodical requests are to be shipped via fax, ARIEL, or mail. Fax requests are marked with a series of "F"s down the margin, ARIEL shipping requests with a series of "A"s down the margin, etc.

The only shortcoming to this program is that it only works on the local PAC; we have not found a way to generalize it to other libraries in the program. However, it has the potential to be developed as another long-range project as time and funding permit.

The time savings that electronic requesting has created for us has allowed us to take advantage of several opportunities. For example, Colorado State is now beta testing the AVISO software package for application in the United States. We are the first location to be doing large scale testing, and we see the potential for enormous possibilities. ILL has traditionally been a paperwork driven process. We see applications with the AVISO software package that will allow us to rely more and more on electronic record keeping, and become less dependent on the paper-and-file records that have been time-consuming as ILL requests have increased in the past several years. The efficiencies of maintaining records in a database environment, without the mediating paperwork, should be a familiar promise to many of us–but the actualization that has seemed so far away is moving ever closer to being a plausible, and timesaving, reality. AVISO allows staff to track data from both borrowing and lending. The statistics package is both flexible and comprehensive, and ISM, parent company to AVISO, has invested heavily in developing a package that interfaces with the OCLC environment.

We also have the opportunity to participate in another pilot project, this time with a package developed by OCLC. The PILLR statistics package promises to be an extremely broad-based application derived from ILL records, however with vastly different functions than the AVISO package. The PILLR statistics program will have the capacity to track requests throughout the OCLC request process, determine the success of specific lender string combinations, and, most important, provide reference and collection development information on a scale that was previously impossible. We are currently in the fifth month of using the package, and the information that we have been able to abstract has already influenced the collection development process at Colorado State. Unlike AVISO, PILLR will not have a direct and immediate impact on the ILL processes that we have developed, but the information is valuable on a scope only recently considered to be of "daydream proportions."

CONCLUSION

The underlying ILL philosophical principle at CSU is stated by Julie Wessling, "The easier it is to request an item, the more acceptable it becomes to rely on access from a remote provider. Therefore, the most important goal of Colorado State's program is to make it easy to use and to encourage active use by all members of the campus community."[2] The ZAP program epitomizes this philosophy. It is also adaptable to a diverse set of library types and library users. While the heaviest users of the program have been academics, small libraries within library systems have found extremely creative ways to utilize the program, and several public libraries have received thousands of requests through ZAP. In the context of service and resource sharing, the use of the ZAP program is as essential to the ILL departments of small, local libraries as it is to the CSU libraries.

At the time that the original "Electronic Remote Requesting Program" was under development in 1990, the use of computer networks was limited primarily to the academic and larger corporate environments. In the past two or three years the necessary technology for networked access has become available, both in price and in relative ease of use, for a much wider audience. As the peculiar syntax of the original networked programming applications has rapidly evolved into an easier-to-use framework in a graphical environment, the impact of these programs to a newly literate computer audience has expanded dramatically.

We are now taking the opportunity to develop electronic requests in the WWW environment. It is possible that with growing accessibility to WWW browsers and higher speed modems, this may become the method of choice for remote requesting. Due to the foresight and planning of the previous ILL department heads and development teams, we have the luxury of constantly finding new ways to 'stay ahead' and provide excellent service; we also have a staff who is familiar with change in the electronic environment and has already overcome the tendency to feel intimidated and insecure at the incorporation of new technology. The result is an increasingly complex system that has helped define networked interlibrary loan procedures. The CSU venture into ILL "electronic requesting" has, over time, evolved into a process of departmental automating. It is a process that has barely begun.[3]

NOTES

1. Jane Smith, Internet Access to ILL at Colorado State University," in Julie Still, Ed. *The Internet Library* (Westport, CT. Meklermedia. 1994): 45-56.

2. Julie Wessling, "Electronic ILL: The User Interface," *Document Delivery World.* 9 no. 3(1993): 24-28.

3. Readers interested in viewing ZAP may telnet to: zap.library.colostate.edu. At the log in prompt enter: sed and then their social security number (without dashes). From this point, the user can create a patron profile, select from main menu, create a mock request for individual material types using ZAP templates— book, article, dissertation, government document, etc. To exit type: X. Requests and patron profiles will be automatically deleted.

Empowering the Patron:
Redesigning Interlibrary Loan Services

Barbara G. Preece
Susan Logue

SUMMARY. Redesigning the interlibrary loan process by empowering the patron at Southern Illinois University at Carbondale's Library Affairs has involved a number of projects. These include patron initiated interlibrary loan for items held by members of the Illinois Library Computer Systems Organization (ILCSO); introduction of the interlibrary loan link on FirstSearch, and implementation of web-based interlibrary loan request forms. This article will explore the Access Services Department's success in meeting three of the objectives outlined by the Association of Research Library's North American Interlibrary Loan & Document Delivery (NAILDD) Project. It will provide descriptions of three projects designed to empower patrons, explain the role of institutional support and interdepartmental collaboration in these efforts, and discuss the impact on services. *[Article copies available from The Haworth Document Delivery Service: 1-800-342-9678. E-mail address: getinfo@haworth.com]*

Barbara G. Preece is Associate Professor and Assistant Access Services Librarian, Southern Illinois University at Carbondale, Carbondale, IL.

Susan Logue is Assistant Professor and Assistant Instructional Support Services Librarian at Southern Illinois University at Carbondale, Carbondale, IL.

The authors wish to acknowledge the support of Carolyn A. Snyder, Dean of Library Affairs, and the contributions of the library staff and faculty to the projects described in this paper.

[Haworth co-indexing entry note]: "Empowering the Patron: Redesigning Interlibrary Loan Services." Preece, Barbara G., and Susan Logue. Co-published simultaneously in *Journal of Library Administration* (The Haworth Press, Inc.) Vol. 23, No. 1/2, 1996, pp. 155-166; and: *Interlibrary Loan/Document Delivery and Customer Satisfaction: Strategies for Redesigning Services* (ed: Pat L. Weaver-Meyers, Wilbur A. Stolt, and Yem S. Fong) The Haworth Press, Inc., 1996, pp. 155-166. Single or multiple copies of this article are available from The Haworth Document Delivery Service [1-800-342-9678, 9:00 a.m. - 5:00 p.m. (EST). E-mail address: getinfo@haworth.com].

INTRODUCTION

Libraries have changed the way they acquire materials and how they provide access to their collections. A leveling off or a decline in funds earmarked for acquisitions, the escalating price of materials, and a fluctuating exchange rate have changed the collecting patterns of libraries worldwide. Economics has prompted some of the changes but technology also has had an impact on information access and delivery. Today, patrons can access full-text articles, library catalogs, and databases from their home computers. This change in access methods has forced libraries to reevaluate how they supply information to their patrons. Members of the Association of Research Libraries (ARL) noted an increase in interlibrary borrowing of 108 percent between 1981 and 1992. This increase has required libraries to review, and frequently, redesign their interlibrary loan operations. ARL initiated the North American Interlibrary Loan and Document Delivery (NAILDD) Project to improve the interlibrary loan process for patrons and to make it more cost effective for libraries. The NAILDD Project's "Vision and Overview Statement" addresses the future direction of access and delivery of library materials.[1] It places particular emphasis on patron initiated interlibrary loans. This article will describe three innovative projects implemented by the Access Services Department of Southern Illinois University at Carbondale in response to the ARL document. The projects include patron initiated interlibrary loan from libraries of the Illinois Library Computer Systems Organization (ILCSO); implementation of the First-Search interlibrary loan link, and introduction of web-based interlibrary loan forms. The article also will explain the role of institutional support and interdepartmental collaboration in these efforts, and discuss the impact of these projects on delivery services.

BACKGROUND

Southern Illinois University at Carbondale's Library supports the University's baccalaureate programs and graduate education through the doctorate. It serves more than 20,000 students and 5,000 faculty and staff. The Library contains more than 2.2 million volumes, 3.6 million units of microform, and approximately 14,000 periodical subscriptions. It is a member of ARL and several library consortia including the Greater Midwest Research Library Consortium (GMRLC), a group of 18 libraries located throughout the Midwest; the Illinois Library and Information Network (ILLINET), a network of 2,600 Illinois libraries; and the Illinois Library Computer Systems Organization (ILCSO), a group of 45 libraries that use the Illinois state wide online catalog, ILLINET Online (IO), for both local and interlibrary operations.

The mission of Library Affairs stresses a commitment to the patron's access to instructional and research materials.

> . . . Library Affairs will assume a leadership role in providing intellectual, bibliographic, instructional, and physical access to information resources. Service to users is the first priority of the library.[2]

In many ways the mission reflects the "ARL Statement on Information Access & Delivery Services."

> [U]sers may exercise choice and responsibility; A.R.L. research libraries serve as sources for comprehensive collections, centers of instruction and advice, and providers of gateway services to other libraries or information sources.[3]

Libraries that provide access to a variety of resources can support "user-centered services."[4] SIUC's Library Affairs embraces the philosophy of providing access to a wide variety of information resources to its patrons which eases the transition to user-centered services. An environment that empowers the user can be achieved by meeting the objectives listed in the ARL NAILDD "Overview and Vision Statement."[5] Library Affairs' Access Services Department reviewed the statement and identified three objectives that could be implemented locally to improve access to information and delivery services. The three objectives are:

1. Search a variety of local and remote library catalogs, citation databases, union catalogs, and other electronic sources of bibliographic resources.
2. Transfer a citation into an electronic request or order.
3. Direct a request or order to one of a range of suppliers, including commercial document delivery suppliers, or a local or remote library ILL/document delivery department.[6]

Success in achieving the three objectives would be dependent upon a redesign of the interlibrary loan process. Baker and Jackson in their discussion of the interlibrary loan system note that the interlibrary loan system is more than library to library and should evolve to end-user-to-supplier.[7] SIUC's Access Services Department agreed that changes were needed to achieve the stated objectives. The desired goal was the development of an environment where patrons could exercise choice and responsibility.

The redesign of interlibrary loan is an ongoing and evolving process. The NAILDD Project describes the ideal interlibrary loan comprehensive management system. The Library has made some changes in its interlibrary loan operation to achieve this ideal but more importantly it has taken the first steps in empowering its patrons. The next few sections describe some of the projects implemented as part of the redesign process. "Patron Initiated Borrowing" describes a project where patrons initiate a loan from another Illinois library. "FirstSearch Interlibrary Loan Link" explains a process where bibliographic citations are transferred into electronic requests. "Interlibrary Loan on the Web" explains the transfer of patron initiated interlibrary loan web-based requests to the OCLC Interlibrary Loan Review File.

PATRON INITIATED BORROWING

ILLINET Online (IO) is a WLN-based system that serves as the online catalog for more than 2,600 member libraries of the Illinois Library and Information Network (ILLINET). The catalog contains more than nine million bibliographic records and is based on the OCLC cataloging data of more than 800 Illinois libraries. One component of the catalog serves as the local circulation system for 45 members of the Illinois Library Computer Systems Organization (ILCSO). These libraries include each of the state-supported universities, private colleges and universities, five community colleges, a state-supported high school for gifted students in mathematics and the sciences, and the Illinois State Library. IO's circulation module also serves as the interlibrary loan system for ILCSO members, the regional library systems, and other ILLINET members. ILLINET members transacted more than 600,000 interlibrary loans on IO in 1995.

A patron-initiated interlibrary loan option on ILLINET Online allows ILCSO patrons (and staff from other ILLINET member libraries) to charge items from other ILCSO libraries. Southern Illinois University at Carbondale (SIUC) provided their patrons access to this feature beginning in the fall of 1993. Individuals affiliated with SIUC charge items from other ILCSO libraries regardless of their location. Patrons can charge, renew, or recall items from other ILCSO libraries using the online catalog from PCs in the Library, their dorm, office, or home. Patrons who prefer to complete a paper request for items held by ILCSO libraries may still do so, although our patrons are encouraged to self-initiate a charge. The patron initiated interlibrary loan option was introduced during the fall semester

1993. Workshops, handouts, and a notice in the school's newspaper advertised this enhancement to the interlibrary loan process.

Once a patron charges an item from another ILCSO school, a page slip is generated at the lending library where it is searched and retrieved. The lending library sends the requested item to the patron's home library by the Intersystems Library Delivery System (ILDS), a state-supported delivery system. The patron is responsible for the item's return and is billed if an item is not returned promptly or if it is lost. If the item is unavailable, the lending library discharges it, and sends the page slip to the patron's home library noting that the item is unavailable. What impact has this had on the interlibrary loan process at SIUC? Loans from ILCSO libraries have increased significantly and new procedures have been implemented to handle the increased volume. This service has proven very popular with our patrons. While only 426 items were direct charged during January 1994, the number increased to 1,119 items direct charged in January 1996. Chart 1 shows a comparison between the number of items charged during 1994 and 1995. These charges represent 68 percent of the filled returnable interlibrary loan requests in 1994 and 75 percent of the filled returnable interlibrary loan requests in 1995 (Chart 2). Also, a database was designed that generates patron notification letters

CHART 1. Items Charged Through ILLINET Online

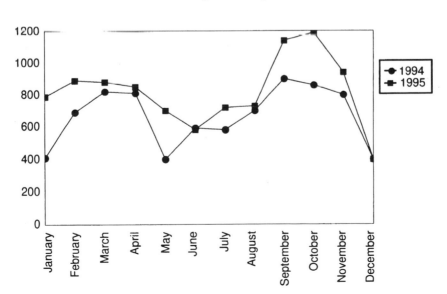

and tracks items received. Page slips that show an item is unavailable are mailed to the patron.

FIRSTSEARCH AND THE INTERLIBRARY LOAN LINK

The Illinois State Library administered a grant that provided free access to nine FirstSearch databases beginning in October 1994. The first phase of the grant ran from June 30, 1995 and was extended through June 30, 1996. Library Affairs implemented the project in January 1995 by providing Internet access to the state-supported FirstSearch databases on all public and staff terminals located in the Library. The grant provides access to ArticleFirst, FastDoc, ContentsFirst, PapersFirst, Proceedings First, WorldCat, ERIC, GOP Monthly Catalog, and MEDLINE. A few of the FirstSearch databases, ArticleFirst, FastDoc, PapersFirst, WorldCat, and MEDLINE provide the patron with an interlibrary loan link after retrieving a bibliographic citation. Bibliographic information is transferred to a form that prompts the patron for personal data such as address and identification number. Once submitted, the request is transferred to the library's OCLC ILL Review File. Library Affairs opened access to the FirstSearch Interlibrary Loan Link at the beginning of fall semester 1995. Training sessions were held for the public services staff and the general public. Requests received from the interlibrary loan link have grown steadily since its introduction. While only seven requests were initiated during the first month of use more than 70 requests were generated through the link in January 1996 (Chart 3).

INTERLIBRARY LOAN ON THE WEB

Library Affairs has made significant progress toward its goal of empowering the patron in the interlibrary loan arena with the implementation of the patron initiated borrowing option in ILLINET Online and the interlibrary loan link in FirstSearch. Next, the Access Services Department investigated the issues involved in placing interlibrary loan forms on the web. Librarians from Access Services and Instructional Support Services worked collaboratively on this project from its inception. Both agreed that the forms should be used to automate the interlibrary loan process. Access Services staff held brainstorming sessions to articulate their vision of the interlibrary loan process. Everyone agreed that the ideal was a situation where a patron-initiated request was processed and tracked automatically. The librarians developed a proposal and presented it to the Dean of Library

CHART 2. Items Borrowed

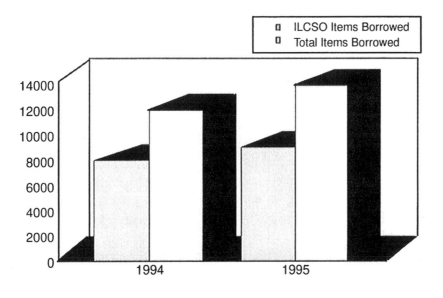

CHART 3. FirstSearch ILL Requests

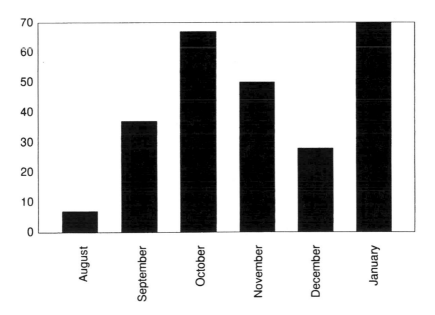

Affairs and the Director of Technical and Automated Services who agreed to support the project with staff and other resources as necessary. The project had five objectives:

1. Create a web based interlibrary loan form.
2. Eliminate the rekeying of data into the OCLC interlibrary loan sub-system.
3. Transfer the request to the OCLC review file.
4. Automate the searching process.
5. Develop a tracking system for all interlibrary loan requests.

The primary goal of the project was to let the patron initiate an interlibrary loan request from any PC that supported a web browser. Other libraries had designed electronic interlibrary loan messaging systems but none had developed web based forms that interacted with OCLC. A review of the chapter, "ILL PRISM Transfer," in OCLC's Interlibrary Loan User Guide prompted a phone call to OCLC where Tony Melvyn and Jim McDonald agreed to offer their support of this project.[8]

A beta version of the forms was placed on the web in the summer of 1995. A selected group of faculty used the forms during this test period. The forms were modified based on comments received from this group and the Access Services staff. The staff also contributed information for a home page that contained information about the interlibrary loan process. A link to this information was added to the Library Affairs Home Page (http://www.lib.siu.edu) at the beginning of fall semester 1995. The page included four links: (1) Interlibrary Loan General Information (2) Frequently Asked Questions (3) ILLINET Online (a reminder to patrons to check this resource before requesting items) and (4) Interlibrary Loan Request Forms (Loans and Articles). No publicity announced the forms other than a notice in the "What's New" section of the Library's Home Page. While anyone could access the forms, a valid SIUC identification number was required to submit a request to the Library. The number of requests received through the web has remained fairly steady since its introduction (Chart 4). They represent about 20 percent of the requests received by the interlibrary loan Unit (Chart 5).

Once the project was approved a team was identified to work on its development. Team members included librarians and staff from Instructional Support Services, Cataloging, and Access Services. Instructional Support Services staff were responsible for web development, an individual from Cataloging offered expertise in OCLC processing, and the Access Services staff addressed workflow and standards.

When a patron submitted an interlibrary loan request during the initial

CHART 4. Requests Received

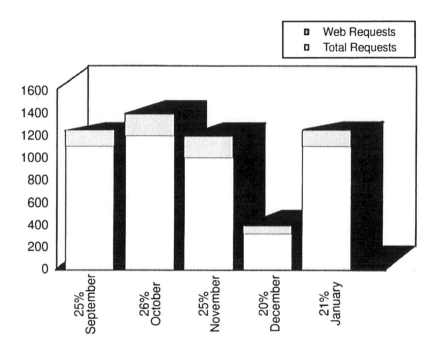

phase of the project request, a script converted the data to an e-mail file that was formatted to display and print. Next, a C program converted the incoming records to the BER (Basic Encoding Rules) format for OCLC. The records were then sent by FTP to OCLC which sent the records to the Library's OCLC Interlibrary Loan Review File.

The Access Services staff processed the incoming records along with records generated through the FirstSearch databases. While this was a step toward automating the process, the team members decided that there must be other avenues that would further speed up the process. Again, driving the redesign was the goal of better service to the patron. A revised process was implemented in January 1996. In the new process, the patron saw no change to the request forms but much had been done behind the scenes. Now, a successfully submitted interlibrary loan was automatically converted and formatted by a Perl script into a web form. Staff open a concurrent session in ILLINET Online and OCLC. If an item cannot be charged from an ILCSO library an OCLC accession number is added, the form is reviewed for accuracy, edited if necessary, and then submitted. A Perl

CHART 5. Web Requests

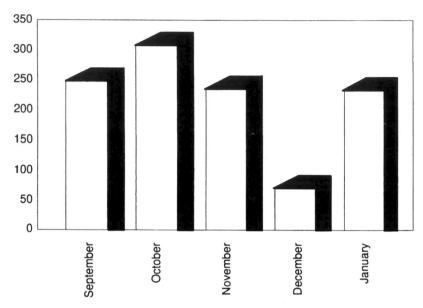

script then creates a record for an Expect program. This launches a Telnet session in which the record is transferred to the OCLC Review File.

This process has had a significant impact on the interlibrary loan process. The project has met three of its objectives: (1) interlibrary loan requests are on the web; (2) data is not rekeyed; (3) requests are transferred to the Library's OCLC Interlibrary Loan Review File. The team continues to refine the project. Progress is being made in the last two areas including the development of an Access based database that will track the progress of an interlibrary loan request, copyright compliance, and provide collection development data. Another feature under development is the process that automates searching of ILLINET Online.

ADMINISTRATIVE SUPPORT AND INTERDEPARTMENTAL COLLABORATION

Three areas of support have been essential for the success of the projects. These include: (1) administrative support; (2) technological support; and (3) human resources. Administrative support has allowed the Access Services Department the opportunity to explore the possibilities and achieve some of the objectives outlined in the NAILDD Project's "Overview and Vision Statement." The first two projects described were opportunities offered by the state's commitment to resource sharing. The web project provided Library Affairs with a unique opportunity. Staff transcended traditional departmental boundaries in the development and implementation of this project. The Library's administration endorsed the idea of a collaborative effort by staff from a variety of areas with the goal of providing better service to our patrons. The team members included a librarian and staff from Instructional Support Services who guided the web development, a staff member from Cataloging with expertise in the management of workflow and OCLC, and a librarian and staff from Access Services who addressed content, design, and workflow. The Systems Support Staff provided technological support. The success of this project was achieved by the collaborative efforts of these individuals. It is efforts such as these that will provide better access to and delivery of information to the Library's patrons.

IMPACT ON SERVICES

The three projects implemented by Access Services had a positive impact on interlibrary loan services. Patrons can generate requests from any location with a PC and modem. Requests received by the new methods continue to increase while the number of paper requests continues to decrease. The patron-initiated interlibrary loan project has been enthusiastically received by our patrons. Use of the FirstSearch databases has increased each month since the project was implemented as has the number of interlibrary loan links generated by the system. Finally, the response to the interlibrary loan web forms has been very positive. As new services are implemented the staff must reassess its workflow and ask the questions, "Why are we doing this?" "What can we do differently?" and finally, "What can we do to make it better and easier for the patron?" Also, we must continually review the ARL statement and ask "Are we taking full advantage of the technology to access and deliver information to our patrons?" "A User-Centered View of Document Delivery and Interlibrary Loan" describes a scenario that to some may have seemed unbelievable a few years ago.[9] The patron in this article performs a number of document delivery and interlibrary loan transactions from her office. Articles from a CD-ROM database are sent to a local printer, an article is ordered from a document supplier and is sent to her Internet address, and a book is charged from the university's library and held for her at the circulation desk. We have come very close to this ideal and may achieve it in the near future.

CONCLUSION

The patron initiated services adopted by Library Affairs at Southern Illinois University at Carbondale have had a significant impact on providing access to information and delivery of services. The use of technology and a redesign of library operations supports this initiative. Patrons can transfer citations into electronic requests either through the interlibrary loan web forms or the FirstSearch interlibrary loan link. Patron generated requests are transferred to the library's online system to remote interlibrary loan departments. Technological innovations such as the web interface with OCLC have transformed the interlibrary loan process. An increase in items borrowed, prompted by the patron initiated interlibrary loan module on the statewide catalog also has impacted the process. New and faster methods to process materials have been adopted. The library to library connection may never disappear but the redesign of the interlibrary loan process has empowered our patrons and provided them increased access to information and better delivery of services.

REFERENCES

1. Association of Research Libraries. *North American Interlibrary Loan & Document Delivery Project: Overview & Vision* (Washington, DC: The Association; 1994).

2. Library Affairs. Southern Illinois University at Carbondale. *Mission Statement,* 1992.

3. Association of Research Libraries. *Information Access & Delivery Services: A Strategic Direction for Research Libraries* (Washington, DC: The Association; 1994).

4. Association of Research Libraries. *North American Interlibrary Loan & Document Delivery Project: Overview & Vision.*

5. Ibid.

6. Ibid.

7. Baker, Shirley K. and Mary E. Jackson. "Maximizing Access, Minimizing Cost: A First Step Toward the Information Access Future. *Public Library Quarterly.* 13 no. 3 (1993): 3-20.

8. OCLC. *Interlibrary Loan User Guide* (Columbus, Ohio: OCLC; 1992, rev. 1994).

9. Harry S. Martin and Curtis L. Kendrick. "A User-Centered View of Document Delivery and Interlibrary Loan: A Scenario Envisioning Faculty Research with Little Intervention by Library Staff." *Library Administration and Management.* 8 (Fall 1994): 223-7.

A Manager's Viewpoint:
Opportunities for Radical Paradigm Shifts

Brice G. Hobrock

SUMMARY. Academic libraries have accepted the consequences of a variety of uncontrollable financial, technological and political conditions for the past ten years with only incremental action. The usual resource-addition and cooperative solutions are not sufficient. The time has come for more radical, global solutions. The regional academic library consortium's application to document access is examined as a mechanism for resolving long-term problems. Radical paradigm shifts and library reengineering targeting resource sharing, document acquisition, and user interfaces are outlined. These strategies are presented as a giant step toward solving the problems of this decade and the next century. *[Article copies available from The Haworth Document Delivery Service: 1-800-342-9678. E-mail address: getinfo@haworth.com]*

INTRODUCTION

Isn't it time for radical solutions to the hard problems affecting medium-sized and larger academic libraries? Academic libraries and their parent universities too easily accept the harsh realities of hyperinflation of information materials, technology growth, and loss of funding support at every level. In coping with these realities, only marginal, seldom radical,

Brice G. Hobrock is Professor and Dean of Libraries at Kansas State University, Manhattan, KS (E-mail address: hobrock@ksuvm.ksu.edu).

[Haworth co-indexing entry note]: "A Manager's Viewpoint: Opportunities for Radical Paradigm Shifts." Hobrock, Brice G. Co-published simultaneously in *Journal of Library Administration* (The Haworth Press, Inc.) Vol. 23, No. 1/2, 1996, pp. 167-187; and: *Interlibrary Loan/Document Delivery and Customer Satisfaction: Strategies for Redesigning Services* (ed: Pat L. Weaver-Meyers, Wilbur A. Stolt, and Yem S. Fong) The Haworth Press, Inc., 1996, pp. 167-187. Single or multiple copies of this article are available from The Haworth Document Delivery Service [1-800-342-9678, 9:00 a.m. - 5:00 p.m. (EST). E-mail address: getinfo@haworth.com].

innovation is attempted. Money, alone, is never enough. We must seek radical solutions.

> The significant problems we face cannot be solved at the same level of thinking we were at when we created them.

> —Albert Einstein[1]

Thus, let's not blame somebody else for our problems. We librarians have the best chance to find solutions. So, let's start thinking at another level, as conventionally incremental thinking will not discover the innovative solutions we must have.

Do library consortia, one of our finest inventions which frequently serve as synergy points for problem solving, provide the level of innovative thinking required to solve today's academic library plight? Consortia are part of a cooperative landscape with which we are very comfortable and from which we derive great benefits, but, will they survive in their present form? What happens when a member library can no longer carry its fair share of the [cost-neutral] give-and-take that is required in the conventional consortium? With technologies offering alternate access to text, what is the future of the consortium and the conventional interlibrary loan process?

Interlibrary loan is under great stress because of user demand, declining local holdings, expanded worldwide output, and so forth. Zemsky and Massy's references to "expanding perimeters, melting cores, and sticky functions" are useful metaphors in describing our libraries and the document acquisition predicament.[2] Clearly, to serve customers, interlibrary loan (document acquisition) must be reinvented to solve the problems faced by the consortium and the individual academic library member.

Herein conditions are examined that lead the library manager to expand thinking and planning beyond conventional, marginal improvements, or consortial dependencies now employed. Marginal performance improvement is not good enough; we need to reinvent our libraries such that dramatic increases in performance are forthcoming.

Thus, Reengineering, a corporate invention, is discussed as an application for the radical reinvention of the academic library and its key processes, including document acquisition–interlibrary loan. By definition, reengineering requires a dramatic improvement in performance through process reinvention. But, it must be accompanied by paradigm and cultural shifts. The consortium is subsequently reexamined for its role in the reengineered library.

Management and leadership are synonymous in the context of this paper. It is presumed that the manager with an adequate understanding of problems, management tools, and desired outcomes will exert the leadership (ability to persuade others of the rightness of the goal) necessary to achieve radical change. However, leadership is discussed as an essential component of successful reengineering.

EXCUSES, EXCUSES

What is the problem? For the most part, it is that the majority of academic libraries' collections can no longer pretend to be comprehensive or to serve a majority of user needs. The voluminous output and cost of scholarly information have outstripped a library's ability to maintain a comprehensive collection, particularly of current information. Of course, there is so much information available in every subject that the beginning scholar has a difficult time getting a grip. Even the established scholar can only follow a fraction of available information. There is also increasing concern that scholarship of the future may consist of reordering old information, rather than creating new information. Since the researcher can't reasonably read it all, how does the scholar identify what is relevant? How does the library with scarce funds identify relevant materials for the scholar? How are other resources obtained? The existing model must be changed.

We librarians apologize to our faculties and students and protest that we can do nothing because we are insignificant consumers in an irrational, fragmented and unconventional economic system dominated by predatory publishers. We say, "it is not a 'library' problem," "it is really a faculty and university problem, and the scholarly research culture must change the dissemination and reward system," before a solution is possible. Don't count on it! Governors, Legislators, Regents and Boards everywhere are demanding "businesslike practices," "everybody working harder and doing more with less." The work of Barr and Tagg, for example, suggests that curriculum redesign is very much on the minds of administrators and faculty.[3] Thus, librarians cannot depend on the slowness of change in the university to shield our own inability to bring ourselves to undertake radical change. Are libraries going to lead radical change in the university, or are we going to be bystanders?

It has been ten years since the U.S. Dollar was allowed to float free against European and Japanese currencies and average annual serial inflation of almost 15 percent entered our vocabularies. So, why haven't academic librarians taken more radical individual or cooperative action against the problems that threaten to make us marginal players in our universities? Why aren't individual library leaders taking action to reform the processes that we as leaders can control?

The answer is because we are "librarians." By most accounts, we are a logical bunch who care about users and think in terms of "rational" processes and "deliberate" change. We assume radical action can only put us in a situation of beginning to make choices and put us outside the mainstream. We are "herd animals" committed to cooperation and agreements that multiply our assets. We are reluctant to do anything that is not a "trend" previously tested and ratified by our guiding consortium or organizational attachments as good for the whole. Consortia are hallmarks of the good things about libraries. Our selflessness and commitment to sharing, however, may inhibit individual leadership toward radical institutional change.

This library manager's intention, therefore, is to introduce issues that might lead an individual librarian to consider radical change through reinvention of library processes, including shifts of individual and organizational thinking and structures. Reinvention should lead to internal changes of attitude, beliefs, and cultural norms that make us able to lead change. Interlibrary loan reinvention, as a microcosm of document access opportunity, could serve as a catalyst for further significant institution-wide change.

CURRENT CONDITIONS

The conditions that require us to consider radical change are not new to academic library leaders. However, it is not clear that rank and file librarians are aware of these matters. Typical responses to calls for radical change bring old answers. "We've been changing how we do things all along, why are you bothering us with yet another planning effort?" "Why don't you leave us alone and let us deal with our users?" "What do you mean, 'radical?'"

Academic library problems have not changed much in the past five years. The intensity, the tools and the determination by which we must seek innovative solutions, however, are increasing. Haven't we run out of excuses? Our parent universities today face changing global conditions:

- growing resource constraints that increase competition for funds, both public and private;
- increasing demand for services and pressures to offer a vastly different product;
- changing consumer base for higher education, requiring service to different age distributions and geographically place-bound adults;

- increasing responsibility to anticipate educational and employment demands and to change curriculum accordingly;
- increasing accountability for the use of public resources and expected outcomes;
- decreasing value of higher education among public priorities compared to other pressing social problems such as crime, welfare, and health care;
- reinventing of government at all levels;
- increasing pressure on universities to become more businesslike;
- adoption of corporate models that drive thinking;
- the growing role of technology and advanced telecommunications in how and where work is done;
- increasing belief in government that there are easy solutions to complex problems and they are best managed at the lowest possible level;
- increasing belief that most problems will go away without continuing commitment of public funds which are easily replaced by private funding.

It is not expected that these conditions will soon abate. Libraries are under the gun by governing entities to do something more than marginal change, and to do it quickly. Some myths and misinformation harbored by users, legislators, educators and even some librarians contribute to the difficulties:

- electronic information and computers have replaced the need for print formats and librarians as interpreters and guides;
- access to the Internet and the "Web" solves all information needs;
- electronic information is free and libraries should have no more financial problems;
- scholarly information has too small a customer base to be really in demand, and thus, to have real commercial value;
- information technologies develop rapidly but one-time funding of hardware, software, and database licenses is sufficient to bring a library to a sufficient level of technological development;
- faculty really don't need the library anymore as they can talk to colleagues via electronic mail on the Internet;
- electronic publications will soon be readily accepted as sufficient evidence of scholarship for faculty tenure and promotion;
- archiving information published in electronic format is not necessary;

- just freeze the library acquisitions budget and let the print collections decline by attrition, we can borrow whatever we need from other libraries;
- for-profit scholarly publishers have the best interests of scholars and libraries in mind;
- the majority of our users want to become truly educated about information and how to find it.

PAST LIBRARY PLANNING

Common sense serves managers well with conventional planning methods, especially goal/objective setting and strategic planning. There is really not a lot to learn, other than the daunting task of how to move the organization collectively and willingly toward a set of planning choices that will be implementable.

This author has previously discussed the value of strategic planning, assessing the environment and making choices among alternatives that have the greatest impact when scarce funding is the limiting factor.[4] Nevertheless, new planning models are always available. The cynic in all of us believes that the newest model is just a trick to provide employment for management consultants and to divert the staff away from "real work."

However, the Deming total quality management (TQM) method and its variation, continuous quality improvement (CQI) (locally called team training) have become planning methods of choice for many corporations, universities, and libraries. Paradigm shifts, greater reliance on teamwork, accompanied by various analytical tools, all help planning teams solve problems in an existing process or unit, usually increasing productivity by small increments. The TQM and CQI planning models, thus, limit analysis to small, easily-managed processes. Customer orientation, teamwork, moving decision-making to lower levels, flattening the hierarchy, all contribute to a more effective organization. These methodologies are useful to library staff at all levels in achieving improved output with fewer resources.

Nevertheless, TQM and CQI do not provide the transformational planning model we desire to find radical solutions to library problems, to revitalize and reinvent how we approach major library processes. Incremental, small scale change isn't working; it isn't good enough to solve the problems that affect academic libraries today.

PARADIGM SHIFTS–WHAT ARE THEY?

A paradigm shift is needed in order to bring radical change to academic libraries. A paradigm is just a model, a word, or phrase that describes what an organization does. A paradigm may represent philosophy, customer or culture. On the other hand, a paradigm may be an expanded set of statements that represent how individual libraries work. Organizational attitudes are reflected by a "now" statement and a "new," shifted representation. An organizational philosophy, one each for both old and new paradigms, is desirable, but is difficult to come by. Such philosophies for change require radical thinking.

Paradigms may represent many different and detailed facets of a complex system. Barr and Tagg, in developing an academic "instruction" to "learning" paradigm shift model for the university, identify components of the "teaching" process, and show how concepts change from old to new "learning" paradigm.[5] Contrast exercises assist the paradigm shifter in analyzing the processes that must be reinvented. What "we want to become" is especially difficult. Paradigm identification, describing who we are and what we do, in simple, meaningful, and understandable language, is the hardest part of the change process.

Paradigm shifting should be a collective staff activity. Involvement of all stakeholders in the paradigm identification process is essential, because we want cultural shift in the whole organization. It may be approached systematically by brainstorming the categories suggested below.

- similes or "Gumpisms," where comparison of unlike objects is made explicit, e.g., "a library is like . . . " as in, "life is like a box of chocolates. You never know what you are going to get";[6]
- metaphors or models, figures of speech in which one's library is compared to another different thing, as if it were the other, "John Dough Library, your information hotline";
- translate a statement about our most encompassing and essential business by triage, where one identifies the sorely wounded and the healthy—those processes that are to receive heroic resuscitation;
- focus on the customer as in TQM or reengineering which both identify a paradigm shift to the library's users;
- take in outside viewpoints—if the customer is our most important business, what do our customers think about us? Old paradigm: "can't find anything in that place." New paradigm: "guaranteed success in meeting your information needs";
- irritations as paradigm identifiers, "The thing that irritates me most about this library is. . . ."

PARADIGM SHIFTS–A MEDICAL CARE MODEL

From this author's experience in identifying a paradigm shift for Kansas State University Libraries, the medical care system simile is the most useful approach. The direct comparison of the two systems, since both need radical modification, opens thinking about how they can be reinvented. "Library care is like medical care." Both economic systems are product-driven rather than demand-driven; total costs are determined by the quantity of product and the number of organizational and service provider units drawing economic advantage from the system. There is no economy of scale. There is no competition. Every scholarly unit (case) is unique. Every customer (patient) and his information (health care) needs are unique. The library acquisitions budget (Medicare) is a faculty (patient) entitlement to everything that is available, without consideration of cost (expensive science journals). Thinking about medical insurance (or lack of it) and HMOs suggests that libraries will become rationers of information and its access, if we are to survive. A scarce product that must be rationed has user cost implications for libraries.

Scholars are like kidney donors, giving away a valuable commodity (copyright), with services (the journal) for the patient (other scholars) being repurchased by insurance (library acquisitions budget) with health care (information) providers (publishers) of the service profiting handsomely. The scholar has given up rights to the product and the acquisition budget is bankrupt. The middle providers (publishers) laugh all the way to the bank. The kidney donor (scholar) gets nothing but stitches, and our thanks and recognition (tenure). Thus, we see that the comparisons are apt. But we may profit from the medical care comparison exercise by understanding that the *old library paradigm = critical information care,* meaning that today's library is like a hospital emergency room. The library has stocked critical information supplies and staff (librarians) are waiting for patients to randomly appear for critical care. The customer arrives with an urgent need for assistance (the undergraduate whose paper is due tomorrow), but realizing that every patient (user) is unique, the best efforts of a professional team are required. The nature of the patient's problem may not be critical at all, leading us to conclusions that the care system (information care) is not rationally constructed to meet user needs, and that significant service and economic gains can be obtained by rethinking the model (paradigm). The comparison suggests that the *new library paradigm = managed information care,* creating a model for change and reinvention of libraries (and health care) that will insure future quality services (care) at a price the customer can afford. This new paradigm should lead to immediate identification of library processes that are subjects for radical reinvention, such as interlibrary loan.

Our interlibrary loan units have increased productivity incrementally, creating many happy customers, through addition of personnel and adoption of the technologies. But, with constraints outlined above and declining resources, we seek radical changes to interlibrary loan and most other library processes.

REENGINEERING: FAD OR FUTURE?

Universities are being asked to "reengineer" their processes as a direct response to the conditions existing in higher education. The corporate derivation of reengineering is proposed as the appropriate model to introduce businesslike practice (read efficiencies) into a most unbusinesslike entity. Corporate "reengineering" is often misinterpreted as "downsizing" the work force and thus, improving the corporate bottom line. That is because some corporations interpret it as such and the cases are widely reported in the press. Consequently, academic candidates for reengineering are skeptical.

What is reengineering and how can it be applied as a useful management model for universities (or libraries)? Management consultants stand ready for our call for assistance to "reengineer our libraries." So, is it just the latest buzzword, the latest management fad? Management literature is full of hundreds of references to reengineering, reinvention and so forth. All refer to a vague process that promises to bring dramatic change to service organizations. Is it surprising that the corporate landscape is littered with failures? Or, is reengineering a breakthrough concept that will allow libraries to significantly change processes and to survive the challenges outlined here?

The author proposes that reengineering is a breakthrough concept for libraries, allowing us to identify processes that can be radically changed. The outcomes could be so significant, that libraries could cease being the victims of conditions that they cannot change.

REENGINEERING THE ACADEMIC LIBRARY

"Engineering" suggests a nuts-and-bolts process, formula-driven, with "one size fits all" outcomes. According to Hammer and Stanton, reengineering is the reinvention of how work is done.[7] In the process, it requires reinvention of the organization, requiring new job designs for staff, new organizational structures, and management systems. But, in its purest application, reengineering is:

> the fundamental rethinking and radical redesign of [library] processes to bring about dramatic improvements in performance. [8]

Dramatic performance improvement means increases of 50 percent or greater, not marginal improvements of five to 10 percent. Performance may be measured as reduced costs, increased processing speed, unit production by staff, more users served, etc. For libraries, putting information in the hands of more customers, providing higher quality information results for users, reducing delays in acquisition of information, are examples of performance improvement. Librarians and staff will be beneficiaries of reduced stress and will develop the pride that comes from greater service to customers, as processes are reinvented.

Reengineering is customer-oriented, with the primary intention to improve outcomes for our library users (customers). However, if the library is inwardly-focused, and reengineering is staff-directed it should not be attempted.

Radical is about throwing away existing processes and reinventing new processes for doing work. It is not about throwing away staff. It is reinvention of how work is done, how the customer gets access, obtains information, how processing is done, or how administrative services are provided. Reengineering is not about improving processes as we do them now. Thus TQM and CQI are not reengineering, nor can they be effectively integrated with the reengineering process.

Reengineering starts from the blank page. If interlibrary loan did not exist today, how would we invent it? Would we invent interlibrary loan as a separate function or an integrated part of the acquisition of information for users?

What are processes, and why is it important to reinvent them? Processes are a "group of related tasks that together create value for a customer."[9] Too many library processes are orphans, fragmented to the extent that they are essentially unmanaged. This is why reinvention of library processes can bring about radical improvement, because total library reengineering can bring unmanaged and unrelated processes together as a more functional whole.

Redesign is really about forgetting how a process is done today and determining how it can be done differently. If the process is poorly designed, even if staff are capable and well-trained, improvement of performance is futile.

A REENGINEERING PROCESS FOR LIBRARIES

What is the formula? If reengineering offers such opportunity for radical change, how do we get started? Well, as Hammer states, there isn't any real process.[10] Nothing universal has been invented. Thus, reengineering is not yet a science. Successful reengineering depends upon organizational commitment, leadership of an individual (a senior person in the organization) who can adapt a variety of methods tried by previous practitioners and guide the library staff to a successful conclusion. Or, consultants may be engaged. What follows is one library's pioneering design of a reengineering process.

- Identify leadership. This must be a senior manager, committed to the process and determined to carry through. The approach is called top-down initiative. The reengineering leader must read extensively in the literature about methodology and case histories of successes and failures, and be able to develop an understandable methodology for his/her organization. The leader must be prepared to convince the entire library staff of the reasons why it must be done—no debates, not whether we will do it or not—and a sense of how it can be completed successfully.
- Select a time period, no more than one year, for completion of the basic reengineering plan.
- Engage all members of the library staff in the process. Begin with key managers and secure their commitment. Meet with small groups of staff on frequent occasions to educate and convert. Answer all questions and keep reengineering on meeting agendas for discussion. Make it clear that nobody is excused from responsibility for reengineering, or they may remain outside the future plans of the library. Implement "bottom-up input" because the actual process reinvention will be done by the staff that are responsible for the work. To successfully implement a reengineered process, ownership must be present.
- Be certain that process and information flow is not hierarchical, but is circular and interactive at all stages.
- Educate library staff to the notion that each person will value them and their assignment in terms of what it does to serve users, and not in terms of title, how many persons are supervised, and where they fall in a hierarchial structure.
- Develop the paradigm shift. Discuss the library's identity, who you are and what you are trying collectively to do over a long period, using small and large group forums. Reengineering is more than pro-

cess reinvention; it is also cultural change to a new model for doing business. Determine who and what the library wants to be and make the new paradigm a guiding principle.

Since reengineering is about radically changing how work is done, there is a systematic process that can be used to identify the procedures to be reengineered.

- Identify the "core functions" of the library. Avoid the existing departmental and unit organization and think globally about everything the library does. Avoid selecting as core functions the things that are seen as quick solutions or panaceas. Specifically avoid the identification of "technology" as a core area, even for process identification. Technology is not a "process" or "outcome." Technology is not our reason for being. Reengineering is not about automating. Technology is not reengineering. Technology may be a part of a process reinvention, however. Technology, along with staff and user education and training, and diversity, should be viewed as an overlay to the entire process reinvention outcome.

  Core functions suggested are:

  - support services;
  - partnerships;
  - the user interface;
  - information sources.

- Develop a "core team" for each "core function," to identify processes to be reengineered or outcomes expected. Leadership will provide a clear charge to each team, but will encourage each to be unconstrained by boundaries. Nothing is off-limits and teams should be urged to think broadly inside and outside the charge. Core teams should include people who are known to think outside normal boundaries, and probably should not include a preponderance of individuals normally associated with the core function. Hammer describes the characteristics of the successful reengineer.[11] Membership should include students, academic faculty, and library staff.
- Bring together core team outputs for sorting and summation. Utilize leadership to determine a unique set of processes and outcomes that will be subject to reinvention. Communicate and discuss so that stakeholders will not become alienated.
- Remand all processes to "process working groups," composed of those individuals who have a stake in the implementation of the

reengineered process. The process groups will take responsibility for process reinvention from the "blank page." Utilize "extended working groups" with special expertise who can solve special problems. Urge the process groups to consult as widely as necessary. Leadership will provide necessary support. Impose realistic resource considerations on the process outcomes. Each process group must identify a method to access performance outcomes.

Serious reengineering will operate a sufficient number of process teams simultaneously, cutting across the functional landscape, such that reengineering will have a coordinated and library-wide outcome.[12] Leave no single permanent staff member outside the reengineering process.

- Curtail any tendencies for teams to exhaustively analyze existing processes. Encourage teams to reach closure quickly. Curtail most other standing meetings in the organization or limit all to very short meeting durations.
- Leadership collects and reviews all process reinventions and subsequently assembles and packages a set of outcomes that best represent the new paradigm. Do not overlook the possibility that many good ideas already exist and have been implemented. Not all current processes should be discarded.
- Deploy processes and resources to appropriate structural models for implementation. Review and seek wide input from staff. Job designs, organizational structure and managment systems are to be identified at this time.
- Assign process development and implementation responsibilities to structural "product and process units" for implementation with timetables. Achieve all process revisions within one year from beginning of process.
- Implement a system of continuous outcome assessment and review.

The efficacy of these procedures cannot yet be assessed because they are currently being tested for use in academic libraries. Figure 1, the "nuclear model" or "another Manhattan project" for reengineering processes, illustrates the circular nature of communications interaction among core teams and the other parts of the process.

REENGINEERING CANDIDATES

Baker's pioneering work for ARL in creating new models for interlibrary loan are of great value.[13] Consider that interlibrary borrowing for a

FIGURE 1. The "Nuclear" Model. "Another Manhattan Project"

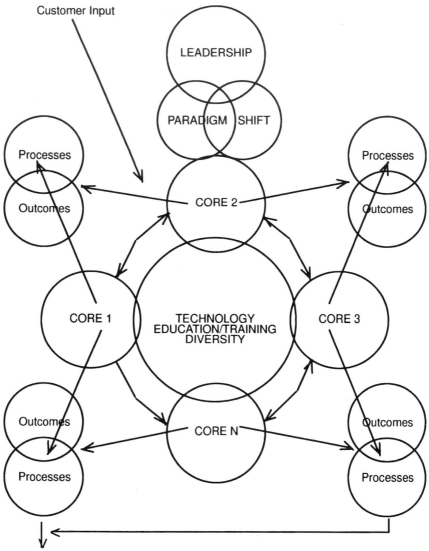

library is just another form of acquiring information for users. Thus, we might reinvent interlibrary loan processes as part of the acquisitions process.

Obtaining information for the collections and for users from all sources and by all means, includes the process known as acquisitions. Current aspects of acquisitions and interlibrary loan such as selection, self-publishing, print- and non-print acquisitions, electronic databases and full-text journals, electronic journals, document delivery providers, consortial agreements, physical delivery systems, and cooperative collection development should all be reinvented as a single process. Fragmentation of these processes in existing library organizations adds up to poor resource deployment. Smith and Johnson propose that (serious) consortial cooperative collection development should be undertaken as a survival tactic, especially since we have the technical means to share information about what we own.[14] The selection process, however, is also clearly integratable with the partnership processes described below.

As the faculty shift their paradigm to "learning," and reinvent how information is accessed and integrated with the curriculum, it will be an omission if librarians are not involved as partners. Librarians should seek university-wide roles in faculty instructional innovation, the use of technologies and electronic information in the classroom. Librarians can partner with developmental and support centers, forming relationships with individual faculty in courseware development.

Faculty partnerships for research are also appropriate. Libraries must invent the process for interaction with research faculty and groups such that information partnerships develop. Outcomes include inclusion of funding for information access in research grant proposals.

As distributed computing and local networks become available in virtually all departments, colleges, and other budget units, it is critical that the library develop linkages (usually easily done through the campus network, but sometimes difficult in data partnering because of individual local network incompatibilities) to avoid duplicative database costs and to aid faculty with bringing library resources into instruction and research.

Librarian-departmental partnerships may develop naturally if librarians are individually active, but the SWAT Team process (sending teams representing selection, databases, instruction, access and technology) shows promise as a process invention. Library-departmental collaboration on subject-based information centers may result, with new resources forthcoming from the department.

"Information care advocacy," the obvious translation of the "managed information care" paradigm into the user interface, is a clear pathway for reinvention of librarians' role in dealing with individual users (customers). Thus, librarians are renamed as "information care advocates," responsible for the individual needs of all incoming user requests, logging, referring, or carrying out to satisfactory conclusion, each request for assistance. "Advocacy" also implies that librarians will not sit and wait for users to appear, but will seek out those in need of information services, and involve themselves widely in instructional, research, and outreach activities of the university.[15]

Our customers desire "one-stop shopping" and do not care to experience the "run-around" from department to department just for the joy of the search. This is the era of instant gratification, and users do not wish to be troubled with multiple interactions, forms, and approvals. While public agencies suffer from "a program to meet every need," reinvention of the user interface process should give us the means to serve customers with available resources.

Since customers want information and they want it now, how do we invent the processes that give it to them? Some librarians believe that learning and instruction is the real library paradigm. Certainly, training and instruction underpin the kind of lifelong learning that we hope students will obtain while under our wing. But is systematic training by traditional methods in libraries able to meet the challenge? Within a few years, our library digital systems will have full voice, data, video capabilities. Collaborations with faculty on instructional design, integrating information access skills into the "learning" process would seem to correlate with a customer-based librarian-as-advocate role.

Although we previously established that "technology" was not an end in itself, and that it affects reinvention of most processes, libraries, universities, and the worldwide scholarly communications system have reached the stage where simple application of technology to problem-solving is a second-tier agenda. It is, however, possible to create a "digital convergence" within a library's access process systems. Digital convergence differs from the "virtual library" in that virtual is an "outcome" that affects the user's perception of information. Digital convergence is a "process" that lends itself to the reengineering concept, the reinvention of access systems for users. With client-server architectures exploding within available integrated systems, the complete convergence of voice, data, video, and networks onto a single interface is imminent, particularly with delivery or access anywhere because of Internet access.

Clearly we have computer hardware, software, and telecommunications technology available or under development, plus the expertise in our libraries and universities to create a convergence of information access systems for our users. NASULGC's briefing paper for university presidents on telecommunications establishes the background set of issues and suggests that emerging university/industry partnerships can lead to reengineered universities through converging information technologies and telecommunications.[16]

Nevertheless, the convergence of digital resources into a single interface creates process opportunities for librarians to invent instructional programs that fit specific user groups. Some libraries, such as Dykes Library, University of Kansas Medical Center, Kansas City, have developed a model for the "procrastinator's dream" where no human intervention is necessary for the user to obtain basic assistance with medical research needs.

The concept of fee for services and information, plus cost sharing on databases for John Dough Library is beginning to be accepted by departments and colleges, under certain circumstances. This is another area ripe for reinvention by librarians in partnership with our academic counterparts.

Reinventing the library's interlibrary loan/document delivery process is a first step to becoming an effective partner in a consortium. All libraries in the consortium will increase dependencies on consortial trading partners. We must place greater reliance on the consortium if we are to meet the expectations of our legislatures, boards, and presidents. However, we must make it very clear that "getting it from another library" does not release one's own library from maintaining the means, the critical mass of owned collections (ownership and willingness to share information materials), to be an effective consortial partner. A number of specific issues must be considered that are unique among reengineered processes for libraries in the consortial environment:

- How does the library manager change local insularity and negative attitudes that remain toward consortiums, e.g., direct loans of journals and special collections materials?
- Do we need to reinvent the premise of "free" documents to faculty and students and become cost-recovery operations? Does the "pass the cost to the user," becoming popular in government, extend to libraries in public institutions? There is some evidence that university colleagues would rather face cost pass-through than face additional reallocation of university budgets to libraries.
- How do we educate administrators and public officials that the "information highway" is filled with chuckholes, is not yet the panacea to information access and does not justify eliminating building of core print collections?

- integrate interlibrary loan borrowing and collection development activities and make reference librarians more effective partners with the faculty in acquiring documents.
- utilize instate library resources more effectively; access to libraries funded from State resources should be free.
- Must there be changes in the financial arrangements among consortium libraries, reimbursing the "haves" for unbalanced services to the "have-nots?"

Have-nots will be obligated to:

- compensate for limited collection assets with "service response." "Service response" is rapid response to the needs of all libraries in the consortium. If the smaller library builds a reputation for effectiveness, requests for loans will grow. While the smaller library may not be the "library of last resort," its reputation for service will make it an effective partner.
- deploy sufficient personnel resources to interlibrary loan to meet growth of borrowing and lending. Insist upon continuing process and organizational effectiveness in a reengineered ILL by use of quality improvement analysis (CQI).
- budget, redeploy funds from acquisitions budgets to meet increasing demands from users for articles purchased from vendors, or be prepared to compensate consortium partners in the future for net-borrower charges.
- effectively invest and budget for access to repository libraries and services—Center for Research Libraries—or establish depository accounts with special libraries to obtain preferential services and rapid access.

Deborah and Frank Popper examined economic and demographic trends on the Great Plains several years ago, and declared that the area east from the Rocky Mountains to the Mississippi River, and south from the Canadian border to Texas, would eventually return to a pre-settlement state, when it was populated principally by buffalo and Native American tribes.[17] This metaphor is aptly applied to the academic libraries of this region. In isolation, we are individually doomed to inhabit the Buffalo Commons. Effective consortial partnerships can create a very different and hopeful future.

Although regional shared-interest, i.e., geographical proximity and shared values and principles are helpful, these factors are becoming somewhat less important. Digital systems and effective overland delivery are reducing the need for geographical proximity. Nevertheless, shared values and principles are often the result of more personalized regional communication, institutional name recognition, and shared principles. Also, building upon other academic or non-academic principles can create an effective consortium.

The Greater Midwest Research Library Consortium (GMRLC) illustrates revitalization of older consortial linkages into more effective partnerships. The libraries of the Big-Eight athletic conference (Kansas, Colorado, Oklahoma, Nebraska, Iowa State, Oklahoma State, Missouri, and Kansas State), and the Western Interstate Consortium on Higher Education (WICHE) (adding Colorado State) have shared resources for more than three decades, using free interlibrary loan agreements to pass print materials among the institutions. Shared geography, characterized by long distances among institutions, and physical isolation from population centers of the U.S. made this limited group effective in a pre-1985 time.

Revitalization became necessary in the late 1980s, however, because the old grouping of institutions and limited agenda was not sufficient to solve the serious problems beginning to be faced by all academic libraries. New leadership in most institutions demanded greater effectiveness and more substantive agendas. That same leadership–virtually all Big-Eight library directors–expanded the agenda of the old consortium to include union listings, overland delivery, digital convergences, and joint applications for external funding. Subsequently, other regional institutions expressed interest in becoming partners, and New Mexico, Arkansas, Wyoming, Southern Illinois were admitted as full members of what became the GMRLC. With the Big-Twelve athletic conference replacing the Big-Eight and Southwest Conferences, Texas, Texas A & M, Baylor, and Texas Tech have become full participating members. Linda Hall Library in Kansas City has been an associate member from the beginning of discussions about expansion. There should not be undue concern about the athletic conference origins of an academic library consortium, because the visionary presidents support a full agenda of academic relationships among the institutions. Geographical proximity and "likeness" among the institutions serve as the basis for an effective and vital regional library consortium.

The list of services that are subject to reinvention or revitalization is large, e.g., security, preservation, recruitment, travel to name a few not examined here. However, the above examples provide an indication of how much work there is to be done to radically reinvent processes that directly affect the delivery of information to the customer. Total reengineering of one's library will require the reengineering czar or czarina to utilize all reasonable processes for which dramatic performance improvement is possible.

FINAL THOUGHTS AND CONCLUSION

The premise of this paper is that individual libraries must take more radical action in confronting the challenges of the '90s and those we can anticipate continuing into the next century. Library managers and library leaders must accept the principles of reengineering, or other new ways of thinking that lead to radical change.

Although paradigm shifting has taken on the label of cliché among some managers and certainly among cynical librarians, who take a dim view of frequent change and new management or planning principles, we need to seriously confront the models and attitudes that we now possess and protect. The problems outlined here all qualify for change. Change of paradigms, models, and culture and how they affect how we provide information to customers, is the process.

Managers must also find a way to effect change within our organizations, and to lead individual library staff through change by making them partners. Managers need to create the next generation of library leaders devoid of frustrations with limited resources, mistrust, weariness with constant change, and general alienation from management.

Interlibrary loan and our entire approach to information sources and document acquisition must be reengineered. Library consortiums play a major role among solutions available to academic libraries, even though libraries have long been committed to the principle of helping each other. We must reexamine our consortiums for effective partnering and for new ways to be effective. Radical improvement in performance must result or we are doomed to muddle along for another ten years.

All librarians must take responsibility for what happens to academic libraries in the next few years. Radical change does not excuse any particular group operating within our organizations. Especially, librarians in the public interface must seek new ways to partner with users and academic departments. They must become more directly responsible for the users' document needs.

We must confront the problems outlined here and not accept the obvious directions planned by outside suppliers of information and our funding infrastructure. We must take charge and change how we deal with these challenges, or we will continue to decline.

NOTES

1. Robert B. Barr and John Tagg, "From Teaching to Learning, A New Paradigm for Undergraduate Education," *Change* 26 (November/December, 1995): 13.

2. Robert Zemsky and William F. Massy, "Toward an Understanding of Our Current Predicaments," *Change* 26 (November/December 1995): 41.

3. Robert B. Barr and John Tagg, p. 13.

4. Brice G. Hobrock, "Creating Your Library's Future Through Effective Strategic Planning," *Journal of Library Administration* 14, no. 2 (1991): 37-57.

5. Robert B. Barr and John Tagg, p. 16.

6. *Forrest Gump* (Paramount Pictures, 1994) film.

7. Michael Hammer and Steven A. Stanton, *The Reengineering Revolution* (New York, Harper Collins Publishers, Inc., 1995).

8. Ibid., 3.

9. Ibid., 4

10. Ibid., xv.

11. Ibid., 59.

12. Ibid., 13.

13. Shirley K. Baker and Mary E. Jackson, "Maximizing Access, Minimizing Cost: A First Step Toward the Information Access Future" (Washington, DC, Association of Research Libraries, February 1993).

14. Eldred Smith and Peggy Johnson, "How to Survive the Present while Preparing for the Future: A Research Library Strategy," *College and Research Libraries* 53 (September 1993): 389-96.

15. Jerry D. Campbell, "Shaking the Conceptual Foundations of Reference: A Perspective," *Reference Services Review* 20 (Winter 1992): 29-35.

16. National Association of State Universities and Land-Grant Colleges, Commission on Information Technologies, *The Changing Telecommunications Marketplace: Issues and Challenges for Higher Education* (Washington, DC, The Commission, 1995): 6.

17. Deborah E. Popper and Frank J. Popper, "The Great Plains: From Dust to Dust," *Planning* (December, 1987): 18.

Appendix

What follows is series of tables that report descriptive and inferential data from the 1995 interlibrary loan customer satisfaction survey among ten of the 18 Greater Midwest Research Libraries Consortium (GMRLC) members. During data analysis, it became obvious that an overview of the data could be valuable to other academic librarians interested in bench marking performance in interlibrary loan. Therefore, the data is organized so that the reader can focus on a specific institution or review survey responses from the entire group of respondents.

As the authors organized this volume, we found ourselves fascinated by the comparative performance of the institutions and by the variation among responses to specific questions. Although some current research efforts are being undertaken to study ILL customer satisfaction among several libraries, most notably the Council on Library Resources (CLR) and Association of Research Libraries (ARL) project coordinated by Mary Jackson, previous studies look at ILL customer satisfaction within one academic institution. This is the only current data available from a group of academic libraries that analyzes ILL customer satisfaction with the same survey instrument.

Because the CLR/ARL project staff will pilot test their study among GMRLC Libraries using a different survey instrument, these findings are particularly timely and valuable. Comparing the results of this survey with the CLR/ARL customer satisfaction survey now underway can reveal valuable insights about survey methodology and customer response. The timely coincidence of both studies creates opportunities for comparison that would not be possible had the studies been separated by years. The rapid pace of change in interlibrary loan offices quickly redefines work-flow, procedures and performance expectations, often outdating comparisons. Even so, we believe these appendices may also provide future researchers with an historical record that can be used in future research efforts about customers' satisfaction with all types of library services.

[Haworth co-indexing entry note]: "Appendix." Co-published simultaneously in *Journal of Library Administration* (The Haworth Press, Inc.) Vol. 23, No. 1/2, 1996, pp. 189-253; and: *Interlibrary Loan/ Document Delivery and Customer Satisfaction: Strategies for Redesigning Services* (ed: Pat L. Weaver-Meyers, Wilbur A. Stolt, and Yem S. Fong) The Haworth Press, Inc., 1996, pp. 189-253. Single or multiple copies of this article are available from The Haworth Document Delivery Service [1-800-342-9678, 9:00 a.m. - 5:00 p.m. (EST) E-mail address: get info@haworth.com].

189

LIST OF TABLES

FIGURE A.1. Interlibrary Loan Services (ILL)—Survey 1995

The item attached is the result of a request you made for an interlibrary loan. We are interested in your opinion of the quality of service. Please take a few moments and respond to the questions below. Your input will help the Libraries improve. If you have already completed this form for another item, please complete this form AGAIN! Your opinion of each transaction is an important part of our study. When you are done, fold the completed form in half, staple closed and return in campus mail or use the self-addressed stamped envelope provided. All responses are anonymous.

Thank you.

1) When did you receive the attached interlibrary loan item? _____/_____/_____.

2) In the past year, about how many books or articles have you requested from ILL?___ .

Please answer the following by selecting the rating which most represents your opinion of the statement and write that rating in the space provided.

1 = strongly agree   2 = agree   3 = neutral   4 = disagree   5 = strongly disagree

3) _____ I received this item in a timely manner.

4) _____ I am satisfied with telephone interactions I have had with interlibrary loan staff.

5) _____ Based on this transaction, I am satisfied with interlibrary loan service.

6) _____ Because it took so long to receive this item, it was no longer useful to me.

7) _____ I will be using interlibrary loan services in the future.

8) _____ The item I received is the item I requested.

9) _____ This item was valuable to my research.

10) _____ If I could be guaranteed faster delivery, I would be willing to pay a fee of $10 to get this item.

11) _____ I found it convenient and easy to place a request.

12) _____ The interlibrary loan staff are readily available to answer my questions.

13) _____ It is convenient for me to pick up books I receive on interlibrary loan at the library.

14) _____ I currently order some materials I need directly from commercial vendors on the internet (CARL, FirstSearch, UMI, etc.)

15) _____ The average cost of ILL transactions to the library is about $18. This material was worth that investment.

Comments?

_____

_____

Item requested via: _____ OCLC _____ RLIN _____ MAIL _____ FAX _____ ARIEL
Item transmitted via: _____ mail _____ in-state courier _____ Ariel _____ fax _____ FedEx
Date Requested:_____ Date Received: _____
Type of notification: _____ phone _____ mail _____ e-mail   Date notified:_____/_____/_____
Status: faculty _____ grad _____ undergrad _____ other _____

TABLE A.1 GMRLC Statistics

Reporting Institutions

INSTITUTION	Size of Collection	Number of ILL- Lending	Number of ILL-Borrowed	Total	Expenditures for Serials
Arkansas**	1,212,417	13,909	11,544	25,453	$1,502,987
Baylor**	1,174,059	9,318	3,666	12,984	$867,339
Colorado*	2,575,290	32,318	13,162	45,480	$3,560,773
Colorado State*	1,553,346	33,616	22,796	56,412	$1,976,492
Iowa State*	2,011,189	24,546	8,297	32,843	$2,720,353
Kansas*	3,292,923	43,150	19,307	62,457	$2,999,669
Kansas State**	1,307,731	20,091	17,806	37,897	$1,719,173
Linda Hall**	675,000	23,798	66	23,798	$1,700,000
Missouri*	2,683,566	38,428	17,034	55,462	$2,418,517
Nebraska*	2,278,154	12,276	15,270	27,546	$2,872,015
New Mexico*	1,949,583	25,458	21,458	46,916	$2,870,546
Oklahoma*	2,484,094	30,459	23,789	54,248	$2,719,542
Oklahoma State*	1,758,337	20,338	12,652	32,990	$1,882,152
Southern Illinois*	2,280,457	33,652	14,117	47,769	$2,360,408
Texas*	7,019,508	34,916	19,322	54,238	$3,677,907
Texas A&M*	2,226,104	35,882	21,217	57,099	$3,159,915
Texas Tech**	1,257,234	23,873	33,599	57,472	$1,395,347
Wyoming**	1,112,034	20,627	9,081	29,708	$1,800,376

*ARL STATISTICS 1993-94
**American Library Directory 1995-96 and self-reporting

TABLE A.2. Survey Reliability

All Institutions

Institution	Cronbach Coefficient Alpha*
A	0.7427
B	0.6956
C	0.7182
D	0.6876
E	0.7997
F	0.4187
G	0.6942
H	0.7637
I	0.7366
J	0.7657
All Institutions	0.7183

* Alpha calculations required the reversal of responses to negatively worded variables, i.e., "because it took so long receive this item, it was no longer useful to me." Positive ratings of these questions require the respondent to disagree.

TABLE A.3. Useable Surveys Returned

By Institution

Institution	Frequency	Percent
A	79	10.30
B	101	13.10
C	57	7.40
D	101	13.10
E	65	8.40
F	70	9.10
G	84	10.90
H	81	10.50
I	78	10.10
J	54	7.00

N = 770

TABLE A.4. Means for Responses to Questions with Numerical Answers

All Institutions

Variable	N	Mean	Std Dev
		(No Scale)	
Delivery Speed	714	15.4691	16.3265
Number of Requests	702	29.0071	53.6404
		(Scale 1-5)	
Timeliness	750	1.6986	0.9372
Telephone Interactions	628	1.6066	0.8260
Satisfaction	745	1.4563	0.7430
Delivery Took Too Long	713	4.4221	0.9148
Will Use in the Future	751	1.1770	0.5052
Received the Correct Item	751	1.1358	0.4763
Value of ILL	732	1.3456	0.6315
Willingness to Pay $10	728	3.9478	1.0358
Convenient to Place Request	751	1.6085	0.8204
Staff Availability	734	1.4482	0.6725
Pick Up Convenience	729	1.8641	1.0051
Vendor Use	674	4.0459	1.1288
Worth $18 Investment	703	2.0099	1.1341

Scale

1 = Strongly Agree, 2 = Agree, 3 = Neutral, 4 = Disagree, 5 = Strongly Disagree

TABLE A.5. Patron Status

All Institutions

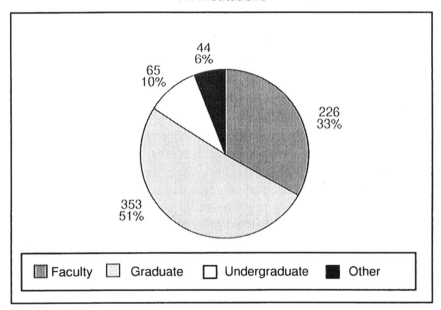

44
6%

65
10%

226
33%

353
51%

▨ Faculty ☐ Graduate ☐ Undergraduate ■ Other

N = 688

TABLE B.1. Means for Responses to Survey Questions with Numerical Responses

Institution A

	N	Mean	S.D.	Min.	Max.
Delivery Speed	71	18.9437	17.1770	7	97
Number of Requests	76	26.2500	31.7440	1	150
Timeliness	79	1.8608	1.1063	1	5
Telephone Interactions	71	1.8451	0.9358	1	5
Satisfaction	79	1.5570	0.8733	1	5
Delivery Took Too Long	76	4.2500	1.0214	1	5
Will Use in the Future	77	1.2208	0.5988	1	5
Received the Correct Item	79	1.1519	0.3612	1	2
Value of Interlibrary Loan	79	1.3671	0.6637	1	4
Willingness to Pay $10	76	3.8289	0.9985	1	5
Convenient to Place Request	78	1.8845	0.9395	1	5
Staff Availability	78	1.7051	0.8391	1	4
Pick Up Convenience	75	1.9200	0.9831	1	5
Vendor Use	74	3.6400	1.2432	1	5
Worth $18 Investment	73	1.9863	1.2303	1	5

TABLE B.2. Means for Responses to Survey Questions with Numerical Responses

Institution B

	N	Mean	S.D.	Min.	Max.
Delivery Speed	101	18.3465	31.2539	1	313
Number of Requests	97	15.6907	22.1761	1	175
Timeliness	101	1.6237	0.9258	1	5
Telephone Interactions	74	1.7568	0.8884	1	4
Satisfaction	101	1.4059	0.6660	1	4
Delivery Took Too Long	98	4.3878	0.9485	1	5
Will Use in the Future	101	1.1782	0.4560	1	4
Received the Correct Item	101	1.0990	0.3318	1	3
Value of Interlibrary Loan	100	1.3600	0.7180	1	5
Willingness to Pay $10	101	3.9901	1.1269	1	5
Convenient to Place Request	101	1.4257	0.5890	1	4
Staff Availability	100	1.3100	0.5064	1	3
Pick Up Convenience	98	1.7346	0.8916	1	4
Vendor Use	88	4.2159	1.0875	1	5
Worth $18 Investment	93	2.0107	1.0784	1	5

TABLE B.3. Means for Responses to Survey Questions with Numerical Responses

Institution C

	N	Mean	S.D.	Min.	Max.
Delivery Speed	37	12.8900	8.3192	4	48
Number of Requests	52	24.5000	24.5940	1	100
Timeliness	57	1.8421	0.9218	1	5
Telephone Interactions	42	1.9762	0.9497	1	4
Satisfaction	56	1.5893	0.8480	1	5
Delivery Took Too Long	54	4.4074	0.8131	2	5
Will Use in the Future	56	1.2500	0.6396	1	4
Received the Correct Item	56	1.1429	0.5855	1	5
Value of Interlibrary Loan	55	1.4545	0.6890	1	3
Willingness to Pay $10	55	4.0182	0.9524	2	5
Convenient to Place Request	57	1.4737	0.7345	1	4
Staff Availability	54	1.6111	0.7871	1	4
Pick Up Convenience	55	1.9455	0.9510	1	5
Vendor Use	52	3.8462	1.1612	1	5
Worth $18 Investment	55	1.8909	0.9164	1	4

TABLE B.4. Means for Responses to Survey Questions with Numerical Responses

Institution D

	N	Mean	S.D.	Min.	Max.
Delivery Speed	93	18.6200	15.2614	4	126
Number of Requests	88	20.4770	23.2848	1	100
Timeliness	92	1.4565	0.0717	1	5
Telephone Interactions	88	1.3295	0.6383	1	4
Satisfaction	93	1.3225	0.5142	1	3
Delivery Took Too Long	88	4.6477	0.7278	1	5
Will Use in the Future	94	1.1702	0.5213	1	5
Received the Correct Item	94	1.1489	0.3868	1	3
Value of Interlibrary Loan	92	1.3261	0.6132	1	5
Willingness to Pay $10	89	4.2584	0.9597	1	5
Convenient to Place Request	93	1.6667	0.9247	1	4
Staff Availability	92	1.3370	0.5981	1	4
Pick Up Convenience	93	1.7742	0.9905	1	5
Vendor Use	87	4.2069	1.0690	1	5
Worth $18 Investment	90	1.8111	0.9586	1	5

TABLE B.5. Means for Responses to Survey Questions with Numerical Responses

Institution E

	N	Mean	S.D.	Min.	Max.
Delivery Speed	59	11.2203	5.8606	1	28
Number of Requests	53	15.7925	13.6358	1	55
Timeliness	61	1.7869	0.9851	1	5
Telephone Interactions	50	1.6800	1.0774	1	5
Satisfaction	61	1.3443	0.6554	1	4
Delivery Took Too Long	61	4.4098	0.8037	1	5
Will Use in the Future	62	1.1452	0.3986	1	3
Received the Correct Item	62	1.0806	0.4168	1	4
Value of Interlibrary Loan	60	1.2500	0.5712	1	4
Willingness to Pay $10	61	3.7377	0.9815	1	5
Convenient to Place Request	62	1.5645	0.6173	1	3
Staff Availability	61	1.3934	0.5561	1	3
Pick Up Convenience	61	1.6230	0.8975	1	5
Vendor Use	56	4.0893	1.0318	1	5
Worth $18 Investment	60	1.9667	1.2069	1	5

TABLE B.6. Means for Responses to Survey Questions with Numerical Responses

Institution F

	N	Mean	S.D.	Min.	Max.
Delivery Speed	66	15.5758	8.1090	5	53
Number of Requests	61	53.2623	108.9217	1	800
Timeliness	70	1.7571	0.9237	1	5
Telephone Interactions	53	1.6038	0.7426	1	3
Satisfaction	67	1.4925	0.7662	1	5
Delivery Took Too Long	62	4.4355	0.7814	1	5
Will Use in the Future	70	1.1571	0.5551	1	·5
Received the Correct Item	70	1.1143	0.3205	1	2
Value of Interlibrary Loan	64	1.3594	0.5453	1	3
Willingness to Pay $10	64	3.9688	1.0230	1	5
Convenient to Place Request	70	1.6143	0.7282	1	3
Staff Availability	68	1.5147	0.6346	1	3
Pick Up Convenience	67	2.2045	1.0318	1	4
Vendor Use	53	3.9811	1.1005	1	5
Worth $18 Investment	61	2.0984	1.1648	1	5

TABLE B.7. Means for Responses to Survey Questions with Numerical Responses

Institution G

	N	Mean	S.D.	Min.	Max.
Delivery Speed	78	15.1795	10.2637	5	63
Number of Requests	77	47.8831	92.2071	1	400
Timeliness	81	1.7531	1.1128	1	5
Telephone Interactions	71	1.4648	0.7527	1	3
Satisfaction	79	1.5063	0.9320	1	5
Delivery Took Too Long	76	4.3684	1.1295	1	5
Will Use in the Future	81	1.1235	0.3310	1	2
Received the Correct Item	79	1.1392	0.5246	1	5
Value of Interlibrary Loan	78	1.3462	0.5772	1	3
Willingness to Pay $10	79	3.8987	0.9418	2	5
Convenient to Place Request	81	1.5432	0.7913	1	5
Staff Availability	77	1.2468	0.4633	1	3
Pick Up Convenience	77	1.9351	1.1278	1	5
Vendor Use	70	3.9857	1.1609	1	5
Worth $18 Investment	74	1.8919	1.0925	1	5

TABLE B.8. Means for Responses to Survey Questions with Numerical Responses

Institution H

	N	Mean	S.D.	Min.	Max.
Delivery Speed	77	8.3896	5.9497	1	32
Number of Requests	75	26.1600	23.1353	1	100
Timeliness	78	1.4615	0.6585	1	4
Telephone Interactions	75	1.5067	0.6852	1	3
Satisfaction	79	1.3544	0.6413	1	4
Delivery Took Too Long	77	4.5844	0.8789	1	5
Will Use in the Future	78	1.1538	0.3631	1	2
Received the Correct Item	79	1.1519	0.5086	1	4
Value of Interlibrary Loan	78	1.3205	0.5697	1	3
Willingness to Pay $10	77	4.0000	0.9868	1	5
Convenient to Place Request	79	1.6076	0.8385	1	4
Staff Availability	79	1.3924	0.6488	1	3
Pick Up Convenience	78	1.5641	0.8153	1	4
Vendor Use	75	3.9467	1.3038	1	5
Worth $18 Investment	77	2.1299	1.3313	1	5

TABLE B.9. Means for Responses to Survey Questions with Numerical Responses

Institution I

	N	Mean	S.D.	Min.	Max.
Delivery Speed	78	13.8974	12.2343	1	67
Number of Requests	74	40.7432	60.1979	1	250
Timeliness	77	1.7273	0.9547	1	5
Telephone Interactions	65	1.4154	0.6822	1	3
Satisfaction	77	1.4156	6.1453	1	4
Delivery Took Too Long	70	4.3000	1.0405	1	5
Will Use in the Future	78	1.1282	0.3365	1	2
Received the Correct Item	77	1.1169	0.5374	1	5
Value of Interlibrary Loan	75	1.2533	0.5949	1	5
Willingness to Pay $10	75	3.6667	1.2118	1	5
Convenient to Place Request	76	1.5658	0.8056	1	4
Staff Availability	74	1.4730	0.8146	1	5
Pick Up Convenience	75	2.1467	1.1353	1	5
Vendor Use	72	4.2222	1.0101	1	5
Worth $18 Investment	70	2.2429	1.1849	1	5

TABLE B.10. Means for Responses to Survey Questions with Numerical Responses

Institution J

	N	Mean	S.D.	Min.	Max.
Delivery Speed	54	19.1481	14.0664	6	101
Number of Requests	49	20.8163	26.0068	1	100
Timeliness	54	1.9074	0.9370	1	5
Telephone Interactions	39	1.7949	0.7671	1	3
Satisfaction	53	1.7170	0.8853	1	5
Delivery Took Too Long	51	4.3725	0.8237	1	5
Will Use in the Future	54	1.2963	0.8156	1	5
Received the Correct Item	54	1.2407	0.7994	1	5
Value of Interlibrary Loan	51	1.4706	0.7577	1	4
Willingness to Pay $10	51	4.0588	1.0278	2	5
Convenient to Place Request	54	1.7963	1.1223	1	5
Staff Availability	51	1.6863	0.7346	1	3
Pick Up Convenience	50	2.0200	1.1156	1	5
Vendor Use	47	4.2766	0.9017	2	5
Worth $18 Investment	50	2.1400	1.1250	1	5

TABLE C.1. Delivery Speed in Days

Mean and Standard Deviation by Institution

Institution	N	Mean	Std Dev
A	71	18.9437	17.1771
B	101	18.3465	31.2539
C	37	12.8919	8.3193
D	93	18.6237	15.2614
E	59	11.2203	5.8606
F	66	15.5758	8.1090
G	78	15.1795	10.2637
H	77	8.3896	5.9497
I	78	13.8974	12.2343
J	54	19.1481	14.0664

TABLE C.2. Number of Requests

Mean and Standard Deviation by Institution

Institution	N	Mean	Std Dev
A	76	26.2500	31.7444
B	97	15.6907	22.1761
C	52	24.5000	24.5944
D	88	20.4773	23.2848
E	53	15.7925	13.6259
F	61	53.2623	108.9217
G	77	47.8831	92.2071
H	75	26.1600	23.1353
I	74	40.7432	60.1979
J	49	20.8163	26.0069

TABLE C.3. Timeliness

Mean and Standard Deviation by Institution

Institution	N	Mean	Std Dev
A	79	1.8608	1.1063
B	101	1.6238	0.9258
C	57	1.8421	0.9218
D	92	1.4565	0.7173
E	61	1.7869	0.9851
F	70	1.7571	0.9237
G	81	1.7531	1.1128
H	78	1.4615	0.6585
I	77	1.7273	0.9547
J	54	1.9074	0.9370

Scale
1 = Strongly Agree, 2 = Agree, 3 = Neutral, 4 = Disagree, 5 = Strongly Disagree

TABLE C.4. Satisfying Telephone Interactions

Mean and Standard Deviation by Institution

Institution	N	Mean	Std Dev
A	71	1.8451	0.9358
B	74	1.7568	0.8884
C	42	1.9762	0.9497
D	88	1.3295	0.6383
E	50	1.6800	1.0774
F	53	1.6038	0.7426
G	71	1.4648	0.7527
H	75	1.5067	0.6852
I	65	1.4154	0.6822
J	39	1.7949	0.7671

Scale
1 = Strongly Agree, 2 = Agree, 3 = Neutral, 4 = Disagree, 5 = Strongly Disagree

TABLE C.5. Satisfaction with Transaction

Mean and Standard Deviation by Institution

Institution	N	Mean	Std Dev
A	79	1.5570	0.8733
B	101	1.4059	0.6660
C	56	1.5893	0.8480
D	93	1.3226	0.5142
E	61	1.3443	0.6554
F	67	1.4925	0.7662
G	79	1.5063	0.9320
H	79	1.3544	0.6413
I	77	1.4156	0.6145
J	53	1.7170	0.8853

Scale
1 = Strongly Agree, 2 = Agree, 3 = Neutral, 4= Disagree, 5 = Strongly Disagree

TABLE C.6. Delivery Took Too Long

Mean and Standard Deviation by Institution

Institution	N	Mean	Std Dev
A	76	4.2500	1.0214
B	98	4.3878	0.9485
C	54	4.4074	0.8131
D	88	4.6477	0.7278
E	61	4.4098	0.8037
F	62	4.4355	0.7814
G	76	4.3684	1.1295
H	77	4.5844	0.8789
I	70	4.3000	1.0405
J	51	4.3725	0.8237

Scale
1 = Strongly Agree, 2 = Agree, 3 = Neutral, 4 = Disagree, 5 = Strongly Disagree

TABLE C.7. Will Use in the Future

Mean and Standard Deviation by Institution

Institution	N	Mean	Std Dev
A	77	1.2208	0.5988
B	101	1.1782	0.4560
C	56	1.2500	0.6396
D	94	1.1702	0.5213
E	62	1.1452	0.3986
F	70	1.1571	0.5552
G	81	1.1235	0.3310
H	78	1.1538	0.3631
I	78	1.1282	0.3365
J	54	1.2963	0.8156

Scale
1 = Strongly Agree, 2 = Agree, 3 = Neutral, 4 = Disagree, 5 = Strongly Disagree

TABLE C.8. Received the Correct Item

Mean and Standard Deviation by Institution

Institution	N	Mean	Std Dev
A	79	1.1519	0.3612
B	101	1.0990	0.3318
C	56	1.1429	0.5855
D	94	1.1489	0.3868
E	62	1.0806	0.4168
F	70	1.1143	0.3205
G	79	1.1392	0.5246
H	79	1.1519	0.5086
I	77	1.1169	0.5374
J	54	1.2407	0.7994

Scale
1 = Strongly Agree, 2 = Agree, 3 = Neutral, 4 = Disagree, 5 = Strongly Disagree

TABLE C.9. Value of Item to Research

Mean and Standard Deviation by Institution

Institution	N	Mean	Std Dev
A	79	1.3671	0.6637
B	100	1.3600	0.7180
C	55	1.4545	0.6890
D	92	1.3261	0.6132
E	60	1.2500	0.5712
F	64	1.3594	0.5453
G	78	1.3462	0.5772
H	78	1.3205	0.5697
I	75	1.2533	0.5949
J	51	1.4706	0.7577

Scale
1 = Strongly Agree, 2 = Agree, 3 = Neutral, 4 = Disagree, 5 = Strongly Disagree

TABLE C.10. Willingness to Pay $10.00

Mean and Standard Deviation by Institution

Institution	N	Mean	Std Dev
A	76	3.8289	0.9985
B	101	3.9901	1.1269
C	55	4.0182	0.9524
D	89	4.2584	0.9597
E	61	3.7377	0.9815
F	64	3.9688	1.0230
G	79	3.8987	0.9418
H	77	4.0000	0.9868
I	75	3.6667	1.2118
J	51	4.0588	1.0278

Scale
1 = Strongly Agree, 2 = Agree, 3 = Neutral, 4 = Disagree, 5 = Strongly Disagree

TABLE C.11. Convenient to Place Request

Mean and Standard Deviation by Institution

Institution	N	Mean	Std Dev
A	78	1.8846	0.9395
B	101	1.4257	0.5890
C	57	1.4737	0.7345
D	93	1.6667	0.9247
E	62	1.5645	0.6173
F	70	1.6143	0.7282
G	81	1.5432	0.7913
H	79	1.6076	0.8385
I	76	1.5658	0.8056
J	54	1.7963	1.1223

Scale
1 = Strongly Agree, 2 = Agree, 3 = Neutral, 4 = Disagree, 5 = Strongly Disagree

TABLE C.12. Staff Are Readily Available

Mean and Standard Deviation by Institution

Institution	N	Mean	Std Dev
A	78	1.7051	0.8391
B	100	1.3100	0.5064
C	54	1.6111	0.7871
D	92	1.3370	0.5981
E	61	1.3934	0.5561
F	68	1.5147	0.6346
G	77	1.2468	0.4633
H	79	1.3924	0.6488
I	74	1.4730	0.8146
J	51	1.6863	0.7346

Scale
1 = Strongly Agree, 2 = Agree, 3 = Neutral, 4 = Disagree, 5 = Strongly Disagree

TABLE C.13. Pick Up Convenience

Mean and Standard Deviation by Institution

Institution	N	Mean	Std Dev
A	75	1.9200	0.9831
B	98	1.7347	0.8916
C	55	1.9455	0.9510
D	93	1.7742	0.9905
E	61	1.6230	0.8975
F	67	2.1045	1.0318
G	77	1.9351	1.1278
H	78	1.5641	0.8153
I	75	2.1467	1.1353
J	50	2.0200	1.1156

Scale
1 = Strongly Agree, 2 = Agree, 3 = Neutral, 4 = Disagree, 5 = Strongly Disagree

TABLE C.14. Currently Use Commercial Vendors

Mean and Standard Deviation by Institution

Institution	N	Mean	Std Dev
A	74	3.6486	1.2434
B	88	4.2159	1.0875
C	52	3.8462	1.1612
D	87	4.2069	1.0690
E	56	4.0893	1.0318
F	53	3.9811	1.1005
G	70	3.9857	1.1609
H	75	3.9467	1.3038
I	72	4.2222	1.0101
J	47	4.2766	0.9017

Scale
1 = Strongly Agree, 2 = Agree, 3 = Neutral, 4 = Disagree, 5 = Strongly Disagree

TABLE C.15. Worth $18.00 Investment

Mean and Standard Deviation by Institution

Institution	N	Mean	Std Dev
A	73	1.9863	1.2303
B	93	2.0107	1.0784
C	55	1.8909	0.9164
D	90	1.8111	0.9586
E	60	1.9667	1.2069
F	61	2.0984	1.1648
G	74	1.8919	1.0925
H	77	2.1299	1.3313
I	70	2.2429	1.1849
J	50	2.1400	1.1250

Scale
1 = Strongly Agree, 2 = Agree, 3 = Neutral, 4 = Disagree, 5 = Strongly Disagree

TABLE D.1. Pearson Correlation Coefficients

Institution A

	Q-1	Q-2	Q-3	Q-4	Q-5	Q-6	Q-7	Q-8	Q-9	Q-10	Q-11	Q-12	Q-13	Q-14	Q-15
Delivery Speed (Q-1)	--		.4055		.2842	-.3068									
Number of Requests (Q-2)		--													
Timeliness (Q-3)	.4055		--		.7249	-.6246	.4303	.3723			.3045	.2799	.2919		.3180
Telephone Interactions (Q-4)				--						-.2338		.2945	.3447		.4000
Satisfaction (Q-5)	.2842		.7249		--	-.7513	.5452	.3936			.4915	.4855			.3641
Delivery Took Too Long (Q-6)	-.3068		-.6246		-.7513	--	-.5405	-.4213			-.2943				-.3477
Will Use in the Future (Q-7)			.4303		.5452	-.5405	--	.3816			.2423				
Received the Correct Item (Q-8)			.3723		.3936	-.4213	.3816	--	.5463		.4003	.3472			.4215
Value of Interlibrary Loan (Q-9)								.5463	--						.3856
Willingness to Pay $10 (Q-10)				-.2338						--					
Convenient to Place Request (Q-11)			.3045		.4915	-.2943	.2423	.4003			--	.7204	.4289		.3372
Staff Availability (Q-12)			.2799	.2945	.4855			.3472			.7204	--	.5169		.2832
Pick Up Convenience (Q-13)			.2919	.3447							.4289	.5169	--		
Vendor Use (Q-14)														--	
Worth $18 Investment (Q-15)			.3180	.4000	.3641	-.3477		.4215	.3856		.3372	.2832			--

p = < .05

n = 53

sas = proc corr no miss alpha

TABLE D.2. Pearson Correlation Coefficients

Institution B

	Q-1	Q-2	Q-3	Q-4	Q-5	Q-6	Q-7	Q-8	Q-9	Q-10	Q-11	Q-12	Q-13	Q-14	Q-15
Delivery Speed (Q-1)	--	.3605													
Number of Requests (Q-2)	.3605	--								.2661					
Timeliness (Q-3)			--	.3866	.6935	-.5506	.3982		.2614		.2640	.2585			.2837
Telephone Interactions (Q-4)			.3866	--	.3448				.2619			.2858	.3955		.3207
Satisfaction (Q-5)			.6935	.3448	--	-.5398	.4931	.2643	.4036		.3362	.3266			.2730
Delivery Took Too long (Q-6)			-.5506		-.5398	--	-.2553		-.3550						-.2842
Will Use in the Future (Q-7)			.3982		.4931	-.2553	--	.3468	.5167			.2724			.2902
Received the Correct Item (Q-8)					.2643		.3468	--	.4480						
Value of Interlibrary Loan (Q-9)			.2614	.2619	.4036	-.3550	.5167	.4480	--		.2970	.3254			.3697
Willingness to Pay $10 (Q-10)		.2661								--					
Convenient to Place Request (Q-11)			.2640		.3362				.2970		--	.3190	.4104		
Staff Availability (Q-12)			.2585	.2858	.3266		.2724		.3254		.3190	--	.4681		.6186
Pick Up Convenience (Q-13)				.3955							.4104	.4681	--		.3192
Vendor Use (Q-14)														--	
Worth $18 Investment (Q-15)			.2837	.3207	.2730	.2842	.2902		.3697			.6186	.3192		--

p < .05

n = 63

sas = proc corr no miss alpha

TABLE D.3. Pearson Correlation Coefficients

Institution C

	Q-1	Q-2	Q-3	Q-4	Q-5	Q-6	Q-7	Q-8	Q-9	Q-10	Q-11	Q-12	Q-13	Q-14	Q-15
Delivery Speed (Q-1)	--	.4258					.5127								
Number of Requests (Q-2)	.4258	--													
Timeliness (Q-3)			--	.8381		-.6096									
Telephone Interactions (Q-4)			.8381	--		-.6322		.4732		-.6226					
Satisfaction (Q-5)					--	-.5894			.4803	-.5330					
Delivery Took Too Long (Q-6)			-.6096	-.6322	-.5894	--	-.6150	.5300	-.5300	-.4468					
Will Use in the Future (Q-7)	.5127					-.6150	--								
Received the Correct Item (Q-8)				.4732		.5300		--			.6423				
Value of Interlibrary Loan (Q-9)					.4803	-.5300			--	.5878					
Willingness to Pay $10 (Q-10)				-.6226	-.5329	-.4468			.5878	--					
Convenient to Place Request (Q-11)								.6423			--	.5052			
Staff Availability (Q-12)											.5052	--			
Pick Up Convenience (Q-13)													--		
Vendor Use (Q-14)														--	
Worth $18 Investment (Q-15)															--

p = < .05

n = 22

sas = proc corr no miss alpha

TABLE D.4. Pearson Correlation Coefficients

Institution D

	Q-1	Q-2	Q-3	Q-4	Q-5	Q-6	Q-7	Q-8	Q-9	Q-10	Q-11	Q-12	Q-13	Q-14	Q-15
Delivery Speed (Q-1)	--		.6793												
Number of Requests (Q-2)		--								.2366	-.2712	-.2472	-.2567		
Timeliness (Q-3)	.6793		--	.2480	.5562						.2385	.3678			.2409
Telephone Interactions (Q-4)			.2480	--	.5189			.4843			.3639	.4002	.3884		
Satisfaction (Q-5)			.5562	.5189	--	-.3426		.5143			.4202	.5096			
Delivery Took Too Long (Q-6)					-.3426	--		-.3124			-.2450				
Will Use in the Future (Q-7)							--	.3339							
Received the Correct Item (Q-8)				.4843	.5143	-.3124	.3339	--	.4073		.2504	.4031			
Value of Interlibrary Loan (Q-9)								.4073	--						.2688
Willingness to Pay $10 (Q-10)		.2366								--				.2589	
Convenient to Place Request (Q-11)		-.2712	.2385	.3639	.4202	-.2450		.2504			--	.6480	.6366		
Staff Availability (Q-12)		-.2471	.3678	.4002	.5096			.4031			.6480	--	.5993		
Pick Up Convenience (Q-13)		-.2567		.3884							.6366	.5993	--		
Vendor Use (Q-14)										.2589				--	
Worth $18 Investment (Q-15)			.2409						.2688						--

p = < .05

n = 72

sas = proc corr no miss alpha

TABLE D.5. Pearson Correlation Coefficients

Institution E

	Q-1	Q-2	Q-3	Q-4	Q-5	Q-6	Q-7	Q-8	Q-9	Q-10	Q-11	Q-12	Q-13	Q-14	Q-15
Delivery Speed (Q-1)	--				.3307										
Number of Requests (Q-2)		--													
Timeliness (Q-3)			--	.5624	.8670	-.7074	.6520	.3749	.3366			.5249	.3959		.4231
Telephone Interactions (Q-4)			.5624	--	.6415	-.4960	.3363					.5874	.5873		
Satisfaction (Q-5)	.3307		.8670	.6415	--	-.6364	.6243				.4102	.5270	.4060		.3401
Delivery Took Too long (Q-6)			-.7074	-.4960	-.6364	--	-.8103	-.4712	-.3386						-.4547
Will Use in the Future (Q-7)			.6520	.3363	.6243	-.8103	--	.6972	.5858						.4531
Received the Correct Item (Q-8)			.3749			-.4712	.6972	--	.8664						
Value of Interlibrary Loan (Q-9)			.3366			-.3386	.5858	.8664	--						.3354
Willingness to Pay $10 (Q-10)										--					
Convenient to Place Request (Q-11)					.4090						--	.5332	.3935		
Staff Availability (Q-12)			.5249	.5874	.5270						.5332	--			
Pick Up Convenience (Q-13)			.3959	.5873	.4060						.3935		--		
Vendor Use (Q-14)														--	
Worth $18 Investment (Q-15)			.4231		.3401	-.4547	.4531		.3354						--

p = < .05

n = 38

sas = proc corr no miss alpha

214

TABLE D.6. Pearson Correlation Coefficients

Institution F*

	Q-1	Q-2	Q-3	Q-4	Q-5	Q-6	Q-7	Q-8	Q-9	Q-10	Q-11	Q-12	Q-13	Q-14	Q-15
Delivery Speed (Q-1)	--														
Number of Requests (Q-2)	.4049	--													
Timeliness (Q-3)	.4049		--		.5798	-.3706					.3405				
Telephone Interactions (Q-4)				--											
Satisfaction (Q-5)			.5798		--										
Delivery Took Too Long (Q-6)			-.3706				-.3338			.3335	-.3837				
Will Use in the Future (Q-7)						-.3338	--				.3406				
Received the Correct Item (Q-8)								--							
Value of Interlibrary Loan (Q-9)									--						
Willingness to Pay $10 (Q-10)						.3335				--					
Convenient to Place Request (Q-11)			.3405			-.3837	.3406				--				
Staff Availability (Q-12)												--			
Pick Up Convenience (Q-13)													--		
Vendor Use (Q-14)														--	
Worth $18 Investment (Q-15)															--

p = < .05

n = 49

sas = proc corr no miss alpha

* Institution F has an alpha value below acceptable levels, therefore reliability is low.

TABLE D.7. Pearson Correlation Coefficients

Institution G

	Q-1	Q-2	Q-3	Q-4	Q-5	Q-6	Q-7	Q-8	Q-9	Q-10	Q-11	Q-12	Q-13	Q-14	Q-15
Delivery Speed (Q-1)	--		.5637		.3898						.5136	.3690			
Number of Requests (Q-2)		--												-.2920	
Timeliness (Q-3)	.5637		--	.3921	.8375		.5432	.4499	.3968		.4450	.6727	.3626		
Telephone Interactions (Q-4)			.3921	--	.5948		.3599				.2911	.5606	.3451		
Satisfaction (Q-5)	.3898		.8375	.5948	--		.7642	.5721	.2949		.4473	.7365	.3767		
Delivery Took Too long (Q-6)						--									
Will Use in the Future (Q-7)			.5432	.3599	.7642		--	.6382			.2970	.4738			
Received the Correct Item (Q-8)			.4499		.5721		.6382	--	.3136			.5358			
Value of Interlibrary Loan (Q-9)			.3968		.2949			.3136	--			.3444		-.3494	
Willingness to Pay $10 (Q-10)										--			-.2847		
Convenient to Place Request (Q-11)	.5136		.4450	.2911	.4473		.2970				--	.3911			
Staff Availability (Q-12)	.3690		.6727	.5606	.7365		.4738	.5358	.3444		.3911	--	.3039		
Pick Up Convenience (Q-13)			.3626	.3451	.3767					-.2847		.3039	--	-.2830	.3373
Vendor Use (Q-14)		-.2920							-.3494				-.2830	--	
Worth $18 Investment (Q-15)													.3373		--

p = <.05

n = 49

sas = proc corr no miss alpha

TABLE D.8. Pearson Correlation Coefficients

Institution H

	Q-1	Q-2	Q-3	Q-4	Q-5	Q-6	Q-7	Q-8	Q-9	Q-10	Q-11	Q-12	Q-13	Q-14	Q-15
Delivery Speed (Q-1)	--		.4513		.2844	-.2754	.2069	.3005			.3092				
Number of Requests (Q-2)		--	-.2760							.2557					
Timeliness (Q-3)	.4513	-.2760	--	.3103	.7863	-.5315	.6120	.5170	.4570		.6516	.5313	.5728		
Telephone Interactions (Q-4)			.3103	--	.3385			.2826			.4148	.5834	.2534		
Satisfaction (Q-5)	.2844		.7863	.3385	--	-.3223	.4997	.6123	.4056		.6786	.5318	.5576		
Delivery Took Too Long (Q-6)	-.2754		-.5315		-.3223	--	-.2948	-.4433	-.3328					.2512	-.2574
Will Use in the Future (Q-7)	.2069		.6120		.4997	-.2948	--	.4022	.3085		.4136	.4045			
Received the Correct Item (Q-8)	.3005		.5170	.2826	.6123	-.4433	.4022	--	.4321						
Value of Interlibrary Loan (Q-9)			.4570		.4056	-.3328	.3085	.4321	--		.2882		.2729		
Willingness to Pay $10 (Q-10)		.2557								--					
Convenient to Place Request (Q-11)	.3092		.6516	.4148	.6786		.4136		.2882		--	.7773	.6560		
Staff Availability (Q-12)			.5313	.5834	.5318		.4045				.7773	--	.5766		
Pick Up Convenience (Q-13)			.5728	.2534	.5576				.2729		.6560	.5766	--		
Vendor Use (Q-14)						.2512								--	.2641
Worth $18 Investment (Q-15)						-.2574								.2641	--

p = < .05

n = 62

sas = proc corr no miss alpha

217

TABLE D.9. Pearson Correlation Coefficients

Institution I

	Q-1	Q-2	Q-3	Q-4	Q-5	Q-6	Q-7	Q-8	Q-9	Q-10	Q-11	Q-12	Q-13	Q-14	Q-15
Delivery Speed (Q-1)	--		.4235			-.2979				-.3370					
Number of Requests (Q-2)		--													
Timeliness (Q-3)	.4235		--	-.3772	.6784	-.5871			.4774						
Telephone Interactions (Q-4)			-.3772	--	.6606	-.3712	.2982	.3248			.3288	.7174	.4341		
Satisfaction (Q-5)			.6784	.6606	--	.3213	.3273		.4680		.3025	.5128	.3566		
Delivery Took Too Long (Q-6)	-.2979		-.5871	-.3712	.3213	--	-.2976					-.3755		.3163	
Will Use in the Future (Q-7)				.2982	.3273	-.2976	--					.4849	.3075		
Received the Correct Item (Q-8)				.3248				--					.4791		
Value of Interlibrary Loan (Q-9)			.4774		.4680				--						
Willingness to Pay $10 (Q-10)	-.3370									--	.3247	.2875	.3627		
Convenient to Place Request (Q-11)				.3288	.3025					.3247	--	.3248		-.3208	
Staff Availability (Q-12)				.7174	.5128	-.3755	.4849			.2875	.3248	--	.4546	-.3434	
Pick Up Convenience (Q-13)				.4341	.3566		.3075	.4791		.3627		.4546	--	-.2847	
Vendor Use (Q-14)						.3163					-.3208	-.3434	-.2847	--	
Worth $18 Investment (Q-15)															--

p = < .05

n = 50

sas = proc corr no miss alpha

TABLE D.10. Pearson Correlation Coefficients

Institution J

	Q-1	Q-2	Q-3	Q-4	Q-5	Q-6	Q-7	Q-8	Q-9	Q-10	Q-11	Q-12	Q-13	Q-14	Q-15
Delivery Speed (Q-1)	--				.4145							.3782			
Number of Requests (Q-2)		--											.4171		
Timeliness (Q-3)			--	.4778	.4305	-.7317									
Telephone Interactions (Q-4)			.4778	--	.4831	-.4514	.3913	.3750							
Satisfaction (Q-5)	.4145		.4305	.4831	--	-.5874	.6659	.6621			.4808	.6567			.4328
Delivery Took Too long (Q-6)			-.7317	-.4514	-.5874	--			-.5750			-.4404			-.5373
Will Use in the Future (Q-7)				.3913	.6659		--	.9449			.6018				.4600
Received the Correct Item (Q-8)				.3750	.6621		.9449	--			.6059				
Value of Interlibrary Loan (Q-9)						-.5750			--						.8292
Willingness to Pay $10 (Q-10)										--	-.4596				
Convenient to Place Request (Q-11)					.4808		.6018	.6059		-.4596	--	.5506			
Staff Availability (Q-12)	.3782				.6567	-.4404					.5506	--			
Pick Up Convenience (Q-13)		.4171											--		
Vendor Use (Q-14)														--	
Worth $18 Investment (Q-15)					.4328	-.5373	.4600		.8292						--

p = <.05

n = 28

sas = proc corr no miss alpha

219

TABLE E.1. Delivery Speed in Days

All Institutions

	Number of Days	Frequency	Percent
Short	0-8	190	26.60
Medium	9-12	164	23.00
Long	13-18	174	24.30
Longest	19 or More	186	26.10

N = 714

TABLE E.2. Number of Requests

All Institutions

Number of Requests	Frequency	Percent
0-2	89	12.70
3-5	99	14.10
6-10	121	17.20
11-20	126	18.00
21-30	125	17.80
31-60	80	11.40
61 and over	62	8.80

N = 702

TABLE E.3. Timeliness

All Institutions

Variable	Frequency	Percent
Strongly Agree	391	52.10
Agree	261	34.80
Neutral	49	6.50
Disagree	31	4.10
Strongly Disagree	18	2.40

N = 750

TABLE E.4. Telephone Interactions

All Institutions

Variable	Frequency	Percent
Strongly Agree	370	58.90
Agree	148	23.60
Neutral	100	15.90
Disagree	7	1.10
Strongly Disagree	3	0.50

N = 628

TABLE E.5. Satisfaction

All Institutions

Variable	Frequency	Percent
Strongly Agree	483	64.80
Agree	211	28.30
Neutral	32	4.30
Disagree	11	1.50
Strongly Disagree	8	1.10

N = 745

TABLE E.6. Delivery Took Too Long

All Institutions

Variable	Frequency	Percent
Strongly Agree	20	2.90
Agree	17	2.40
Neutral	33	4.60
Disagree	209	29.40
Strongly Disagree	432	60.80

N = 713

TABLE E.7. Will Use in the Future

All Institutions

Variable	Frequency	Percent
Strongly Agree	641	85.40
Agree	100	13.30
Neutral	2	0.30
Disagree	3	0.40
Strongly Disagree	5	0.70

N = 751

TABLE E.8. Received the Correct Item

All Institutions

Variable	Frequency	Percent
Strongly Agree	673	89.60
Agree	66	8.80
Neutral	5	0.70
Disagree	2	0.30
Strongly Disagree	5	0.70

N = 751

TABLE E.9. Value of Item to Research

All Institutions

Variable	Frequency	Percent
Strongly Agree	528	72.10
Agree	166	22.70
Neutral	30	4.10
Disagree	5	0.70
Strongly Disagree	3	0.40

N = 732

TABLE E.10. Willingness to Pay $10.00

All Institutions

Variable	Frequency	Percent
Strongly Agree	19	2.60
Agree	44	6.00
Neutral	164	22.50
Disagree	230	31.60
Strongly Disagree	271	37.20

N = 728

TABLE E.11. Convenient to Place Request

All Institutions

Variable	Frequency	Percent
Strongly Agree	415	55.30
Agree	251	33.40
Neutral	55	7.30
Disagree	24	3.20
Strongly Disagree	6	0.80

N = 751

TABLE E.12. Staff Are Readily Available

All Institutions

Variable	Frequency	Percent
Strongly Agree	468	63.80
Agree	213	29.00
Neutral	45	6.10
Disagree	6	0.80
Strongly Disagree	2	0.30

N = 734

TABLE E.13. Pick Up Convenience

All Institutions

Variable	Frequency	Percent
Strongly Agree	332	45.50
Agree	244	33.50
Neutral	85	11.70
Disagree	56	7.70
Strongly Disagree	12	1.60

N = 729

TABLE E.14. Currently Use Commercial Vendors

All Institutions

Variable	Frequency	Percent
Strongly Agree	29	4.30
Agree	50	7.40
Neutral	90	13.40
Disagree	197	29.20
Strongly Disagree	308	45.70

N = 674

TABLE E.15. Worth $18.00 Investment

All Institutions

Variable	Frequency	Percent
Strongly Agree	302	43.00
Agree	207	19.40
Neutral	110	15.60
Disagree	53	7.50
Strongly Disagree	31	4.40

N = 703

TABLE E.16. Item Requested Via
All Institutions

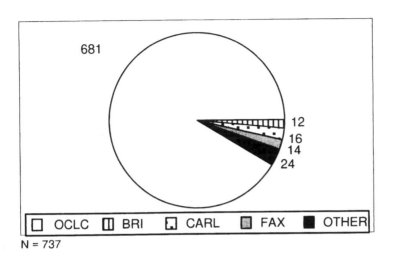

N = 737

TABLE E.17. Item Transmitted Via
All Institutions

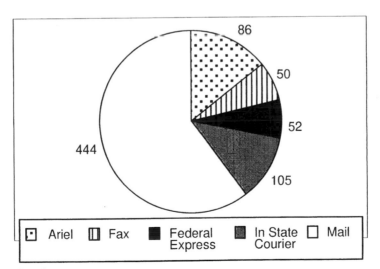

N = 737

TABLE E.18. Type of Notification

All Institutions

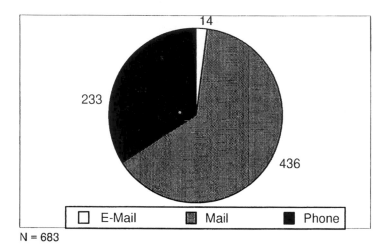

N = 683

TABLE F.1. 1995 ILL Customer Satisfaction Survey Comments

Ranked by Category Type for All Institutions

Speed	Value	Staff Interactions	Request Process	Delivery	Reliability	Communication	Access v. Acquisition	Cost	Satisfaction	Comments
X	X	X							X	Your service, knowledge, and courtesy of staff and quick turn around time are invaluable, thank you.
X	X	X							X	The staff is helpful and pleasant, and materials usually arrive in a timely manner. I deeply appreciate the super service; as a grad student I don't know how I would afford the necessary ILL materials.
X	X	X								I was really impressed with the service I received when my articles were rushed. I was still able to use them and I only had to pay $3 for each article. It worked out well.
X	X						X			Sure wish we had enough journals that we didn't need ILL or that it all was available on-line for a reasonable price. Speed would be nice too.
X	X							X		It took over 2 months to get this article. I finally wrote the author and he faxed a copy to me and I've been doing research from this information for 6 weeks now. ILL is not useful to me. A fee of $10 is pretty steep!
X	X							X		I would like to have next-day service!! If I had to pay a fee, I would not be able to use the service. I could certainly not afford $10 no matter how fast!! $18 is very high, but I needed the material.
X	X							X		In this particula' case, I was able to supply only very sketchy information about the book I needed. I received the book much sooner than I expected. I would be willing to pay for such fast service in the future.
X	X								X	I love ILL!! I think you do a great job. Since I do my research on time, I do not need, want faster delivery, I'm not willing to pay for it either.
X	X								X	Your office does a great job. The changes are great because those of us in the state are in great need of material and we must get it in a timely manner. Thank you.
X	X								X	Previous ILL transactions have been fast, good, and very useful. I would pay a fee for use of ILL for a semester, but in no way think all students should pay a fee.

TABLE F.1. (continued)

Speed	Value	Staff Interactions	Request Process	Delivery	Reliability	Communication	Access v. Acquisition	Cost	Satisfaction	Comments
X	X									I would like faster service, but I do not intend to pay fees.
X	X									This specific book took longer than usual. Other requests I placed in the past arrived earlier. Still, it was useful to me, no matter what.
X	X									As a doctoral student in a heavily research-driven field, I would find myself at a virtual stand-still without ILL. This item was received with unusual swiftness.
X	X									Sometimes slow, but worth it. Maybe if we had a time frame in which we were guaranteed a time for the book to come in–that might help. Also, if some materials could be copied instead of sending the whole book.
X	X									Since the library's budget is so limited and many books are rarely used, ILL is essential. The key for patrons like me is to start planning early in order to get the material on time, since it does take a while.
X	X									This book was late because I ordered it too late. I like the service of ILL but it is not worth $18.
X	X	X			X					ILL should have notified me that it would take such a long time. However, I still appreciate the effort and time ILL put into my request.
X	X	X					X			I love the ILL staff! Everything I've needed for my research has been received in a timely fashion. I only regret that out library didn't already have these items.
X	X	X								The time it took to get this particular item does not reflect the usual speedy service I get from ILL. FirstSearch is a great service. ILL staff is excellent, give them all big raises.
X		X								Although I have had problems with ILL in the past, this request was handled smoothly and promptly.
X		X								The service is rapid, efficient and user-friendly.

						Comment
X						I have always received the items in a timely manner. The system seems efficient and the staff are very helpful.
X	X					Very helpful and prompt.
X	X					Thank you for the fast and hassle-free service. Everyone I dealt with was knowledgeable and effective, especially the young student worker.
X	X	X				This item took over 2 months to be loaned, not because of the diligent and persistent efforts of the staff, but because of the obscurity of the item. Service would be greatly improved if you could have student employees drop off forms and pick up books.
X	X					This could have been faster, but understandable. I requested by computer, not very obvious on how to use it but extremely convenient.
X	X					I use ILL a lot—filling out the same info over and over is really a pain. Usually "speed" is not important to my research, so that's not really important or valuable.
X		X				I made most of my ILL requests pretty late in the semester and have been very pleased with the speedy service I've had. I also appreciate getting some items sent in the mail to my house.
X		X				I was pleasantly surprised at how quickly these materials were received; mailing them to me was even more helpful. Thanks much!
X	X				X	I have only recently started using ILL, but I have been pleased with the service and feel that the requests have been attended to promptly.
X		X			X	I want faster delivery. I have used ILL four times. I could get 2 items I requested. Just 50%.

Comments	Satisfaction	Cost	Access v. Acquisition	Communication	Reliability	Delivery	Request Process	Staff Interactions	Value	Speed
ILL is fast, efficient, dependable and willing to go the extra mile to obtain needed material.					X					X
Although this transaction took a long time and needed to be reordered, usually service is very good, although slow at times.					X					X
I've been very happy with ILL services. They have saved me in more than one occasion with the quick response.					X					X
I don't believe this request could have been handled more rapidly. There have been a couple of requests in the past which seem to have gotten lost in the shuffle. Most things arrive in a couple of weeks, though.					X					X
The material was correct but I almost did not receive the item in time.					X					X
This request was handled promptly and was "in time." I have made previous requests that never were completed and was disappointed.					X					X
I had good luck this time, but my last ILL request was returned without me ever being contacted and had to be re-requested (a 6-week wait).				X						X
Service was extremely slow. I requested a few articles and it took over 3 weeks to get here. I was not notified when some materials came in.				X						X
This item was very long in coming but you kept track of the process. Thanks.				X						X
Although 3 of 4 requested books were quickly received, I placed a request over 3 weeks ago and still have not been notified—it is now too late to be useful to me.				X						X
Since no new books have been ordered in my area of research, I am forced to use ILL. It would be more convenient if a fax were used than mail—I think it would get to me quicker.			X							X
Sometimes I would like to pay for faster delivery.		X								X

								Comment
X	X							If a fee should be charged, it should be reasonable. Say $2-$5 per book. Or, add it onto tuition say $30 per student per semester. Also sometimes the wait is too long. Two weeks to get a book is a little long.
X		X						I am amazed at how quickly I received the material and am extremely pleased with service and cost, thank you.
X			X					Very helpful, speedy and courteous service.
X								This was the first time have used the ILL service. It was much easier than I expected, and I was very happy when the articles arrived so quickly.
X								Although this item took a long time in coming, I requested at the same time several other items. Those items arrived in a much more timely manner.
X								I would like to have faster service, when the book or article is in other countries.
X								I am very much impressed by having fast delivery of this material. Thank you.
X								The book came due two weeks after I ordered it. It came in on Friday. My paper was due on Monday. I'll not sleep tonight. Speedier delivery would be helpful, but not crucial.
X								Sometimes requests take too long.
X								I hope there is a way to get dissertations faster.
X								I hope the remaining articles requested also arrive quickly.
X								Why are faculty requests processed faster than graduate student requests? I requested the same article as a grad student and never got it. This time I put my professor's name on it and got the article.
X								Proposal deadlines are rigid and absolute—was need prompt service, and by and large we get it!
X								The speed with which I have received requested items has improved recently. In the past, it seemed as though things took much longer.

TABLE F.1. (continued)

Speed	Value	Staff Interactions	Request Process	Delivery	Reliability	Communication	Access v. Acquisition	Cost	Satisfaction	Comments
X										Information requested other than books was received in a timely manner.
X										The service would be better if the lead time could be reduced.
X										I made some article requests 2 or 3 months ago. I still have not yet received them. But, generally I receive what I requested within reasonable time.
X										Many of the articles could not get to me on time.
X										Sometimes it takes too long, but this one was fine.
X										I've only just started using ILL here—my first two requests arrived in about 1 week—it was very good service.
	X	X			X				X	I am usually very pleased with the service at ILL and it is a necessary part of my research. The only difficulty I have had is at extremely busy times when no libraries will respond.
	X	X				X				You might find a way to let us know this cost. That would reduce unnecessary ILL requests. I really appreciate the service, and I think the staff is great. I was confused using OCLC to find the books because the instructions were incomplete.
	X	X					X			ILL is extremely important for my research because this library does not carry many of the journals critical for my specific area. ILL overcomes this obstacle—efficiently and courteously—Thank You!
	X	X							X	I have always found the staff very helpful. I really wish the campus budget would allow the library enough funds to cut down on the cost of ILL, yet I feel that "A" has an excellent ILL dept.
	X	X							X	ILL staff are great; the service is convenient enough and certainly indispensable.
	X	X							X	The interlibrary loan staff and the services they provide have made research at this university possible . . . without ILL I may as well give up finding materials necessary for real research.

							Comment
X	X					X	I didn't know ILL cost $18 a shot! But it's a wonderful service, and I couldn't get by without it. The staff here is excellent.
X	X						The ILL program as well as the entire library is exceptional. A top strength for the university. Thanks for your professional and courteous service.
X	X						The ILL staff is very courteous, efficient and diligent. I cannot thank them enough for their help. As a matter of fact, I may not be able to do some of the research without their help. Thank you very much.
X	X						The ILL service and staff are absolutely superb! Without their courteous, friendly and efficient assistance, I would have difficulty pursuing my research. Kudos! For a job well done.
X	X						This service is very useful and is the best on campus. Staff is friendly and efficient.
X	X						ILL has been indispensable, the staff has always been extremely helpful. Thank you.
X	X						I highly appreciate ILL staff's work. I won a Graduate School Dean's Small Grant. Most of the materials I needed for this project were supplied by ILL. Every staff is very kind to me.
X	X						I feel fortunate to have received this service gratis. It would be worth a few dollars to me even at this point as an impoverished grad student. People have always been helpful in person and on the phone. Great work.
X	X						ILL is a very valuable resource for my dissertation research. My special thanks to the staff. Keep up the good work.
X		X					Materials are worth $18 if it will help research. I suggest that the form be changed so the loan item only has to be entered once. That way we don't have to rewrite some information so many times.
X				X			Very convenient. It makes my resources endless. I could have picked up my articles at the library to save the cost of postage.
X				X			Good service. It's really helpful to my research. Suggestion: Extended hour for picking up materials will be more convenient.

Comments	Satisfaction	Cost	Access v. Acquisition	Communication	Reliability	Delivery	Request Process	Staff Interactions	Value	Speed
Although I will point out that the book probably didn't cost that much, I am generally happy with interlibrary loan, which I have only begun to use extensively this semester, although I have had some trouble with works of Canadian origin being received.	X				X				X	
Except for the time ILL lost my request, I have had good experiences with ILL. I appreciate the low cost of service for me and other students.	X	X			X				X	
$18 to photocopy an article seems excessive—however, I can see how mailing a book / staff time could add up. ILL is very helpful for me, especially since our library has little material that is helpful to my research.		X	X						X	
I cannot be sure how valuable a book or article will be until I see it. If I had to pay for requests, I would mostly not use interlibrary loan. Students & faculty should not be charged because "C" Library's collection is inadequate in areas.		X	X						X	
There should be no cost to faculty. The university ought to do that much in support of our research. We don't get paid enough to afford $10 an item and the library's holdings are insufficient for cutting edge research.		X	X						X	
ILL is the only way that I can perform a comprehensive literature review. I would prefer immediate access to journals, but I can live with the inconveniences of ILL. Thank you for providing service.			X						X	
Because my dept. is very small and does not have many of the resources I need, and because the library is also lacking in materials, I find that I must rely on ILL. Their service is vital to me and they have always been excellent. Thank You.			X						X	
In my area of research, "A's" library does not have a lot of references, and because of this the ILL services have been very helpful. Without it, my research would be very difficult.			X						X	
I enjoy the service and really appreciate the efforts you have made. This service is extremely useful to me and maybe many other researchers because our library doesn't have a lot of liberal art books and journals.			X						X	

						Comment
X			X			Definitely ILL helps my research tremendously. Yet $18 a book, we may be able to buy more books for the library with the budget for ILL. In any event, ILL is wonderful.
X			X			$18 is a lot of money—you could buy many of the books for that price. Still, as a faculty member and author, I need to read all the relevant literature—even if the library does not own the book or article.
X			X			Many of the materials I am requesting would be vital for any research on the subject. I hope that the needs in terms of requested books are being passed on to book ordering departments.
X			X			This service is an important one since many journals that are not "main-stream" journals are being dropped.
X			X			It's worth it to me because I can't get it anywhere else. If our library had a better collection, I wouldn't need to use ILL so much—we're also losing journals I now have to use ILL to get articles from.
X			X			I believe ILL is one of the most valuable services that the library offers. This is especially true for students in less popular fields, which often translates into the fact that the library holdings are very weak in that area.
X			X			ILL service is valuable because the libraries don't have a lot of journals that I need.
X					X	Charges for ILL requests probably wouldn't hurt faculty, but would make student research almost impossible.
X					X	It is difficult to place a dollar amount of worth on these materials. It is worthwhile having access to materials not held by the library. However, one cannot tell how useful the article will be until it is received.
X					X	It is worth $18 to me, due to the nature of my research.
X					X	I thought the cost is much less than $18. I really appreciate your services. ILL is a very important part of my student life. Keep up the good work. Thank you.

TABLE F.1. (continued)

Speed	Value	Staff Interactions	Request Process	Delivery	Reliability	Communication	Access v. Acquisition	Cost	Satisfaction	Comments
	X							X		It is a shame that it costs so much to get items that don't always prove to be as useful as one hoped, but that's the way research goes.
	X								X	Great service, please continue.
	X								X	A great service when needed.
	X								X	Very satisfied. Excellent resource.
	X								X	This is a great service. It makes the library global. Please keep offering the service.
	X								X	ILL has been very useful in all respects.
	X								X	I have usually been happy with my ILL service. I would not want to see a change initiated for ILL materials.
	X								X	Thanks so much for all your help over the past two years. I couldn't have made it through my master's program without you!!
	X								X	I am pleased with the services the ILL is providing. I hope this continues, thank you for your valuable service and I will be using them quite often in the future.
	X								X	You do a great job. The service has been very valuable to me in working on my dissertation. Keep up the great work.
	X								X	YEAH–Great work! You're a life saver to a nursing grad student.
	X								X	If not for ILL, I would not be able to complete any research that I have thus far undertaken. Thank you immensely for the service.
	X								X	I appreciate this service. Invaluable to my work.
	X								X	I have been extremely pleased with the ILL program. It has definitely helped my study and I will use it in the future.

				Comment
			X	I appreciate your service, but I wonder whether this type of survey is really necessary. I think that once is a good measurement, several times will bias the result.
			X	This system is very convenient to my research, without this, I think it's very difficult for me to follow up the information.
			X	Document Delivery is a very important service because of the isolation of our building.
			X	I appreciate the service.
			X	Material directly related to my research.
			X	I appreciate ILL's help with my research.
			X	ILL is the backbone of research.
			X	I do lots of health psychology research for myself and my graduate adviser. We would be at a great disadvantage without ILL.
			X	ILL service of "C" Library is playing a vital role in advancement of scientific knowledge of students, faculty, and teachers at campus. Thanks and congratulations.
			X	I think this service is quite helpful for research.
			X	ILL is essential to my research as many of the modern (newer) journals in Glycobiology and Medicinal Chemistry are not well represented in this library.
			X	The biggest problem I've had with ILL is that I have ordered things that end up being useless because I had too little information when I ordered it ... It is very difficult to tell what titles to order on the online abstracts or synopsis.
			X	The ILL service has been key for me because "C" has had few of the books I need for my research. However, because I have ordered so many books, there is no way I could pay $10 each. I'd have to stop using the service.

TABLE F.1. (continued)

Speed	Value	Staff Interactions	Request Process	Delivery	Reliability	Communication	Access v. Acquisition	Cost	Satisfaction	Comments
	X									Very necessary service.
	X									ILL is vital to my research and I feel that they do a great job. I only wish they would have gotten a CD that I also needed.
	X									I rely very much on ILL. In point of fact, it would be very difficult for me to complete my research and publications without this key service.
	X									The ILL program has been essential to my research, and I am very grateful to the extremely helpful staff.
	X									ILL is a great service! As a doctoral student, working on my dissertation, the service is extremely valuable. Only more valuable would be full-text retrieval for scholarly journals like law reviews in Lexis/Nexis with access from home on our new system.
	X									This article turned out to be just what I expected–gives me a summary of the writing of the author, with a reference list to the entire body of works. Thank you.
	X									Our library has inevitably limited holding, so ILL is essential for teaching and research.
	X									The ILL service is very useful and helpful to me.
	X									Do they all cost so much? This is a critical service for us–without a med. school half of our literature is unavailable.
	X									I use ILL frequently and my only comment is sometimes the material is not as helpful as I thought it would be. Maybe better descriptions would help.
	X									Without this service, I could not do necessary research.
	X									Thank you–this service is the lifeline of my research.
	X									I have always, especially when working on my book and earlier research, found ILL service excellent.

						Comment
X						I got excellent grades last semester due to being able to order things my professor had not seen before.
X						This article was important to my research—I use ILL for dozens of mostly articles. Given that our library has limited serials available—ILL has done fine for me.
X						Over 95% of what I order on ILL is well worth it. This item was not but one cannot always tell by looking.
X						I had no idea that these orders were so expensive. I appreciate the much needed services of the ILL office. It's too bad that our enrollment fees aren't used more for this service.
	X	X				With the extensive number of requests I have placed, it takes a lot of time to fill out cards (& I don't have a computer by which to make requests). However, I don't have any suggestions how to make this easier. I've appreciated all of ILL help!
	X	X				My interactions with the ILL staff have left me very impressed with their dedication and service. If there is any way to reduce the time it takes to fill up multiple ILL forms, that would be very helpful.
	X		X			I drive 50 miles to campus. Closing at 5 PM meant I couldn't pick up the items that came in. The staff is very helpful in mailing out and calling to expedite matters.
X				X		My first order for this book, which is the third of a three volume series was canceled because vol. 2 was found. They then disagreed with me that they found Vol. 2 This was extremely disconcerting.
X				X		ILL staff is very friendly and apparently tries very hard. But they also seem to be very much overworked and not very knowledgeable about how to obtain some types of materials, especially microfilm.
X				X		I have done a lot of business with ILL and have been impressed with the service. Many of the items I ordered are difficult to find, but the staff has always done their best to find it.

TABLE F.1. (continued)

Speed	Value	Staff Interactions	Request Process	Delivery	Reliability	Communication	Access v. Acquisition	Cost	Satisfaction	Comments
		X			X				X	I am very very satisfied with the ILL service here. I frequently order materials through ILL, some of them in non-roman scripts, and have always received good, considerate service.
		X								Staff is very helpful and ILL is very convenient to use.
		X								The only inconvenience is due to the construction; and, sometimes I'm busy and have trouble finding the time to get to ILL. The ILL staff are excellent and always pleasant. I've never been dissatisfied with ILL service.
		X								Sometimes I have the impression that the staff feel hassled by interlibrary loan requests and would rather not have patrons make them.
		X								Great Staff, raises for everyone.
		X								How many of these forms must I fill out? Y'all do super work.
		X								I love the people and the work they do!!!
		X								Reference Librarians could be more instructive and more helpful in facilitating ILL requests.
		X								I would have put a 5 for service on account of a full-time employee who was super nice to me, but another guy wasn't as nice or more importantly, as patient.
		X								Really helpful to locate and find the materials that I need. Especially the staff are so kind to help me any way at all.
		X								Everyone I talked to in the office was very helpful and friendly, a welcome change from some of the other services on campus. Thanks.
		X								This is the best ILL staff I've ever dealt with.
		X								You folks do a super job. Thanks.
		X								ILL staff are absolutely fabulous! I've been very happy that we can get books from other institutions. It's helped a lot for research and personal stuff.

					Comment
			X		Friendly staff.
			X		ILL staff is always helpful and friendly. I'm very satisfied with their service.
			X		The staff in the department are very pleasant and efficient.
			X		You all do a nice job. Your staff always goes "the extra mile" when I have questions or problems. Thanks.
			X		Staff is great! They are always very willing to assist me in any way.
			X		The staff in the ILL dept. are always friendly and helpful. They are doing a great job.
			X		Keep up the superb job. All the ILL staff deserve hefty pay raises and boxes of chocolates or an occasional night out on the town. Sorry, I'm too poor to contribute.
			X		The ILL staff have frequently gone out of their way to be helpful. I find their work superior to several other college and university libraries I have used.
			X		Very pleasant and helpful staff.
			X		A wonderful helpful group of professionals.
			X		The friendly and efficient ILL staff are a credit to our university's library.
		X	X		The ILL staff seem to go to great lengths to locate material I requested, and keep me informed of their progress.
			X		I have always had a good relationship with the ILL staff. I have never had a problem that couldn't be solved. I very much appreciate your help.

TABLE F.1. (continued)

Speed	Value	Staff Interactions	Request Process	Delivery	Reliability	Communication	Access v. Acquisition	Cost	Satisfaction	Comments
		X								The staff really seems to care about helping faculty members get what they need. I would only say thank you and congratulations for a job well done.
		X								Thank you for all of your courteous help.
		X								Staff has been wonderful.
		X								The staff was very helpful and courteous—Thanks!!
		X								The staff have been very helpful—even when I have come in desperate and it makes them leave their present work. I am very pleased with their services.
		X								ILL is by far the most helpful department at the library. When all research librarians act as if they could care less I can always count on ILL to assist me.
		X				X				Office assistant communicates with interlibrary loan staff and reports no problems.
		X							X	The service and response are exemplary. Excellent!!
		X				X				I am requesting materials to replace pages which are missing. I specifically request ads also, but end up having to request the material again. The staff should make these requests more clear to the lending library.
		X								Will the ILL transactions cost less if ordered through the internet? I like ILL services. I found the office area to be very user un-friendly.
		X								I have nothing but praise to the ILL staff for making ILL so efficient.
		X							X	I'm so glad we have ILL services. I really appreciate these people. They do an excellent job.
		X								I enjoy using ILL to get the articles or books I want. I thank you for the service. Everyone in the ILL is very nice.
			X							I would like to be able to place orders through e-mail. Otherwise, I am very happy with the ILL service.

							Comments
X							It would be helpful to request items over campus e-mail.
X							Could requests be made on e-mail?
		X					It would be useful to have a way to order ILL material by using the Internet (campus network). I think $18 is fairly high. How can it be this expensive?
X							Ordered using ILL on lamar--very convenient!
X							Computerized interactions are nice and would be nice to see expanded. (e.g., being able to take ref. directly from database search to request, rather than writing so much on form.)
X							I like the facility that allows students to request books through ILL using INTERNET.
X		X					With the new ZAP system it is not convenient to check on ongoing loan requests. There is no need to notify the recipient via 'regular mail at his/her private address. How about e-mail or campus mail?
X							I hope easier way. Filling up the sheets takes time if there're two or three articles which I want. Can we use our ID?
X							I use ILL primarily for journal articles--it is time consuming to full out the "card" with the same information time after time.
X							This is a very useful service. One way to improve the process for regular users would be to get rid of a lot of questions on the form. If a list of the regular users is created, then all that is needed is your ID #.
X							I appreciate the e-mail service. I found the old forms somewhat inconvenient, but the ability to use e-mail requests will greatly increase my ILL use.
X							I like that I can request ILL at branch libraries. I am doing my best to inform other students to do the same thing.
X							The requests should be on computer. So a student would fill out his name and it would be faster.
	X						It would be nice if I could pick up ILL books at engineering library instead of the main library.
X	X						Might be better to pick up stuff from dept. rather than library. Access to compendex from dept. Better interface for ILL should be on UNIX as well (or PC machines).

TABLE F.1. (continued)

Satisfaction	Cost	Access v. Acquisition	Communication	Reliability	Delivery	Request Process	Staff Interactions	Value	Speed	Comments
					X					Now that you have extra space and personnel, why not return to the practice of checking out ILL materials directly to clients rather than using Circulation. Clerks are frequently confused.
					X					Can the material be delivered to branch libraries?
					X					If the books were sent to the branch library it would be more convenient.
					X					I would prefer notification through e-mail, even if it meant going to the office to pick it up, if I would receive the information a few days earlier by doing this.
					X					Why not send it through inter-campus mail?
	X				X					Could save money by having us pick up the photocopies here at the library for those of us who frequently visit the library.
	X				X					It would be nice to have choice about paying for expedited service (sometimes time is more of an issue), and to be able to drop off / pick up ILL requests at business library.
			X							I have a hard time understanding the foreign students who leave messages on my answering machine regarding the arrival of my order.
		X	X	X						I never have received some requested items. Requests returned because name of researcher was 3 letters (not initials). If research is worth anything, the publications need to be available.
			X	X						With multiple requests it is difficult to keep track with the current system. Notification varies, sometimes I get a call, sometimes the article is mailed. On at least one occasion the page header was cut off and I didn't have the full citation.
				X						Copy quality of articles sometimes poor, which is the fault of the lending library.
				X						As an art history student, I am frustrated with the poor quality reproduction from Xerox copies of articles. I am surprised that "A" doesn't already own these materials.

		Comment
X		Some articles I have received were poorly photocopied by the lending library. Articles sent by FAX are much less desirable than photocopies, however.
X		Screwed Up! Please get this right the next time.
X		I am very pleased with the service I received. Keep up the great work.
X		I got what I need. Thank you very much.
X		Poor photocopy at times.
X		Quality of the reproduction of material has to be improved.
X		Quality of source of the Faxed articles is too poor for use.
X		Article was missing internal pages.
X		Most items I get are correct. However, 2 of the current 4 were incorrect. I requested "only this edition" and I received earlier editions that were too old to use.
X		I requested three items through ILL. Two arrived perfectly, but one was incorrect. But overall I was impressed.
X	X	Can we keep a copy of ILL request? Sometimes no response of some ILL. In this case, please also call and explain why you can't find these sources. Okay?
X	X	I appreciate the services I receive from ILL. But, some materials I requested earlier this semester have not been located. Why? My request cards were fully completed.
X		On most occasions this service works very well. This was one where it didn't.

TABLE F.1. (continued)

Comments	Satisfaction	Cost	Access v. Acquisition	Communication	Reliability	Delivery	Request Process	Staff Interactions	Value	Speed
Some of the articles never came to me.					X					
The ILL department does an A+ job with anything I send them.					X					
Keep up the good work! I am extremely satisfied with the ILL especially since it has become available on-line.	X			X						
You may let me know the status of the requested item(s).				X						
Just curious: I've supplied my e-mail address on virtually all requests, but have never received a notification via e-mail. Would this help you?				X						
My only criticism is when I'm informed that a book isn't available for loan, but that certain libraries do have it, I would greatly appreciate a note on the form telling me where the book is to be found.				X						
Instead of sending me notification that my books have arrived via postal mail, it could save money and time by simply e-mailing or telephoning me.				X						
On-line access very convenient. Bring back document delivery service!!!				X						
Convenience issues should be partly resolved once I get on e-mail.				X						
I would like to be notified of the progress of my other requests.				X						
Is it possible to do this by e-mail?				X						
She woke me up by calling me at 7:30 in the morning! Was this really necessary? As a grad student, my sleep is an important and rare commodity–Don't do this again!!				X						
I thought I had canceled this request. We finally decided to purchase it.				X						
At this cost, possibly consider providing reimbursement of / or access to certain # of commercial vendor deliveries??		X	X							

							Comment
X							Based on the $18 per ILL transaction, I hope that the library has a system to monitor/track ILL requests for each book, say, per year, and to indicate when the library would save money by purchasing the book.
X							Wouldn't it make more sense to keep these fundamental sources in our library so everyone can use them with no $18 charge?
X							Regarding average cost, etc., I do not believe I, as the patron, should be charged or penalized due to the unavailability of material in this library.
X							If the average per-book cost is $18, I would suggest trying to acquire for the "C" Library any books that are repeatedly requested instead of paying the probable cost of book for repeated short-term loans.
X							A fee of $10 would put this service out of my reach. Many of the books I order (and articles) should be in our library. A better investment of your money would be to buy and process books in a timely manner.
X							This (the $18) is something the library has to determine. Can it do more requesting of materials through ILL than purchasing journals?
X							That seems like an outrageous overcharge rip-off ($18) by somebody. Why does this administration not give a fixed % of grant indirect cost directly to the library? That would provide positive incentive to write grant proposals.
X							If the cost for ILL transactions is higher, it will be better to (re)subscribe to some frequently used journals. One way might relieve the burden of ILL, that is, ask each dept. to list the journals it subscribed and put them on the list.
X							If the cost is this high, we should be receiving the journal, but it is so hard to convince the library that they should start getting a new journal.
X							$18? That's insane. If I and a few other faculty request 10 or so articles per year it would cost more than the journal subscription. Why so expensive?
X							Why is the price so high? With library cutbacks, I suspect my use of ILL will go up. The question for all of us is where is the break-even point? Does it cost more for ILL than we gain by subscription cuts?
						X	This service is great, although I wish the library had more of the journals I needed.
						X	Keep up the good work. I hope the Library will enlarge the stock of books.
						X	Although the books I need are "held" by the library, I have been unable to locate them and the ILL will not order these, this severely complicates my ability to get these articles.

TABLE F.1. (continued)

Comments	Satisfaction	Cost	Access v. Acquisition	Communication	Reliability	Delivery	Request Process	Staff Interactions	Value	Speed
It may be more efficient, and less costly in the long run, if the library subscribed to more journals. It certainly would be more convenient for patrons.			X							
Thanks: could I request our library to buy the material I need?			X							
We should have the materials on hand so that we have the opportunity to view the materials with our own eyes. Titles tell us very little. The university will lose "serious" students to better funded institutions.			X							
I would not want faster and cheaper delivery if it meant that there would be fewer journals on the shelf.			X							
Tell the Dean to get his act together and acknowledge there are serious problems with our library!!			X							
Since "A's" library collection is so poor, ILL is the only way to sustain a reasonable research capability.			X							
Would be more cost effective to just keep up our journal subscriptions, especially if it costs $18 per transaction.			X							
Given the Library's poor collection, investment in databases and ILL is the only practical way to maintain a research capability. It is a prudent resource investment.			X							
If your department could get together with acquisitions and place orders for heavily requested materials, you may be able to cut down on the use and cost of ILL usage.			X							
Some books look like key references. Why and how does the library decide on which books to buy and not to buy?			X							
I requested many things from a journal you discontinued. Wouldn't it be better to resubscribe to this journal?			X							
Subscription to Journal would be more cash effective.			X							
Library needs to look at costs of ILL vs. having complete collection—I have to use ILL often with this journal because library doesn't have some years.			X							

	Comment
X	I think the library, as a whole, might do better to monitor texts requests on ILL, then order them for the permanent collection.
X	The best way to lower the cost and burden of ILL in a long term, I think, is to expand our library, both the building and the collection.
X	There are a number of times I have had to order items that should have been part of the regular collection.
X	Consider running a database and diverting funds to acquire journals that experience high demand. Either buy back issues on microfilm or subscribe to current issues. This would benefit students and the university and its budget.
X	Order the material. Especially the journals.
X	This and one other book recently ordered ILL, are both missing from the library. Perhaps it would be almost as cheap to order new copies.
X	I presume it could cost a lot more to have all of the journals in the library. If this is correct the answer is yes.
X	Since the cost of ILL transactions is expensive for the library, why don't you subscribe to the journals?
X	If people are willing to pay for an overnight ILL request, we should be willing to do more than one a day.
X	I don't understand why it would cost $18 to receive this book. Surely, postage and handling can't cost that much.
X	I believe there are ways to cut this cost down, such as limit the fedex system and use faxes, this would save a lot of time and dollars.

Comments	Satisfaction	Cost	Access v. Acquisition	Communication	Reliability	Delivery	Request Process	Staff Interactions	Value	Speed
There was a mix-up about a similarly titled book that the library had. The book itself would have cost the library $100, so it would take at least five requests of the same volume to make the ILL service for it uneconomical.		X								
This item did not cost me anything. I'd be willing to pay for photocopying costs.		X								
I didn't know the average cost is this high.		X								
Not all items are worth $18.		X								
I understand cost is a factor, and I regret it is so very expensive. Perhaps students should be allowed to designate part of their fees for this service.		X								
Not all material is worth $18. Rare or hard-to-find books—very definitely!		X								
I don't know if there are cheaper ways to get books our library doesn't have. If so, please let me know about them.		X								
I'm concerned abut the expense to the library and have informed my clients that ILL really isn't free.		X								
Xeroxing large format microfiche is hugely expensive for graduate student budgets. Would rather receive hard copy of microfiche items.		X								
$18 seems high.		X								
A resource more directly related would probably be worth $18.		X								
45% of indirect cost is provided on research grants to this university to provide library services to researchers. No service charge should ever be charged against to researchers.		X								
$18 per article seems pretty excessive.		X								
Who pays this fee?		X								
I only had photocopies sent—do they cost $18 too?		X								

					X	I am surprised that ILL doesn't cost me anything unless I request "RUSH." The previous institution I was at charged anywhere from 10 cents to 25 cents per page, depending upon the source.
					X	I don't think it is worth $18 for every item. But, I thought these items were "free" as long as each library is requesting material.
					X	What is the $18 spent on—subdivision of cost? The ILL should remain open after 5PM on certain days as well as during the weekend. Subject area specialists can further help in locating the materials.
					X	$18 seems a shame since this library was supposed to have this book, but it cannot be located.
					X	I am not aware of any cost of ILL transactions which I have done so far.
					X	It's somewhat hard to put a monetary value on articles like this.
					X	Why does it cost so much?
				X		Thank You for your service.
				X		Thank you, thank you, thank you. Carry on Library soldiers.
				X		I found this service every helpful.
				X		Good Service. I'm satisfied.
				X		Doing a great job.
				X		Very good service. I am satisfied.
				X		I am very satisfied with ILL services.
				X		Overall performance of ILL dept. is satisfactory.
				X		I am very satisfied with my ILL service. Thanks for your help.
				X		Very good service.
				X		The ILL service here is excellent. I was at UC Berkeley for 7 years and always had problems with their ILL. "B's" is far more efficient.

TABLE F.1. (continued)

Speed	Value	Staff Interactions	Request Process	Delivery	Reliability	Communication	Access v. Acquisition	Cost	Satisfaction	Comments
									X	I am extremely pleased with ILL. I am here on an almost daily basis and the service has been outstanding.
									X	Thank you, I will be using this service in the future.
									X	Great work.
									X	I greatly appreciate the ILL services on this campus.
									X	Excellent service.
									X	Thanks, excellent service.
									X	First-rate service: Much appreciated.
									X	Very helpful.
									X	Service is excellent in all possible ways.
									X	Excellent service.
									X	Thank you for having such a nice service.
									X	Very good! Thank you very much.
									X	I appreciate a lot for this ILL service. Thanks.
									X	I appreciate the service you offer very much.
									X	ILL has always been the brightest spot in the library and on campus as well.
									X	Thank you.
									X	It's a good service.

252

	X	The general service is great. Please keep up the good job.
	X	The program is first-rate in all facets. It's one of the best features of the library.
	X	ILL provides excellent service.
	X	I am very pleased and impressed with the work of ILL. I make many requests, and have always been quite satisfied.
	X	I am pleased with the overall service I have received from ILL.
	X	Thank you for your service.
	X	It has been most helpful.
	X	Excellent service in all respects. Thanks!
	X	ILL is doing an outstanding job.
	X	Excellent service being made available to faculty.
	X	I have been impressed with the service. I would definitely use it next year, but I am graduating.
	X	Very pleased with ILL services, don't change a thing.
	X	I enjoy the current system.
	X	Good stuff (research)! This means we are making progress and trying to find problems. Keep going.
	X	My request was sent on 9-1-94 not 4-13-95.

Index

Haworth
DOCUMENT DELIVERY
SERVICE

This valuable service provides a single-article order form for any article from a Haworth journal.

- *Time Saving:* No running around from library to library to find a specific article.
- *Cost Effective:* All costs are kept down to a minimum.
- *Fast Delivery:* Choose from several options, including same-day FAX.
- *No Copyright Hassles:* You will be supplied by the original publisher.
- *Easy Payment:* Choose from several easy payment methods.

Open Accounts Welcome for . . .
- Library Interlibrary Loan Departments
- Library Network/Consortia Wishing to Provide Single-Article Services
- Indexing/Abstracting Services with Single Article Provision Services
- Document Provision Brokers and Freelance Information Service Providers

---

MAIL or *FAX* THIS ENTIRE ORDER FORM TO:

Haworth Document Delivery Service
The Haworth Press, Inc.
10 Alice Street
Binghamton, NY 13904-1580

or FAX: 1-800-895-0582
or CALL: 1-800-342-9678
9am-5pm EST

PLEASE SEND ME PHOTOCOPIES OF THE FOLLOWING SINGLE ARTICLES:

1) Journal Title: _____

    Vol/Issue/Year: _____ Starting & Ending Pages: _____

    Article Title: _____

_____

2) Journal Title: _____

    Vol/Issue/Year: _____ Starting & Ending Pages: _____

    Article Title: _____

_____

3) Journal Title: _____

    Vol/Issue/Year: _____ Starting & Ending Pages: _____

    Article Title: _____

_____

4) Journal Title: _____

    Vol/Issue/Year: _____ Starting & Ending Pages: _____

    Article Title: _____

(See other side for Costs and Payment Information)

COSTS: Please figure your cost to order quality copies of an article.

1. Set-up charge per article: $8.00

    ($8.00 × number of separate articles) _____

2. Photocopying charge for each article:

    1-10 pages: $1.00 _____

    11-19 pages: $3.00 _____

    20-29 pages: $5.00 _____

    30+ pages: $2.00/10 pages _____

3. Flexicover (optional): $2.00/article _____

4. Postage & Handling: US: $1.00 for the first article/

    $.50 each additional article _____

    Federal Express: $25.00 _____

    Outside US: $2.00 for first article/

    $.50 each additional article _____

5. Same-day FAX service: $.35 per page _____

GRAND TOTAL: _____

METHOD OF PAYMENT: (please check one)

❑ Check enclosed   ❑ Please ship and bill. PO # _____
(sorry we can ship and bill to bookstores only! All others must pre-pay)

❑ Charge to my credit card: ❑ Visa; ❑ MasterCard; ❑ Discover;
    ❑ American Express;

Account Number:_____ Expiration date:_____

Signature: *X*_____

Name: _____ Institution: _____

Address: _____

_____

City: _____ State:_____ Zip:_____

Phone Number: _____ FAX Number: _____

MAIL or *FAX* THIS ENTIRE ORDER FORM TO:

Haworth Document Delivery Service   or FAX: 1-800-895-0582
The Haworth Press, Inc.   or CALL: 1-800-342-9678
10 Alice Street   9am-5pm EST)
Binghamton, NY 13904-1580